OUTLINES

OF

A MECHANICAL THEORY OF STORMS,

CONTAINING

THE TRUE LAW OF LUNAR INFLUENCE,

WITH

PRACTICAL INSTRUCTIONS TO THE NAVIGATOR, TO ENABLE HIM APPROXIMATELY TO CALCULATE THE COMING CHANGES OF THE WIND AND WEATHER, FOR ANY GIVEN DAY, AND FOR ANY PART OF THE OCEAN.

BY T. BASSNETT.

Η δε μεσοτης εν πασιν ασφαλεςερα.

NEW YORK:
D. APPLETON & COMPANY,
346 & 348 BROADWAY,
AND 16 LITTLE BRITAIN, LONDON.
1854.

CONTENTS.

SECTION FIRST.

SECTION SECOND.

SECTION THIRD.

SECTION FOURTH.

SECTION FIFTH.

SECTION SIXTH.

PREFACE.

On presenting to the public a work of this novel character, overstepping, as it does, the barriers erected by modern systems to the further progress of knowledge, a few words of explanation may not be inappropriate. Early imbued with a desire to understand the *causes* of natural phenomena, the author devoured with avidity the interpretations contained in the elementary works of orthodox science, until reason and observation rendered him dissatisfied with the repast. To him it appeared that there was an evident tendency in scholastic instruction, to make the knowledge of nature inaccessible to the many, that the world might be made more dependent on the few; while many of the *established principles*, on which the learned rested, seemed to be at variance with the simplicity and consistency of truth. Thus situated, he ventured to think for himself, and looking back on the history of the past, and finding so many cases in which the philosophy of to-day was supplanted by a different system on the morrow, he was led to suspect the possibility of future revolutions, and was thus determined to be no longer embarrassed by previous systems, nor deterred by opinions however learned, which conflicted with a rational recognition of the mechanical nature of all physical phenomena.

The science of meteorology, to which the following pages are devoted, is, and always has been, a confessedly complex subject; and on this account, any suggestions and facts which observation gleans,—no matter how humble the source may be, should not be denied a hearing by those professedly engaged in the pursuit of truth. Step by step, the author became more and more confirmed in his doubts of the soundness of many modern theories; and in 1838 he had attained a position which enabled him to allege in the public prints of the day, that there did exist certain erroneous dogmas in the schools, which stood in the way of a fuller development of the causes of many meteorological phenomena. This annunciation was made in general terms, and no notice was taken of it. Subsequently, he forwarded to the British Association of Science, then convened at Birmingham, a communication of similar tenor; and at a later date still, a more particular statement of the advantages of his discoveries to the navigator and agriculturist, was sent to the British admiralty. The first of these communications was treated with silent contempt; the last elicited some unimportant reply. In 1844 a memorial was presented to Congress, accompanied with a certified copy of *predictions* of the weather, written several weeks before the event, and attested in due form by two impartial witnesses; but neither did this result in any inquiry as to its truth. During the time since elapsed, he has been engaged in pursuits which prevented him from pressing the subject elsewhere, until the spring of 1853, he brought his theory under the notice of the Smithsonian Institution. This led to a correspondence between himself and the gentlemanly Secretary of the Institution, whose doubts of the truth of his allegations were expressed with kindness, and whose courtesy was in strange contrast with the conduct of others. In the communications which he forwarded to that Institution, he gave a detailed statement of the difficulties he had met with, and expressed the hope that an Institution, created for the purpose of increasing and diffusing knowledge, would feel justified in lending the influence of its name to facilitate the completion of a theory which was yet undeniably imperfect. In view of this, a test was proposed. *"Give us, for example, a prediction of the weather for one month in each season of the year 1854, for the City of Washington." This test the author refused, for the reason that he did not consider it necessary to wait so long; but he informed the Secretary of the Institution, that he would prepare an outline of his theory, which would enable him to decide upon the merits of the discoveries claimed. This outline is contained in the following pages. During the summer of 1853 he called upon Professor Henry, then at Chicago, with his manuscript; but a sudden indisposition prevented that gentleman from having it read. He, however, strongly recommended its publication from such impressions he then received.† This the author had

* Extract from a letter from Professor Henry.

† This gentleman kindly offered to contribute from his own private means, to forward the publication, but he could do nothing officially without submitting the manuscript to three different censors. He who claims a new discovery, will seldom be satisfied to have it judged by

resolved on, from a sense of duty to the world at large, although the promise was rather of prospective loss than of present benefit. The peculiar form under which the theory appears, is, therefore, a result of the circumstances above stated, and of the author's present inability to enter into the minute details of a subject, which embraces in its range the whole visible creation.

In extending the theory to other phenomena, he has only fearlessly followed out the same principles which have conducted him to a knowledge of a disturbing cause, to which atmospheric storms owe their origin, and in doing so he has conferred with no one. For whatever of merit or of blame may therefore justly attach to these views, he alone is responsible. If he has charged the scientific with inconsistency, or with sometimes forgetting that the truth of their unnecessarily abstruse investigations depends on the truth of the data, he at least is conscientious; for he is too well aware that to provoke an unfavorable verdict by contending against such fearful odds, is not the surest way to either wealth or fame, or even to an acknowledgment of at least *the mite*, which he cannot but feel that he has contributed to the treasury of knowledge. That the scientific organizations of the day do tend to curb the aberrations of a fanciful philosophy, cannot be denied;

men who are engaged in the same investigations, however pure and honorable they may be. Is this Institution adopting the best plan of aiding truth, in its struggles against error? Should any man sit as judge in his own trial? If there had been a powerful Institution to stand between Galileo and the scientific of his day, his doctrines would not have been condemned, and the world would have been fifty years more in advance.

but at the same time there is engendered such a slavish subordination as checks the originality of thought, and destroys that perfect freedom from the trammels of system, so necessary to success in the pursuit of truth. Of such an influence the author explicitly asserts his entire independence.

In thus introducing his theory, the reader is forewarned that he will not find it dressed in the fascinating garb of the popular literature of the day, whose chief characteristic is to promise much when possessing little. It is, however, a plant of the author's own raising, unpropped, unpruned, with none of the delicate tendrils or graceful festoons of the trellissed vine; yet he flatters himself that its roots are watered by the springs of truth, and hopes that he who is in quest of *that*, will not find, amidst its many clusters, any fruit to set his teeth on edge.

MECHANICAL THEORY OF STORMS.

SECTION FIRST.

PRESENT STATE OF METEOROLOGY.

THE present state of the science of which we are about to treat, cannot be better defined than in the words of the celebrated Humboldt, who has devoted a long life to the investigation of this department of Physics. He says: "The processes of the absorption of light, the liberation of heat, and the variations in the elastic and electric tension, and in the hygrometric condition of the vast aërial ocean, are all so intimately connected together, that each individual meteorological process is modified by the action of all the others. The complicated nature of these disturbing causes, increases the difficulty of giving a full explanation of these involved meteorological phenomena; and likewise limits, or *wholly precludes* the possibility of that predetermination of atmospheric changes, which would be so important for horticulture, agriculture, and navigation, no less than for the comfort and enjoyment of life. Those who place the value of meteorology in this problematic species of prediction, rather than in the knowledge of the phenomena themselves, are firmly convinced that this branch of science, on account of which so many expeditions to distant mountainous regions have been undertaken, has not made any very considerable progress for centuries past. The confidence which they refuse to the physicist they yield to changes of the moon, and to certain days marked in the calender by the superstition of a by-gone age."

The charge thus skilfully repelled, contains, however, much truth; there has been no adequate return of the vast amount of labor and expense thus far devoted to this branch of knowledge. And it is not wonderful that the popular mind should expect a result which is so much in accordance with the wants of mankind. Who is there whose happiness, and health, and comfort, *and safety*, and prosperity, may not be more or less affected by reducing to law, the apparently irregular fluctuations of the weather, and the predetermination of the storm? To do this would be the crowning triumph of the age; and the present theory has pioneered the way for its speedy accomplishment.

ORIGINAL CONDITION OF THE EARTH.

That the present order of things had a beginning, is taught by every analogy around us, and as we have the glaring fact forced upon us, that our globe has experienced a far higher temperature on its surface than obtains at present, and moreover, as it is demonstrated beyond a cavil, that the interior is now of far higher temperature than is due to solar radiation, we are justified in concluding, not only that the condition of the interior of our globe is that of fusion, but that its original temperature was far higher than at present; so that the inference is allowable that there has been a time when the whole globe was *perhaps* in this state. But why should we stop here? There are three states of matter, the solid, the fluid, and the gaseous; and with this passing glance at the question, we will jump at once to the theory of La Place,—that not only our own globe, but the whole solar system, has been once in the nebulous state.

In justice to himself, the author ought to remark, that he

had reasoned his way up to this starting point, before even the name of La Place had reached his ears. He makes the remark in order to disclaim any desire to appropriate that which belongs to another; as he may innocently speak of things hereafter, the idea of which has occurred to others. It is not his intention here to say a word *pro* or *con* on the nebular hypothesis; it is sufficient to allude to the facts, that the direction of rotation and of revolution is the same for all the planets and satellites of our system; and that the planes on which these motions are performed, are nearly coincident. That this concordance is due to one common cause, no one acquainted with the theory of probabilities will pretend to deny.

GREAT OBJECT OF LA PLACE.

The science of Astronomy occupies a pre-eminent rank in the physical circle, not only on account of that dignity conferred upon it in the most remote antiquity, or as being the grand starting point—the earliest born of science—from whence we must contemplate the visible creation, if we would reduce its numerous details into one harmonious whole; but also on account of its practical fruits, of the value of which modern commerce is an instance. Accordingly we will glance at its past history. In the earliest ages there was no doubt a rational view entertained of the movements of the planets in space. From the Chaldeans to the Arabs, a belief prevailed, that space was filled with a pure ethereal fluid, whose existence probably did not rest on any more solid foundation than analogy or tradition. One hundred years after Copernicus had given to the world the true arrangements of our planetary system, Descartes advanced his theory of vortices in the ethereal medium, in which the planets were borne in orbits around the sun, and the satellites around their primaries. This idea retained its ground with various additions, until the Geometry of Newton reconciled the laws of Kepler with the existence of a power pertaining to matter, varying inversely as the squares of the distances, to which power he showed the weight of terrestial bodies was owing, and also the revolution of the moon about the earth. Since Newton's day, those deviations from the strict wording of Kepler's laws, have been referred to the same law, and the avowed object of the author of the "Mechanique Celeste," was to bring all the great phenomena of nature within the grasp of analysis, by referring them to one single principle, and one simple law. And in his Introduction to the Theory of the Moon, he remarks: "Hence it incontestibly follows, that the law of gravitation is the sole cause of the lunar inequalities."

BESSEL'S OPINION.

However beautiful the conception, it must be admitted that in its *à priori* aspect, it was not in accordance with human experience and analogy to anticipate a successful issue. In nature law re-acts upon law, and change induces change, through an almost endless chain of consequences; and it might be asked, why a simple law of matter should thus be exempt from the common lot? Why, in a word, there should be no intrinsic difference in matter, by which the gravitation of similar or dissimilar substances should be affected? But experiment has detected no such differences; a globe of lead and a globe of wood, of equal weight, attract contiguous bodies with equal force. It is evident, therefore, that if there be such differences, human means are not yet refined enough to detect them. Was the issue successful then? Generally speaking, we may say yes. But where there is a discrepancy between theory and observation, however small that may be, it shows there is still something wanting; and a high authority (Professor Bessel) says in relation to this: "But I think that the certainty that the theory based upon this law, *perfectly* explains all the observations, is not correctly inferred." We will not here enumerate the cases to which suspicion might be directed, neither will we more than just allude to the fact, that the Theory of Newton requires a vacuum, in order that the planetary motions may be mathematically exact, and permanent in their stability.

A VACUUM REQUIRED BY MODERN SYSTEMS.

Whatever may be the practical belief of the learned, their fundamental principles forbid the avowal of a plenum, although the undulatory theory of light renders a plenum necessary, and is so far virtually recognized by them, ~~and~~ a correction for resistance is applied to the Comet of Encke. Yet there has been no attempt made to reconcile these opposing principles, other than by supposing that the celestial regions are filled with an extremely rare and elastic fluid. That no definite view has been agreed on, is not denied, and Sir John Herschel speculates on the reality of a resisting medium, by suggesting questions that will ultimately have to be considered, as: "What is the law of density of the resisting medium which *surrounds* the sun? Is it in rest or in motion? If the latter, in what direction does it move?" In these queries he still clings to the idea of Encke, that the resistance is confined to the neighborhood of the sun and planets, like a ponderable fluid. But the most profound analyst the world has ever boasted, speaks less cautiously, (Poisson Rech.) "It is difficult to attribute, as is usually done, the incandescence of aërolites to friction against the molecules of the atmosphere, at an elevation above the earth where the density of the air is almost null. May we not suppose that the electric fluid, in a neutral condition, forms a kind of atmosphere, extending far beyond the mass of our atmosphere, yet *subject to terrestrial attraction*, yet *physically imponderable*, and, consequently, following our globe in its motion?" The incandescence of aërolites must, therefore, be owing to friction against the molecules of the electric fluid which forms an atmosphere around the globe. According to this view, some force keeps it there, yet it is not ponderable. As it is of limited extent, this is not the medium whose undulations brings to light the existence of the stars; neither is Encke's, nor Herschel's, nor any other resisting medium. Where shall we find the present established principles of science? If we grant the Newtonians a plenum, they still cling to attraction of *all matter* in some shape. If we confine them to a vacuum, they will virtually deny it. Is not this solemn trifling? How much more noble would it be to exhibit a little more tolerance, seeing that they themselves know not what to believe? We do not offer these remarks as argument, but merely as indications of that course of reasoning by which we conclude that the upholders of the present systems of science are not entitled to any other ground than the pure Newtonian basis of an interplanetary vacuum.

DIFFICULTIES OF THIS VIEW.

This, then, is the state of the case: Matter attracts matter directly as the mass, and inversely as the squares of the distances. This law is derived from the planetary motions; space is, consequently, a void; and, therefore, the power which gives mechanical momentum to matter, is transferred from one end of creation to the other, without any physical medium to convey the impulse. At the present day the doctrines of Descartes are considered absurd; yet here is an absurdity of a far deeper dye, without we resort to the miraculous, which at once obliterates the connection between cause and effect, which it is the peculiar province of physical science to develop. Let us take another view. The present doctrine of light teaches that light is an undulation of an elastic medium necessarily filling all space; and this branch of science probably rests on higher and surer grounds than any other. Every test applied to it by the refinements of modern skill, strengthens its claims. Here then the Newtonian vacuum is no longer a void. If we get over this difficulty, by attributing to this medium a degree of tenuity almost spiritual, we shall run upon Scylla while endeavoring to shun Charybdis. Light and heat come bound together from the sun, by the same path, and with the same velocity. Heat is therefore due also to an excitement of this attenuated medium. Yet this heat puts our atmosphere in motion, impels onward the waves of the sea, wafts our ships to distant climes, grinds our corn, and in various ways does the work of man. If we expose a mass of metal to the sun's rays for a single hour the temperature will be raised. To do the same by an artificial fire, would consume fuel, and this fuel would generate the strength or force of a horse. Estimate, therefore, the amount of force received from the sun in a single day for the whole globe, and we shall find that nothing but a material medium will suffice to convey this force.

Let us appeal to analogy. The undulations of our atmosphere produce sound; that is, convey to the ear a part of a mechanical force imparted to a solid body—a bell for instance. Let us suppose this force to equal one pound. On account of the elasticity of the bell, the whole of the force is not instantaneously imparted to the surrounding air; but the denser the air the sooner it loses its motion. In a dense fluid like water, the motion is imparted quickly, and the sound is not a ring but a click. If we diminish the density of the air, the loss of motion is retarded; so that we might conceive it possible, provided the bell could be suspended in a *perfect vacuum*, without a mechanical tie, and there was no friction to overcome from the rigidity of its particles, that the bell would vibrate forever, although its sound could never reach the ear. We see, therefore, that the mechanical effect in a given time, is owing to the density of the medium. But can we resort to such an analogy? Every discovery in the science confirms more and more the analogy between the motions of air and the medium of space; the angle of reflexion and incidence follows the same law in both; the law of radiation and interference; and if experiments were instituted, there can be but little doubt that sound has also got its spectrum.

ETHER IMPONDERABLE.

The medium of space, therefore, is capable of conveying a mechanical force from one body to another; it therefore possesses inertia. Does it also possess gravity? If we forsake not the principles of science, it is but right that we expect science shall abide by her own principles. Condensation in every elastic medium is as the compressing power, according to all experiments. In the case of our atmosphere under the law of gravitation, the density of air, (supposing it to be infinitely expansible,) at a height only of ten semidiameters of the earth above its surface, would have only a density equal to the density of one cubic inch of such air we breathe, if that cubic inch was to be expanded so as to fill a globular space whose centre should be the earth, and whose surface should take inside the whole visible creation. Such a medium could convey no mechanical force from the sun, and therefore the medium of space cannot be ponderable. Simple as the argument is, it is unassailable.

ELECTRIC FLUID THE MEDIUM OF SPACE.

Let us take yet another view. All experiments prove that the phenomenon we call electricity, is owing to a disturbance of the equilibrium or natural condition of a highly elastic fluid. In certain conditions of the atmosphere, this fluid is accumulated in the region of the clouds, and by its tension is enabled to force a passage through opposing obstacles, in order to restore the equilibrium. By experiment it is found that dry dense air opposes the greatest obstacle to its escape. As the air is rarefied, this obstacle diminishes, until in a vacuum the transmission may be considered instantaneous. There ought to be, therefore, a greater escape of electricity from the clouds upwards than downwards; and, if space be void, or only filled with an extremely attenuated matter, the electricity of the earth, considered as an elastic fluid without ponderosity, (and no law of condensation from the law of gravity in harmony with its other attributes, will allow us to consider it otherwise,) *would long since have left the earth.* The same objection applies in the case of the galvanic and magnetic fluids. If we entertain the idea that electricity is a mere disturbance of natural condition, wherein two fluids are united, and that an excess of one is necessarily attended by deficiency in the other, we depart from the first rule of philosophy, which teaches us to admit no greater number of causes than are sufficient to explain the phenomenon. For we fearlessly assert that not a single fact exists in electrical science, which can be explained better on Dufoy's theory than on Franklin's; and the former objections would still apply.

NEWTONIAN GRAVITY.

But what is gravity? According to Newton: "Hæc est qualitas omnium in quibus experimenta instituere licet, et propterea per Reg. 3 de universes affirmanda est." *Vide* Prin. Lib. Ter. Cor. 2. Prop. vi.

Now the other primary qualities of matter are unaffected by circumstances. The inertia of a particle of matter is the same at Jupiter as on the earth, so also is its extension; but not so with gravity. It depends on other matter, and on its distance from it; and may be less or greater at different times, and in different places. It is, therefore, not philosophical to say that all matter is necessarily ponderous, inasmuch as it is a virtue not residing in itself alone, but needs the existence of other matter to call it into action. If an atom were isolated in space it would have no weight. If influenced by other matter, there must be some physical medium to convey the influence, or gravity is not in accordance with the laws of force and motion. Which horn of the dilemma shall we take? Let us first admit that there is a principle of gravitation, affecting all planetary or atomic matter, and that there exists a highly elastic medium, pervading all space, conveying to us the light of the most distant stars, and that this medium is not affected by gravity. In this summary way, therefore, we have arrived at the pivot on which this theory turns.

The prominent feature of the theory, therefore, is the necessity it will show for the existence of an all-pervading medium, and that it possesses inertia without ponderosity. That electricity is nothing more than the effects of the condensation and rarefaction of this medium by force. That it also pervades all atomic matter, whose motions necessarily move the medium; and, consequently, that there can be no motion without some degree of electricity. That no change can take place in bodies either by chemical decomposition, by increase or decrease of temperature, by friction or contact, without in some measure exciting electricity or motion of the ether. That galvanism and magnetism are but ethereal currents without condensation, induced by peculiar superficial and internal molecular arrangement of the particles of certain substances. That light and heat are effects of the vibrations of atoms, propagated through this universal medium from body to body. That the atomic motion of heat can be produced by the motion of translation or momentum of bodies in the gross, that is, by friction, by compression, &c.; and can be reconverted into momentum at our pleasure. Hence the latent heat or specific atomic motion of combustibles, originally derived from the sun, is transferred to atoms, which are capable of being inclosed in cylinders, so as to make use of their force of expansion, which is thus converted into momentum available for all the wants of man.

GRAVITY MECHANICAL.

When we come to a full examination of this theory, we shall further reason that this *ether*, so far from being of that quasi spiritual nature which astronomers would have us believe, is a fearfully energetic fluid, possessing considerable inertia and elasticity; that its law of condensation is that of all other fluids, that is, as the compressing force directly; and that its effects are simply a product of matter and motion. We will next endeavor to prove that the gravity of planetary matter could not exist without this ethereal medium, by showing that it is an effect produced by the interference of *opposing waves*, whereby a body is prevented from radiating into space its own atomic motion, from the side opposite which another body is placed, as much as on the opposite side, and consequently it is propelled by its own motion towards the other body. And this effect following the simple law of inertia and radiation, is directly as the mass, and inversely as the squares of the distances.

GREAT PRINCIPLE OF DYNAMICS.

One great principle to be kept in view in this investigation, is that which teaches that the product of matter, angular velocity, and distance from the centre of motion, must ever be a constant quality in every balanced system. Yet this principle does not seem to be observed in the case of the planets. We will, however, endeavor to show that it is rigidly observed. And we will extend the principle further, and contend that all the phenomena of nature are consequences of the constant tendency of matter to conform to this principle of equilibrium, when suffering temporary derangement from the operation of other laws. That throughout the system of nature, equal spaces possess equal force. That what we call temperature, is nothing more than the motion of equilibrium or atomic momentum of space; or, in other words, that if all space were fluid, and in a state of equilibrium, the product of each atom of equal volume, by its motion would be a constant quality. From this it would seem to follow, that the specific heat of bodies should be inversely as their atomic weights; and this does, no doubt, *approximately* obtain as was proved by Dulong and Petit, for metallic substances, more recently by Regnault, and has since been extended by Garnier to other substances. But it is to the gaseous state that we must look for confirmation of the principle that equal spaces possess equal power; and in doing so, it will be necessary to bear in mind, that the ether also is affected by temperature.

SPECIFIC HEAT.

It has been contended by some that the medium which conveys the impression of light through transparent bodies, is necessarily more dense within the body than without; but according to this theory the converse is true. A ray of light is a mechanical impulse, propagated through an elastic medium, and, like a wave in water, tends to the side of least resistance. Within a refracting body the ether is rarefied, not only by the proximity of the atoms of the body (or its density), but also by the motions of those atoms; so that if two *simple* gases of different specific gravity be made equal in density by compression, their refraction will be approximately as their specific heats. In the case of solids and liquids, or even compound gases, there is a continual absorption of motion to produce the cohesion of composition and aggregation. And the specific heats of compound gases will be found greater than those of simple gases, in proportion to the loss of volume by combination, *ceteris paribus.* If impenetrability be a law of matter, the more a portion of atomic matter is condensed, the less ether will be found in the same space. The same is also true when the natural density or specific gravity of a gas is greater than that of another. And the lighter the gas, the more will this circumstance vitiate the experiments to determine its specific heat. There is, therefore, this great source of fallacy in such experiments, viz.: that the ether permeates all fluids and solids, and that *its specific heat probably far exceeds that of all other matter.* This is a fundamental position of the theory, in support of which we will introduce a fact announced by M. V. Regnault, which was published in the Comptes Rendus of the French Academy for April, 1853. He says: "In the course of my researches I have encountered, indeed, at every step, anomalies which appeared to me inexplicable, in accordance with the theories formally recognized. For the sake of illustration I will quote one instance: 1st, a mass of gas, under a pressure of ten atmospheres, is contained in a space which is suddenly doubled; the pressure falls to five atmospheres. 2d. Two reservoirs of equal capacity are placed in a calorimeter; the one is filled with a gas, under a pressure of ten atmospheres; the second is perfectly empty. In these two experiments, the initial and final conditions of the gas are the same; but this identity of condition is accompanied by calorific results which are very different; for while in the former experiment there is a reduction of temperature, in the second the calorimeter does not indicate the slightest alteration of temperature." This experiment tends to confirm the theory. In the first experiment, the sudden doubling of the space causes the either also to expand, inasmuch as the sides of the vessel prevent the instantaneous passage of the external ether. In the second, both vessels are full, one of ether, and the other of air mixed with ether; so that there is no actual expansion of the space, and consequently no derangement of the quantity of motion in that space.

2

LAW OF SPECIFIC HEAT.

From this view it is evident that the specific heat of elastic fluids can only be considered as approximately determined. If equal spaces possess equal momenta, and the ethereal or *tomic* matter be inversely as the weight of the atomic matter in the same space, it follows that the product of the specific gravities and specific heats of the simple gases should be constant; or that the specific heats should be inversely as the specific gravities,—taking pound for pound in determining those specific heats. If we test the matter by the data now afforded, it is best to obey the injunction, "*In medio tutissimus ibis.*" In the following table, the first column are the values obtained by Reynault; in the second, the former values; and in the third, the mean of the two.

Gases.	Reg. specific heats.	Former specific heats.	Mean.
Atmospheric air,	.237	.267	.252
Oxygen,	.218	.236	.227
Nitrogen,	.244	.275	.260
Hydrogen,	3.405	3.294	3.350

The specific gravities of these gases, according to the best tables in our possession, are:

	Specific gravities.		Mean.		Products.
Atmospheric air,	1.0000	×	.252	=	.252
Oxygen,	1.1111	×	.227	=	.252
Nitrogen,	0.9722	×	.260	=	.252
Hydrogen,	0.0745	×	3.350	=	.249

As might be expected, there is a greater discrepancy in the case of hydrogen.

If we test the principle by the vapor of water, we must consider that it is composed of two volumes of hydrogen and one volume of oxygen, and that one volume disappears; or that one-third of the whole atomic motion is consumed by the interference of the vibrations of the ether, necessary to unite the atoms, and form an atom of water. We must therefore form this product from its specific gravity and two-thirds of its specific heat. On no one subject in chemistry has there been so much labor expended, as in determining the specific heat of watery vapor. In relation to this, Regnault observes: "It is important to remark that an immense number of experiments have been made, to find the specific heat of steam, and that it is about one-half of what it was thought to be." He gives its value .475; but this is vitiated still, by the non-recognition of the specific heat of the ether. Former experiments give .847. Perhaps Regnault's numbers are entitled to the most weight. Instead of taking the mean, therefore, we will give double weight to his results; so that we get .600 for the specific heat of vapor, and as its specific gravity is .625, the product $.400 \times .625$ is .250, the same as for hydrogen. Little importance, however, should be attached to such coincidences, owing to the uncertainty of the numbers. If our position be correct, the specific heat of hydrogen should be 16 times greater than of oxygen. The atomic weights are as 1 to 8, while their volumes are as 2 to 1; therefore, for equal spaces, the matter is as 1 to 16. Calling the specific heat 16 to 1, and taking the amount due to half the space, the product becomes as 8 to 16; but in the rarer gas there is 8 *times* as much ethereal momentum or matter, which, added to the atomic matter, renders the spaces equal.* Reynault's results give a ratio of specific heats = 1 to $\frac{3.405}{.218}$ = 1 to 15.6.

* The specific heat of the ether being a constant factor, it may be divided out.

THE GOLDEN MEAN.

The history of science proves how few have practically respected the adage of the ancients, which we have chosen for our motto; words which ought to be written in letters of gold in every language under the sun. Descartes, by considering the mechanical impulse of the ether sufficient to explain the planetary motions, failed to detect the force of gravity in the heavens. Newton, on the other hand, feeling that his law was sufficient to explain them, and requiring a vacuum for its mathematical accuracy, rejected the notion of an ethereal medium. His successors, following too closely in his footsteps, and forgetting the golden law, have forced themselves into a position by no means enviable. The short-period comet has driven them to a resisting medium, which, while according to Encke's hypothesis of increasing density around the sun, it explains the anomalies of one periodical comet, requires a different law of density for another, and a negative resistance for a third.

OUTLINES OF THE PROBLEM.

From the position we now occupy, we can see the outlines of the problem before us, viz.: To reconcile the existence of an ethereal medium with the law of gravitation, and to show the harmony between them. We shall thus occupy the middle ground, and endeavor to be just to the genius of Descartes, without detracting from the glory of Newton, by demonstrating the reality of the Cartesian vortices, and by showing that the ether is not affected by gravitation, but on the other hand is *least dense* in the centre of our system. But what (it may be asked) has this to do with the theory of storms? Much every way. And we may so far anticipate our subject as to *assert* that every phenomenon in meteorology where force is concerned, is dependent on the motions of the great sea of electric fluid which surrounds us, in connection with its great specific, caloric. If we are chargeable with overweening pretensions, let it be attributed to the fact that for the last fifteen years we have treated the weather as an astronomical phenomenon, calculated by simple formulæ, and that the evidence of its truth has been almost daily presented to us, so as to render it by this time one of the most familiar and palpable of all the great fundamental laws of nature. True, we have neither had means nor leisure to render the theory as perfect as we might have done, the reason of which we have already communicated.

MOTIONS OF THE STARS.

In investigating the question now before us, we shall first take the case of an ethereal vortex without any reference to the ponderable bodies which it contains, considering the ether to possess only inertia. If there be a vortex around the sun, it is of finite extent; for if the ether be co-extensive with space, and the stars likewise suns with surrounding vortices, the solar vortex cannot be infinite. That there is an activity in the heavens which the mere law of attraction is incompetent to account for, is an admitted fact. The proper motions of the fixed stars have occupied the attention of the greatest names in astronomy, and motions have been detected, which according to the theory of gravity, requires the admission of invisible masses of matter in their neighborhood, compared with which the stars themselves are insignificant. But this is not the only difficulty. No law of arrangement in the stars can exist that will save the Stellar system from ultimate destruction. The case assumed by Sir John Herschel, of a cluster, wherein the periods shall be equal, cannot be made to fulfil the conditions of being very numerous, without infringing the other condition—the non-intersection of their orbits; while the outside stars would have to obey another law of gravitation, and consequently would be still more liable to derangement from their ever-changing distances from each other, and from those next outside; in brief, the stability of those stars composing the cluster would necessarily depend on the existence of outside stars, and plenty of them. But these outside stars would follow the common law of gravity, and must ultimately bring ruin on the whole. We know such clusters do exist in the heavens, and that the law of gravity alone must bring destruction upon them. This is a case wherein modern science has been instrumental in drawing a veil over the fair proportions of nature. That such collections of stars are not designed thus to derange the order of nature, proves *à priori*, that some other conservative principle must exist; that the medium of space must contain many vortices—eddies, as it were, in the great ethereal ocean, whose currents are sweeping along the whole body of stars. We shall consider, (as a faint shadowing of the glorious empire of Omnipotence,) that the whole infinite extent of space is full of motion and power to its farthest verge; and it may be an allowable stretch of the imagination to conceive that the whole comprises one infinite cylindrical vortex, whose axis is the only thing in the universe in a state of absolute unchangeableness.

VORTICOSE MOTION.

Let us for a moment admit the idea of an infinite ocean of fluid matter, having inertia without gravity, and rotating around an infinite axis. In this case there is nothing to counteract the effect of the centrifugal force. The elasticity of the medium would only oppose resistance in a vortex of finite diameter. Where it is infinite, each cylindrical layer is urged outward by its own motion, and impelled also by those behind. The result would be that all the fluid would at last have left the axis, around which would exist an absolute and eternal void; into which neither sound, nor light, nor aught material, could enter.

The case of a finite vortex is very different. However great the velocity of rotation, and the tendency of the central parts to recede from the axis, there would be an inward current down either pole, and meeting at the equatorial plane to be thence deflected in radii. But this radiation would be general from every part of the axis, and would be kept up as long as the rotation continued. If the polar currents can supply the drain of the radial stream, that is, if the axis of the vortex is not too long for the velocity of rotation and the elasticity of the ether, there will be no derangement of the density, only a tendency. And in this case the periodic times of the parts of the vortex will be directly as the distances from the axis, and the absolute velocities will be equal.

FORMATION OF VORTICES.

There is reason to suspect that Newton looked at this question with a jaundiced eye. To do it justice, we must consider the planetary matter in a vortex, as the exponent of its motion, and not as originating or directing it. If planetary matter becomes involved in any vortex, it introduces the law of gravitation, which counteracts the expulsive force of the radial stream, and is thus enabled to retain its position in the centre. A predominating mass in the centre will, by its influence, retain other masses of matter at a distance from the centre, even when exposed to the full power of the radial stream. If the power of the central mass is harmoniously adjusted to the rotation of the vortex, (and the co-existence of the phenomena is itself the proof that such an adjustment does obtain,) the two principles will not clash or interfere with each other. Or in other words, that whatever might have been the initial condition of the solar vortex, the ultimate condition was necessarily one of equilibrium, or the system of the planets would not now exist. With this view of its constitution, we must consider that the periodic times of the planets approximately correspond to the times of the contiguous parts of the vortex. Consequently, in the solar vortex, the density of the ether is directly as the square roots of the distances from the axis. This is not the place fully to enter into a discussion of the question, or to show that the position of each planet in the system is due to the outstanding, uncompensated, portion of the expulsive force of the radial stream, modified by the density of the ether within the planets, and also by their own densities, diameters, inclinations of axis, and periods of rotation. That Jupiter could not remain in the orbit of Mercury, nor Mercury in that of Jupiter, by merely exchanging periods and distances, but that each planet can only be in equilibrio in its own orbit. That any change in the eccentricities of the planetary orbits will neither increase nor diminish the action of the radial stream of the vortex, and consequently will not interfere with the law of gravitation. In relation to the numerous questions that will spring up from such a position, it is sufficient here to say, that it is believed all objections can be satisfactorily answered; while, by this light, a long range of phenomena that have hitherto baffled the sagacity of the wise, come out plainly, and discover their parentage.

In cometary astronomy we shall find much to substantiate these views. The anomalies in their motions, the discrepancies in their periods, calculated from different sets of observations, their nebulosities and appendages, will all receive a satisfactory solution; and these lawless wanderers of the deep be placed in a more interesting light.

TEST OF A THEORY.

It has been remarked that the best evidence of the truth of a theory, is its ability to refer to some general principle, the greatest number of relevant phenomena, that, like the component masses of the chiselled arch, they may mutually bind and strengthen each other. This we claim to be the characteristic of this theory. At the outset it was not intended to allude to more than was actually necessary to give an outline of the theory, and to introduce the main question, yet untouched. We have exhibited the stones of which the arch is composed; but they may be pasteboard,—for the reader has not handled them. We will now produce the keystone, and put it in its place. This he shall handle and weigh. He will find it hard,—a block of granite, cut from the quarry of observed facts, and far too heavy to be held in its place by a mere pasteboard structure.

ENUNCIATION OF THE THEORY.

Quitting, therefore, the region of the planets, we will come down to the surface of our own globe, to seek for some more palpable evidence of the truth of the following propositions:

1st. That space is filled with an elastic fluid, possessing inertia without weight.

2d. That the parts of this fluid in the solar system circulate, after the manner of a vortex, with a direct motion.

3d. That there are also secondary vortices, in which the planets are placed.

4th. That the earth is also placed in a vortex of the ethereal medium.

5th. That the satellites are passively carried around their primaries, with the ethereal current, and have no rotation relative to the ether, and therefore they always present the same face to their primaries, and have no vortex.

The consideration of these propositions involves many others, many difficulties, many apparent anomalies and contradictions, which should bespeak for such a theory,—the offspring of observation, without the aid afforded by the knowledge of others, and of toil without leisure,—a large share of indulgence. With this we will close these preliminary remarks, and present our theory of the physical cause which disturbs the equilibrium of our atmosphere, and which appears the principal agent in the production of storms, in the following words :

The dynamical axis of the terral vortex passes through the centre of gravity of the earth and moon, and is continually circulating over the earth's surface in both hemispheres, in a spiral,—its latitude and longitude, at any particular time, being dependent,—

1st. On the relative mass of the moon.

2d. On the inclination of the axis of the vortex to the earth's axis.

3d. On the longitude of the ascending node of the vortex on the lunar orbit.

4th. On the longitude of the ascending node of the lunar orbit on the ecliptic.

5th. On the eccentricity of the lunar orbit at the time.

6th. On the longitude of the perigee of the lunar orbit at the time.

7th. On the moon's true anomaly at the time.

MASS OF THE MOON.

Those elements which represent the moon's distance and motion are accurately known, and may be taken from the Nautical Almanac, being all embodied in the moon's parrallax or semi-diameter, and in the declination and right ascension ; but for the most important element,—the moon's mass, we in vain look to astronomy. In fact, it may be averred that the importance attached to astronomical authority, concerning the mass of the moon, has caused more trouble than any other question of the whole theory, until we trusted implicitly to the theory itself to determine it. The determination of three unknown elements, viz. : the moon's mass, the inclination of the axis of the vortex, and the right ascension of that axis, is a more difficult problem than at first sight appears, owing to the nature of the phenomena, which affords the only clue for its solution. There are six principal vortices ever in operation on the surface of the earth, and their disturbing influence extends from 200 to 400 miles. To find the precise centre, by one observer confined to one place, is difficult; and to separate them, so as to be fully assured that you have the right one, is perhaps still more so. Happily this tedious labor is accomplished, and we are able with confidence to give the following important elements, as very close approximations to the truth :

Mass of the moon	$\frac{1}{72.3}$
Obliquity of the axis of the vortex .	15° to 32° variable.
Right ascension of ditto	250° to 290° variable.

It must be borne in mind that we are now discussing the main or central vortex of the earth; but before applying them to the calculation, we will explain the *modus operandi*, waving for the present the consideration of the law of density in the Terral vortex. It is evident at first sight that if the periodic times of the parts of the vortex contiguous to the moon, are equal to the moon's period approximately, that the velocity of the ether is greater at the surface of the earth than the velocity of that surface. Now, we have before argued that the ether possesses inertia, it therefore would under such circumstances exert some mechanical action. Consequently, the aërial envelope of our globe, or its superior stratum, is impelled eastward by *convection** of the more rapidly rotating ether. And from the extreme tenuity of its upper layers, is probably forced into immense waves, which will observe to a certain degree, a general paralellism north and south.

* A term adopted by Prof. Faraday to denote the mode in which bodies are carried along by an electrical current.

ATMOSPHERIC CURRENTS.

It is a well-known fact, that the prevailing current of the atmosphere in high latitudes is from the westward. The cause of this is ascribed by Professor Dove to the transfer of the equatorial portions to a higher latitude, by which the excess of its rotative velocity is made apparent, by outstripping the slower moving surface in its progress eastward. No doubt some effect is due to this, but still a difficulty remains. Let us follow this current. The polar current reaches the surface on the borders of the trades with less rotative velocity than the surface, and is, therefore, met by the surface as a current partaking of both motions. In the northern hemisphere it is north-east deflected to east as it approaches the southern trades. By the same reasoning, coming from the north before it reaches the surface, it ought to be also a north-east wind above the lower westerly currents. Now it is an observed fact, that while in the latitude of New York, for instance, the lower westerly winds are to the easterly, as 3 or 4 to 1, in the highest regions of observed clouds, the ratio is much increased; and according to our own observations in this place,* we have never seen the highest cirrus clouds moving westward. How then is this continual interchange kept up? Assuredly we cannot have a current from the poles without a contrary current to the poles. If we go into the arctic circle, we again find the westerly and northerly winds predominating. If the current from the equator follows the surface, the westerly winds ought to be south-west. If it be above the surface wind, then the surface wind is the polar current, and ought to be north-east. Whereas, from the testimony of all who have visited these regions, the prevailing winds are north-west. How can this be?

Again, it is proved that the upper current near the equator is also from the westward—as near due west as possible. Take

* Ottawa, Ill.

the latitude of St Vincent. The difference between the cosein of 13° and radius applied to the circumference, is about 600 miles, which would give 25 miles per hour to the eastward, in lat. 13°. But to do this, it is necessary to transfer it suddenly from the equator; for by a slow motion the easterly tendency would be lost. Give it 24 hours from the equator to lat. 13°, without any loss of easterly tendency, and it comes to that latitude with a velocity of 38 miles per hour to the northward, and only 25 to the eastward; we have, therefore, a wind from south-west by south. Yet it is known that in the tropics the highest visible clouds move from the westward. But as no such case could occur as a transfer in twenty-four hours without loss, and if we diminish the time, the wind is still more southerly. Meteorologists usually cite the falling of ashes at Jamaica during the eruption of Coseguina, in Guatamala, in February 1835, as coming from south-west, whereas the true direction was about west south-west, and the trade wind below was about north. But do we deny that there is an interchange between the frigid and torrid zones? By no means; but we would show that the great controlling power is external to our atmosphere, and that the relative velocities of the earth and the atmosphere is not alone adequate to account for it. By this view the polar current is a north-west wind (which is impossible by Professor Dove's theory), or is carried eastward by electric convection.

HUTTON'S THEORY,

Whether we adopt the views of Fourier or Poullet, as to the temperature of the planetary spaces, it is certain that it is at least equal to, or less than, the lowest temperature of our globe. It is also a well-known fact, that the capacity of air to hold vapor in solution, increases in a higher ratio than the temperature, so that the intermingling of saturated portions of air, at different temperatures, must *necessarily* be attended by precipitation of moisture. This idea was advanced by Doctor Hutton, and considered competent to account for the prominent meteorological phenomena, until Professor Espy broached a questionable principle, (and which is rendered still more so by the late investigations of Regnault,) in opposition to Hutton's theory. That the theory is deficient, no one can gainsay. That Espy has rendered the question clearer, is equally hazardous to assert. Hutton failed in showing a cause for such intermingling on a sufficient scale; while Espy, it may be suspected, has misinterpreted facts, and incautiously rejected the only element possessing the power of raising the storm.

GREAT SPECIFIC HEAT OF THE ETHER.

Whatever may be the degree of condensation or rarefaction in the terral vortex, there must necessarily be a current down the pole or axis, thence to be deflected along the equatorial plane of the vortex, and this drain will be as perpetual as the rarefaction of the centre, (caused by the centrifugal force of rotation,) which calls it forth. It will now be perceived that the fluid of the vortex, which we shall still term ether, is neither more nor less than the electric fluid,—the mighty energising principle of space,—the source of motion,—the cause of magnetism, galvanism, light, heat, gravity, of the aurora, the lightning, the zodiacal light, of the tails and nebulosities of comets, of the great currents of our atmosphere, of the samiel, the hurricane, and the earthquake. It will be perceived that we treat it as any other fluid, in relation to its law of motion and condensation. But we have no right to base our calculations on its resistance, by the analogies presented by ponderable or atomic matter. Atomic fluids,—even pure air, may be considered viscid and tenacious when compared to an infinitely divisible fluid, between whose particles (if we may use the term) no *attraction* of any kind exists. No ponderable matter can come in close contact without feeling the influence of the gravitating force which, at insensible distances,—such as the breadth of a wave of ether, is increased in power, and becomes a cohering and combining force. We contend that this fluid is the only fluid of space; when condensed it is positive, and seeks to escape; when rarefied it is negative, and receives from the contiguous space a restoration of its power. That it can give and receive, from planetary matter, what we call motion; and consequently can affect the temperature of such matter, and be in turn affected by it. And finally that, for its degree of inertia, it exceeds in elasticity and specific heat all other matter.

PROCESS OF DERANGEMENT.

This premised, we see that as the axis of the vortex traverses the surface of the earth, there is a tendency to derange the electric state of the parts travelled over, by bringing the atmosphere and surface of the earth under the rarefied centre of the vortex. For it is not the ether of the atmosphere alone that is affected. It is called forth from the earth itself, and partakes of the temperature of the crust,—carrying up into the upper regions the vapor-loaded atmosphere of the surface. The weather now feels close and warm; even in winter there is a balmy change in the feelings. The atmosphere then fills with haze, even to the highest regions of the clouds; the clouds themselves are ill defined; generally the wind comes in at E. S-E., or S., getting very fresh by the time it chops round to W. In from six to twelve hours from the time of the meridian passage, in this latitude, the Big Cumuli have formed, and commenced their march eastward. In summer time there is always thunder and lightning, when the passage is attended or followed by a storm. In winter, generally, but not always. In summer, the diameter of the storm is contracted; in winter, dilated; in consequence of this, summer is the best season to trace the vortices of the earth through their revolutions. Let us now attend a little to the results. The ether of the surface atmosphere partakes of the temperature of that atmosphere, so also the ether of the earth's crust partakes of the temperature of the crust; and its escape is rapid, compared with the ascent of the air. When it arrives at the colder layers of air above, its temperature sinks, and, on account of the greater specific caloric, it imparts a much higher temperature to those layers than is due to their position; an elevation consequently takes places,—begetting a drain from below, until the upper regions are loaded with a warm and vapory atmosphere. If the action of the sun conspires at the same time to increase the effect, the storm will be more violent. In twelve hours after the meridian passage of the vortex, the storm is brought under the parts of the ethereal atmosphere of the earth most remote from the axis; a reaction now takes place; the cold ether of space rushes in, and, on account of its great specific caloric, it abstracts from the warm atmosphere more than pertains to the difference of temperature, and there is a great condensation. Rain and hail may form in fearful quantities; and when the equilibrium is restored, the temperature will have fallen many degrees.

As it is important that we should have a clear view of the character of the ether, we will revert to the principle we have advocated, viz.: that in equal spaces there are equal momenta. What the ether wants in inertia, is made up by its motion or specific heat, considering in this case inertia to stand for weight when compared with ponderable matter; so that to raise an equivalent amount of inertia of ether to the same temperature as atmospheric air, will require as much more motion or specific heat as its matter is less. And this we conceive to be a law of space in relation to all free or gaseous matter. To apply it to solids would require a knowledge of the amount of force constituting the cohesion of the solid.

INFLUENCE OF DIMINISHED PRESSURE.

But there is another principle which modifies these effects. We have already adverted to the action of the tangential current of the vortex forcing the outer layers of the atmosphere into waves. These waves will be interfered with by the different vortices, sometimes being increased and sometimes diminished by them.* If these waves are supposed very wide, (which would be the case in the attenuated outside layers of the atmosphere,) the action of the vortex will be greater in its passage over a place, which at the time corresponded to the depression point of the wave, that is, to the line of low barometer; because here there would be less resistance to overcome in the passage of the ether from the surface of the earth into space; so that we may conceive each vortex making a line of storms each day around the earth, separated by less disturbed intervals. After the formation of the storm, it of course has nothing to do with the vortex that produced it; it travels in the general direction of the local atmosphere of the place—in intratropical latitudes westward, in extratropical latitudes eastward. If, therefore, the disturbance forms at the place of observation, there will probably be no storm; but further eastward its action would be more apparent or violent. It is impossible, of course, to lay down any general description which shall meet every case. It is a knowledge that can only be acquired by observation, and then is not readily or easily communicated. There are many contingencies to be allowed for, and many modifying causes to keep sight of, to enter into which would only be tedious; we shall, therefore, confine ourselves to the prominent phenomena.

* The principal cause of these waves is, no doubt, due to the vortices, and the eastern progress of the waves due to the rotating ether; but, at present, it will not be necessary to separate these effects.

ACTION OF THE POLAR CURRENT.

We have seen how the passage of the axis of the vortex may derange the electric tension of the parts passed over; but there is another mode of action not yet adverted to.

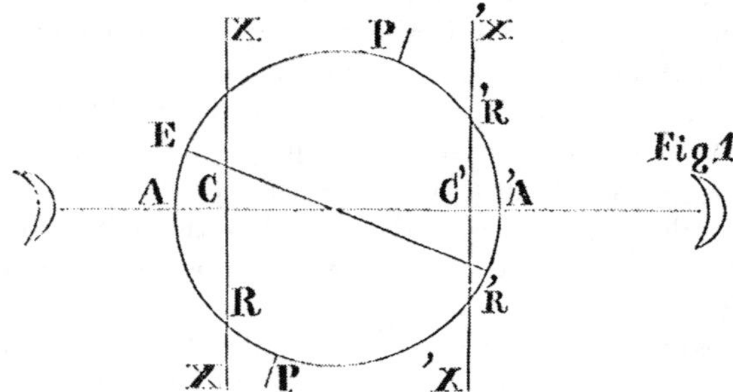

When the moon is at her perigee, the axis of the vortex passes through the centre of gravity of the earth and moon at C, and cuts off the segment R R. At the apogee, on account of her greater distance, and of her consequent power to *push* the earth out from the axis of the vortex X X, the segment R′ R′ is only cut off by the axis; and the angle which the axis makes with the surface will vary with the arcs A R and A′ R′; for these arcs will measure the inclination from the nature of the circle. In passing from the perigee to the apogee the axis will pass over the latitudes intermediate between R and R′ in both hemispheres, neither reaching to the equator E, nor to the pole P. Let us now suppose a meridian of the earth, represented by the line N R S, N being north, and S south, and the surface of the atmosphere by N′ S′; X X still representing the axis of the vortex, ordinarily inclined 34° or 35° to the surface. Let us also conceive the rotation of the earth to cease, (the action of the vortex remaining the same,) thus leaving the axis over a particular longitude. If the ether possesses inertia, there will be an actual

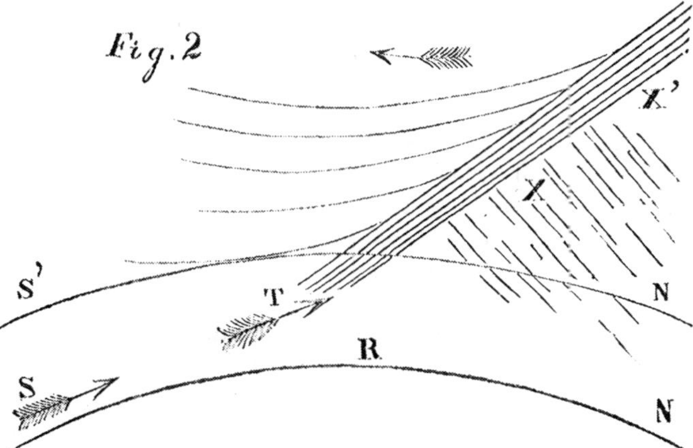

scooping out of the upper portions, driving them southward to a certain distance, where the atmosphere will be piled up above the ordinary level. There will, therefore, be a strong contrary current at the surface of the earth to restore the equilibrium, and if the action be violent, the surface wind will be increased; so that if it be considered tangential to the surface at S, its own momentum will tend to make it leave the surface and mount up to T; and in this way increase the action due to the ether. Now, although the axis is never stationary, but travels round the earth in less than twenty-five hours, yet there is a tendency to this mode of action; and it is even sometimes palpable to the observer when the axis has passed immediately to the northward; for the pinnate shafts and branching plumes of the cirri often reach far to the south of the southern boundary of the storm. These shafts are always longer when radiating from the northward than when proceeding from the southward. The cause is understood by the above figure. At such a time, after dark, the auroral shafts will also be seen over the storm to the northward, but will be invisible to those beneath. There is this to be observed, however, that the visibility of the ethereal current (or the aurora) is more frequent when the passage of the vortex is not attended with any great commotion, its free passage being perhaps obstructed by too dry an atmosphere; hence it becomes more visible. But it may be asserted that a great aurora is never seen except when a vortex is near, and to the northward, and within a few hours of its passage over the meridian. We have, however, seen partial auroras to the south when none existed north, and also cases when the radiation was from west, but they are never as bright as in the north. They are all due, however, to the same cause; and we have frequently followed a vortex for three days to the northward, (that is, seen the effects of its meridian passage,) at 700 miles distance, by the aurora, and even by the lightning, which proves plainly that the *exterior layers* of our atmosphere can reflect a flash of lightning, assisted by the horizontal refraction, otherwise the curvature of the earth would sink it ten miles below the horizon.

LIMITS OF THE VORTEX.

The action of the polar current of the ether, therefore, tends to cause a depression of the barometer, and an elevation to the *northward* and southward, and there is a general set of the wind below to the point of greatest depression. The action of the tangential current works the outer surface of the atmosphere into great ridges and hollows, whose distances apart as well as actual dimensions, are continually changing under the influences of causes not yet alluded to, and it is in the hollows where the action of the polar current will be principally expended. Luckily for the earth, the axis of the vortex is never long in passing over any particular place. In this latitude, whose natural cosine is three-fourths, the velocity *westward* is over 700 miles per hour; but at its extreme limits north, the motion is much slower, and is repeated for two or three days in nearly the same latitude, for then it begins to return to the south; thus oscillating in about one sidereal period of the moon. At its southern limit, the vortex varies but slowly in latitude for the same time, but the velocity is much greater. The extreme latitudes vary at different times with the eccentricity of the lunar orbit, with the place or longitude of the perigree, and with the longitude of the moon's ascending node, but in no case can the *central vortex* reach within 5° of the equator, or higher than about 75° of latitude north or south. Hence there are no storms strictly speaking beyond 83°* of latitude; although a storm may be raging close by, at the turning point south, and draw in a very strong gale from the northward with a clear sky above. So also, although rains and short squalls may be frequent in the vapor-loaded atmosphere of the equator, yet the hurricane does not reach there, owing to the adjustment of the mass and distance of the moon, and the inclination of the axes of the vortices to the axis of the earth. If the temperature of the upper limit or highest latitude of the vortex, was equal to the temperature which obtains at its lowest limit, and the daily extremes of the solar influence as great, the hurricanes would be as violent at the one as the other, and even more so on account of the smaller velocity. But the deficiency of temperature and moisture, (which last is all-important,) prevents the full development of the effect. And even in the tropics, the progress of the sun, by its power in directing the great annual currents of the atmosphere, only conspires in the summer and autumn months, to bring an atmosphere in the track of the vortices, possessing the full degree of moisture and deficiency of electric tension, to produce the derangement necessary to call forth the hurricane in its greatest activity.

* The inner vortex may reach as high as 83° when the moon's orbit is favorably situated.

ROUTINE OF A STORM.

The novelty and originality of this theory will perhaps justify us in dwelling a little longer on what observation has detected. The vortex (and we are now speaking only of the central vortex) does not derange every place alike, but *skips* over large tracts of longitude in its progress westward. We speak here of the immovable axis of the vortex as in motion; in reality it is the rotation of the earth which brings every meridian under its influence in some latitude once every twenty-four hours. The centre of greatest derangement forms the nucleus, towards which the surface currents, under certain restrictions, flow. The strongest current will, however, usually be from the south, on account of the inclination of the axis of the vortex to the surface of the earth.* These currents continuing onwards by their vires inertiæ, according to the first law of motion, assist somewhat in conveying the warm surface wind, loaded with moisture, into the region of cloud; and the diminution of temperature causes the condensation of large masses of vapor, according to Hutton's views; and the partial vacuum thus produced, causes a still greater intermingling. But we have already shown that this is not the sole cause, nor is it ever more than partially accomplished. The ether of the lower atmosphere, and of the crust of the earth, is disturbed, and rushes towards the rarefied axis from the surface, and with the temperature of the surface, thus conveying the surface atmosphere, in a measure, along with it. In the upper regions, this ether (or electric fluid) cools down, or parts with some of its heat, to the air of those regions, and, by its great specific caloric, necessarily and unduly increases the temperature of the air. This, by its expansion and ascension, will cause a further influx from below, until the upper atmosphere becomes loaded with vapor. In twelve hours, at least, a

* The curvature of the earth is more than 10 miles in a distance of 300 miles.

reaction must take place, as that part of the earth's surface is carried six or seven thousand miles from the axis, where the ether is more dense. This in turn descends to the surface, carrying with it the temperature of space, at least 60° below zero; a great condensation must follow; local derangements of the electric equilibrium in the centre of large clouds, when the condensation is active, must now take place, while partially non-conducting masses intervene, to prevent an instantaneous restoration of the equilibrium, until the derangement is sufficient to cause the necessary tension, when all obstacles are rent asunder, and the ether issues forth, clothed in the power and sublimity of the lightning. It is a fearfully-energetic fluid, and, when sufficiently disturbed, competent to produce the most violent tornado, or the most destructive earthquake. That these two phenomena have simultaneously occurred, seems well authenticated; but the earthquake, of course, must be referred generally to derangements of the electric equilibrium of the earth's interior, of which at present we know but little.

The day or morning previous to the passage of the vortex, is frequently very fine, calm, mild, and sleepy weather,—commonly called a weather breeder. After the storm has fully matured, there is an approach of the clouds to the surface, a reduction of the temperature above, and the human body feels the change far more than is due to the fall of temperature. This is owing to the cold ether requiring so much heat to raise its temperature to that of surrounding bodies, or, in other words, is due to its great specific caloric. In summer, this falling of the upper layers in front of the storm is so apparent, that every part is seen to expand under the eye by perspective,—swelling, and curling, and writhing, like the surface of water or oil when just commenced boiling. The wind now partakes of the motion of the external ether, and moves with the storm eastward (in this latitude), or from N-E. to S-E., until the action ceases.

CONDITIONS NECESSARY TO PRODUCE A STORM.

The vortex, in its passage round the earth, may only meet with a few localities favorable for producing a very violent storm; but these nuclei will generally be connected by bands of cloudy atmosphere; so that could we view them from the moon, the earth would be belted like the planet Jupiter. There is reason to suspect, also, that there are variations in the energy of the ethereal motions, independent of the conditions of the earth and its atmosphere, which affects even the radial stream of the sun. For the zodiacal light, which is caused by this radial stream, is at times much more vivid than at others. Also in the case of the aurora, on our own globe. On this point there is much to say, but here is not the place. The conditions favorable for the production of a storm at the *central* passage of a vortex, are a previous exemption from excitement *ceteris paribus*, a high temperature and dew point, a depression of the barometer, and local accumulation of electric tension, positive or negative; and these are influenced by the storms in other places controlling the aërial currents, and thus determining the atmosphere of the place.

LATERAL VORTICES.

We have already alluded to the lateral vortices of the terral system. We must now resort to a diagram.

In the following figure, the arrows represent the ethereal current of the terral vortex; the linear circle, the earth; C the centre of gravity of the earth and moon, and, consequently, the central vortex or axis of the vortex of the earth. *I* represents the position of the inner vortex, and O that of the outer vortex. These two last are eddies, caused by the obstacle presented by the earth in being *pushed* out from the centre by the moon, and are called lateral vortices. There are, therefore, two lateral vor-

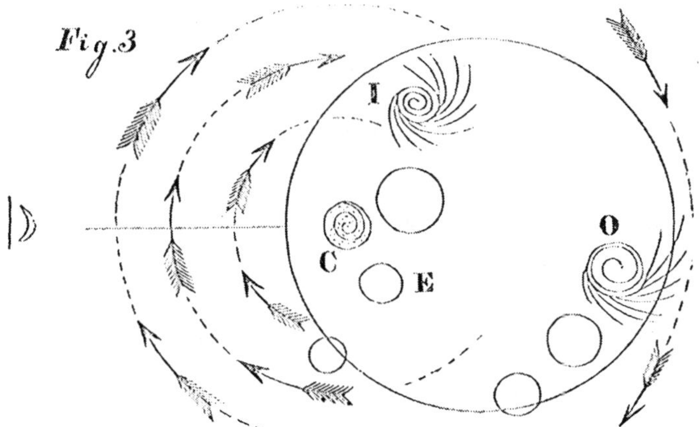

tices, and one central, in both hemispheres, and by this simple arrangement is the earth watered, and the atmospheric circulation produced.

ILLUSTRATION OF THEIR ACTION.

If we place a globe in a vessel of water, so that the vertex shall only just be covered, and place the globe eccentrically in the vessel, so that the centre of the vessel may not be too far from the outside of the globe, and then impart an equable but slow motion to the water, in the manner of a vortex; by viewing the reflected light of the sky from the surface of the water above the globe, we shall be able to trace a succession of dimples, originating at I and O, and passing off with the current, and dying away. The direction of the fluid in these little eddies, will be the same as the direction of the current in the main vortex. If we displace the globe, so as to remove it far from the centre of the vessel, and impart the same motion, the vortex I will be found at E, and the direction of the current will be contrary to the direction of the fluid in the vessel. In the case of the earth and moon, the displacement can never change the position of the inner vortex much. It will always be to the right hand of the central vortex in north latitudes, and in consequence of the ether striking our globe in such a position, the current that is deflected from its true path, by the protuberance of the earth forcing it inside, is prevented by the circular current of the parts nearer the axis of the vortex, from passing off; so that a vortex is formed, and is more violent, *ceteris paribus*, than the vortex at O.

ORDER OF OCCURRENCE.

Whether this mode of action has been correctly inferred, matters little; the lateral vortices follow the law of such a position. The inner vortex always precedes the central from five to eight days, when ascending in this latitude, and comes to the meridian after the moon. The outer vortex, on the contrary, follows the central in its monthly round, and comes to the meridian before the moon. It will be readily understood that if the axes of these lateral vortices be produced through the earth, they will pass through similar vortices in the opposite hemisphere; but as the greatest latitude of the one, corresponds to the least latitude of the other, the same calculation will not answer for both. The same remark applies to the central vortex also.

Thus there are six passages each month over latitude 41°; but as there are intervals of 3° to 6° between two consecutive passages of the same vortex, it may happen that an observer in the middle latitude, would perhaps see nothing of their effects without looking for them. Generally speaking, they are not only seen, but felt. The time of the passage of the outer vortex ascending, corresponds so nearly (in 38° of latitude) at certain times, with the passage of the central vortex descending, that the two may be considered one if attention is not directed to it. The orbits of these lateral vortices depend, like that of the central vortex, on the orbit of the moon for eccentricity, but the longitudes of the perigee will not correspond with the longitude of the moon's perigee. This follows from the theory. As the elements of these orbits are only approximately determined, we shall confine our calculations to the orbit of the central vortex.

REDFIELD'S THEORY OF STORMS.

It will now appear plainly to the reader, that this theory of storms differs in every particular from the rival theories of Redfield and Espy, both as to the cause and the *modus agendi.* It would appear at first sight, as if the discovery of these vortices would at once remedy the great defect in the theory of Redfield, viz.: that no adequate cause is assigned for the commencement and continuation of the vorticose motion, in the great circular whirlwinds which compose a storm. The facts, however, are adverse to such an application. According to Mr. Redfield, the rotation of a circular storm in the northern hemisphere is from right to left, and the reverse in the southern. The author's attention has, of course, been considerably directed to this point; but in every case he has been unfortunate in finding in the clouds a rotation from left to right. Some cases are mentioned in the appended record of the weather. He has also noticed many of those small whirlwinds on arid plains, in Egypt, in Mexico, and in California, which, in the great majority of cases, were also from left to right. His opportunities, however, have not extended to the southern hemisphere. This theory has not, however, been formed on theoretic views, but by looking nature in the face for years, and following her indications. Accordingly, we find that the changes of the wind in a storm forbid the adoption of the circular hypothesis.

WHIRLWINDS VERY LIMITED IN DIAMETER.

The theory, as extended by Col. Reid, rests on a simple rotation around a progressing centre, and is found sometimes supported by evidence of the most violent action at the centre, and sometimes by showing that the central portion is often in a state of calm. We do not attempt to reconcile these views; but would merely observe, that an atmospheric vortex must be subject to the same dynamical laws as all other vortices; and inasmuch as the medium cannot differ greatly in density, from the centre to the circumference, the periodic times of the parts of the vortex, must be directly as their distances from the axis, and consequently the absolute velocities must be equal. If Mr. Redfield resorts to a spirally inward current, it would be a centripetal instead of a centrifugal current, and therefore could not cause the barometer to fall, which was the best feature of the theory in its primitive form. The absolute velocity of the wind is the important element which most concerns us. In the case of a tornado of a few yards in diameter, there is no doubt a circular motion, caused by the meeting of opposing currents; but this may be considered a circle of a very small diameter. The cause is due to a rapid escape of electric or ethereal matter, from the crust of the earth, called forth by the progressing, disturbed space above; this involves the air, and an ascending column in rotation begets the rush on all sides to that column in straight lines: consequently, the velocities will be inversely as the distances from the axis, and the force of the current as the squares of the velocities. On the circular theory, no increase of velocity would be conferred by the approach of the centre, and consequently no increase of power.

OBJECTION TO CIRCULAR STORMS.

Another objection to the circular theory of storms, is the uniformity of phase. If that theory be true, we see no reason why a person should not be sometimes on the northern side of the gale. By referring to a diagram, we perceive that on the northern side the changes of the wind pursue a contrary direction to what they do on the south, yet in nine cases out of ten, each vessel meeting a hurricane will find the same changes of wind as are due to the southern side of the storm. It is true, that if a vessel be to the northward of a great hurricane, there will almost certainly be a north-east gale drawn in, and this might be set down as the outer limits of a circular storm. But when the storm really begins, the wind comes round south-east, south, south-west, ending at north-west, and frequently is succeeded, on the following day, (if in middle latitude,) by a moderate breeze from the northward. Now, if the north-east gale spoken of above, was the outer limits of an atmospheric vortex, a vessel sailing west ought not to meet the hurricane, as a north-east wind is indicative of being already on the west side, or behind the storm.

Again, the characters of the winds, and appearances at the different changes, are opposed to the circular theory. At a distance of fifty miles from the centre of a storm, the wind which passes over a ship as a southerly wind, will have made a rotation and a half, with the hurricane velocity, before the same wind can again pass the ship as a northerly wind, (supposing the progress eastward, and the ship lying to,) that is, the same wind which in another place was a south wind two hours before, and after only going one degree north, becomes a northerly wind,—changed in character and temperature, as every seaman is well aware. In a storm, if the circular theory be true, the character and temperature should be the same, no matter from what point the wind is blowing. This should be a conclusive argument.

Mr. Espy has also changed his ground on the storms of the United States; he does not now contend that the winds blow inwards to a centre, but to a line either directly or obliquely. Thus we see that while Mr. Redfield concedes to Mr. Espy a spirally inward current, the latter also gives up a direct current to the centre, to Mr. Redfield. This shows at least an approximation to the truth.

It is not necessary for the support of this theory, that we should derive any materials from the ruins of others; we shall therefore not avail ourselves of certain discrepant results, which can be found in many of the storms cited by Colonel Reid. With respect to Mr. Espy's *cause* of storms, the experiments of Regnault may be considered as decisive of the question:—1st, because the specific heat of vapor is so much less than Espy assumed it to be; and 2d, because the expansion of air in a free space does not suffer any change of volume by ascending, except what is due to diminished pressure, and the natural temperature of that elevation.

INDICATIONS OF A STORM.

In accordance with our theory, the direction and force of the wind in a storm are due to ascending columns of air, supplied from the upper portion of the atmospheric stratum beneath the clouds. The commotion begins at the highest limits of the cirri, and even at greater elevations. Hence, the hazy appearance of the sky is a legitimate precursor of the coming gale. As a general thing, the wind will blow (at the surface) towards the centre of greatest commotion, but it is too dependent on the ever-varying position and power of temporary nuclei of disturbance, to be long steady, except when the disturbance is so remote that its different centres of induction are, as it were, merged into one common focus. When a vortex is descending, or passing from north to south, and withal very energetic at the time, the southerly wind (which may always be considered the principal wind of the storm in this hemisphere) may blow steadily towards the vortex for three or even four days. When a vortex is ascending, the induced northerly current will be comparatively moderate, and be frequently checked by the southerly wind overblowing the storm, and arriving the day before the vortex which produced it.

The important point for the navigator, is to know the time of meridian passage of the vortex, and its latitude at the time of the passage, and then be guided by the indications of the weather and the state of barometer. If it commences storming the day before the passage, he may expect it much worse soon after the passage; and again, if the weather looks bad when no vortex is near, he may have a steady gale setting towards a storm, but no storm until the arrival of a vortex. Again, if the barometer is low the day before the vortex passes, there may be high barometer to the west, and the passage be attended by no great commotion, as it requires time for the storm to mature, and consequently its greatest violence will be to the east. If at the ship the barometer is high, the vortex may still produce a storm on a line of low barometer to the west, and this line may reach the ship at the time of the passage. In tropical climates the trouble must be looked for to the eastward; as a storm, once excited, will travel westward with that stratum of atmosphere in which the great mass of vapor is lodged, and in which, of course, the greatest derangement of electric tension is produced.

It will now be seen that we do not admit, with Col. Reid, that a storm continues in existence for a week together. Suppose a hurricane to originate in the Antilles at the southern limits of a vortex, the hurricane would die away, according to our theory, if the vortex did not come round again and take up the same nucleus of disturbance. On the third day the vortex is found still further north, and the apparent path of the hurricane becomes more curved. In latitude 30° the vortex passes over 3° or 5° of latitude in a day; and here being the latitude where the lower atmospheric current changes its course, the storm passes due north, and afterwards north-east. Now, each day of the series there is a distinct hurricane, (caused by an increase of energy in a particular vortex, as we have before hinted,) each one overlapping on the remains of the preceding; but in each the same changes of the wind are gone through, and the same general features preserved, as if it were truly a progressive whirlwind, except that each vessel has the violent part of it, as if she was in the southern half of the whirl. The apparent regularity of the Atlantic storms in direction, as exhibited by Col. Reid, are owing in a great degree to the course of the Gulf Stream, in which a vortex, in its successive passages in different latitudes, finds more favorable conditions for the development of its power, than in other parts of the same ocean; thus showing the importance of regarding the established character of storms in each locality, as determined by observation. In this connection, also, we may remark, that the meridians of greatest magnetic intensity are, *ceteris paribus*, also the meridians of greatest atmospheric commotion. The discovery of this fact is due to Capt. Sabine. The cause is explained by the theory.

As it is the author's intention to embody the practical application of this theory to navigation, with the necessary rules and tables, in a separate work, sufficient has been said to familiarize the reader with the general idea of a cause external to the earth, as the active motor in all atmospheric phenomena. We will therefore only allude in a general way to the principal distinguishing feature of the theory. We say, then, that the wind in a storm is not in rotation, and it is a dangerous doctrine to teach the navigator. We also assert as distinctly, that the wind *in* a storm does not blow from all sides towards the centre, which is just as dangerous to believe. If it were wise to pin our faith to any Procrustean formula, we might endorse the following propositions: That at the beginning of a storm the wind is from the equator towards the poles in every part of the storm; that, at a later date, another current (really a polar current deflected by convection) sets in at right angles to the first one; and that at the end of the storm there is only *one* wind blowing at right angles to the direction at the beginning. Outside the storm, considered as a hundred, or two or three hundred miles in diameter, there is, under certain limitations, a surface wind setting towards the general focus of motion and condensation, and this surface wind will be strongest from the westward, on account of the motion of the whole atmosphere in which these other motions are performed being to the eastward.* The whole phenomenon is electrical or magnetic, or electro-magnetic or ethereal, whichever name pleases best. The vortex, by its action, causes a current of induction below, from the equator, as may be understood by inspecting Fig. 2, which in the northern hemisphere brings in a southerly current by convection: the regular circular current, however, finally penetrates below, as soon as the process of induction has ceased; and thus the polar current of the atmosphere at last overcomes the equatorial current in a furious squall, which ceases by degrees, and the equilibrium is restored.

Every locality will have its peculiar features; in each, the prevailing wind will be at right angles to the magnetic meridian, and the progress of the storm will tend to follow the magnetic parallel, which is one reason why the Atlantic and Indian Ocean storms have been mistaken for progressive whirlwinds. When these views are developed in full, the mariner can pretty certainly decide his position in the storm, the direction of its progress, and its probable duration.

* In middle latitudes.

SECTION SECOND.

MECHANICAL ACTION OF THE MOON.

We will now proceed to give the method of determining the latitude of the axis of the vortex, at the time of its passage over any given meridian, and at any given time. And afterwards we will give a brief abstract from the record of the weather, for one sidereal period of the moon, in order to compare the theory with observation.

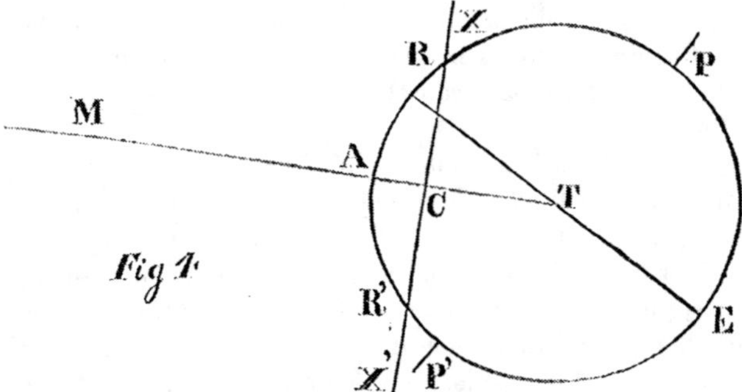

In the above figure, the circle P E R represents the earth, E the equator, P P' the poles, T the centre of the earth, C the mechanical centre of the terral vortex, M the moon, X X' the axis of the vortex, and A the point where the radius rector of the moon pierces the surface of the earth. If we consider the axis of the vortex to be the axis of equilibrium in the system, it is evident that T C will be to C M, as the mass of the moon to the mass of the earth. Now, if we take these masses respectively as 1 to 72.3, and the moon's mean distance at 238,650 miles, the mean value of T C is equal to this number, divided by the sum of these masses,—*i. e.*, the mean radius vector of the little orbit, described by the earth's centre around the centre of gravity of the earth and moon, is equal $\frac{238650}{72.3+1} = 3{,}256$ miles; and at any other distance of the moon, is equal to that distance, divided by the same sum. Therefore, by taking C T in the inverse ratio of the mean semi-diameter of the moon to the true semi-diameter, we shall have the value of C T at that time. But T A is to T C as radius to the cosine of the arc A R, and R R' are the points on the earth's surface pierced by the axis of the vortex, supposing this axis coincident with the pole of the lunar orbit. If this were so, the calculation would be very short and simple; and it will, perhaps, facilitate the investigation, by considering, for the present, that the two axes do coincide.

In order, also, to simplify the question, we will consider the earth a perfect sphere, having a diameter of 7,900 miles, equal to the actual polar diameter, and therefore T A is equal to 3,950 miles.

In the spherical triangle given on next page, we have given the point A, being the position of the moon in right ascension and declination in the heavens, and considered as terrestrial latitude and longitude.

Therefore, P A is equal to the complement of the moon's declination, P being the pole of the earth, and L being the pole of the lunar orbit; P L is equal to the obliquity of the lunar orbit, with respect to the earth, and is therefore given by finding the true inclination of the lunar orbit at the time, equal E L, (E being the pole of the ecliptic,) also the true longitude of the ascending node, and the obliquity of the ecliptic P E.

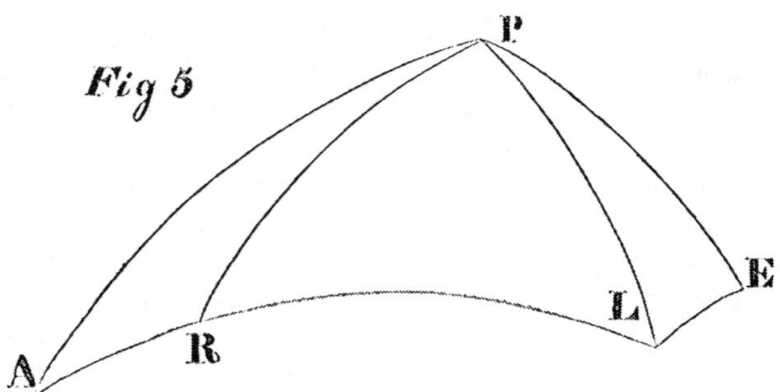

Now, as we are supposing the axis of the vortex parallel to the pole of the lunar orbit, and to pierce the earth's surface at R, A R L will evidently all be in the same plane; and, as in the case of A and L, this plane passes through the earth's centre, A R L must all lie in the same great circle. Having, therefore, the right ascension of A, and the right ascension of L, we have the angle P. This gives us two sides, and the included angle, to find the side L A. But we have before found the arc A R; we therefore know L R. But in finding L A, we found both the angles L and A, and therefore can find P R, which is equal to the complement of the latitude sought.

We have thus indicated briefly the simple process by which we could find the latitude of the axis of the central vortex, supposing it to be always coincident with the pole of the lunar orbit. The true problem is more complicated, and the principal modifications, indicated by the theory, are abundantly confirmed by observation. The determination of the inclination of the axis of the vortex, its position in space at a given time, and the law of its motion, was a work of cheerless labor for a long time. He that has been tantalized by hope for years, and ever on the eve of realization, has found the vision vanish, can understand the feeling which proceeds from frequent disappointment in not finding that, whose existence is almost demonstrated;

and more especially when the approximation differs but slightly from the actual phenomena.

The chief difficulty at the outset of these investigations, arose from the conflicting authority of astronomers in relation to the mass of the moon. We are too apt to confound the precision of the laws of nature, with the perfection of human theories. Man observes the phenomena of the heavens, and derives his means of predicting what will be, from what has been. Hence the motions of the heavenly bodies are known to within a trifling amount of the truth; but it does not follow that the true explanation is always given by theory. If this were so, the mass of the moon (for instance) ought to be the same, whether deduced from the principle of gravitation or from some other source. This is not so. Newton found it $\frac{1}{40}$ of that of the earth. La Place, from a profound theoretical discussion of the tides, gave it as $\frac{1}{58.6}$, while from other sources he found a necessity of diminishing it still more, to $\frac{1}{68}$, and finally as low as $\frac{1}{75}$. Bailly, Herschel, and others, from the nutation of the earth's axis, only found $\frac{1}{80}$, and the Baron Lindenau deduced the mass from the same phenomenon $\frac{1}{88}$. In a very recent work by Mr. Hind, he uses this last value in certain computations, and remarks, that we shall not be very far wrong in considering it as as $\frac{1}{80}$ of the mass of the earth. This shows the uncertainty of the matter in 1852. If astronomy is so perfect as to determine the parallax of a fixed star, which is almost always less than one second, why is it that the mass of the moon is not more nearly approximated? Every two weeks the sun's longitude is affected by the position of the moon, alternately increasing and diminishing it, by a quantity depending solely upon the relative mass of the earth and moon, and is a gross quantity compared to the parallax of a star. So, also, the horizontal parallax—the most palpable of all methods—taken by different observers at Berlin, and the Cape of Good Hope, (a very respectable base line, one would suppose,) makes the mass of the moon greater than its value derived from nutation; the first giving about $\frac{1}{70}$, the last about $\frac{1}{74.2}$. Does not this declare that it is unsafe to depend too absolutely on the strict wording of the Newtonian law of gravitation. Happily our theory furnishes us with the correct value of the moon's mass, written legibly on the surface of the earth; and it comes out nearly what these two phenomena always gave it, viz.: $\frac{1}{72.3}$ of that of the earth. In another place we shall inquire into the cause of the discrepancy as given by the nutation of the earth.

MOTION OF THE AXIS OF THE VORTEX.

If the axis of the terral vortex does not coincide with the axis of the lunar orbit, we must derive this position from observation, which can only be done by long and careful attention. This difficulty is increased by the uncertainty about the mass of the moon, already alluded to, and by the fact that there are three vortices in each hemisphere which pass over *twice* in each month, and it is not *always* possible to decide by observation, whether a vortex is ascending or descending, or even to discriminate between them, so as to be assured that this is the central descending, and that the outer vortex ascending. A better acquaintance, however, with the phenomenon, at last dissipates this uncertainty, and the vortices are then found to pursue their course with that regularity which varies only according to law. The position of the vortex (the central vortex is the one under consideration) then depends on the inclination of its axis to the axis of the earth, and the right ascension of that axis at the given time. For we shall see that an assumed immobility of the axis of the vortex, would be in direct collision with the principles of the theory.

Let the following figure represent a globe of wood of uniform density throughout. Let this globe be rotated round the axis. It is evident that no change of position of the axis would be

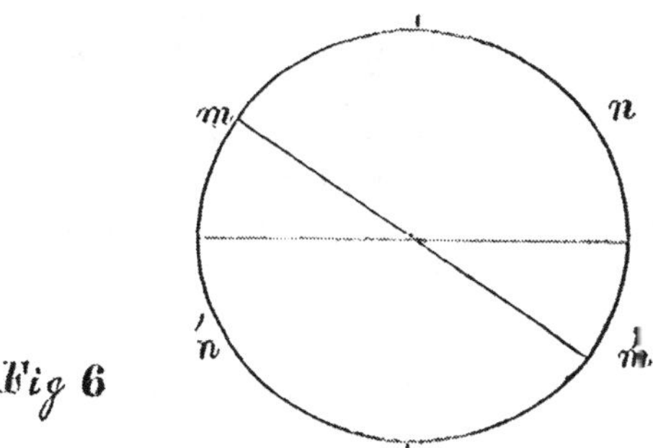

Fig 6

produced by the rotation, If we add two equal masses of lead at m and m', on opposite sides of the axis, the globe is still in equilibrium, as far as gravity is concerned, and if perfectly spherical and homogeneous it might be suspended from its centre in any position, or assume indifferently any position in a vessel of water. If, however, the globe is now put into a state of rapid rotation round the axis, and then allowed to float freely in the water, we perceive that it is no longer in a state of equilibrium. The mass m being more dense than its antagonist particle at n, and having equal velocity, its momentum is greater, and it now tends continually to pull the pole from its perpendicular, without affecting the position of the centre. The same effect is produced by m', and consequently the axis describes the surface of a double cone, whose vertices are at the centre of the globe. If these masses of lead had been placed at opposite sides of the axis on the *equator* of the globe, no such motion would be produced; for we are supposing the globe formed of a hard and unyielding material. In the case of the ethereal vortex of the earth, we must remember there are two different kinds of matter,—one ponderable, the other not ponderable; yet both subject to the same dynamical laws. If we consider the axis of the terral vortex to coincide with the axis of the lunar orbit, the moon and earth are placed in the equatorial plane of the vortex, and consequently there can be no derangement of the equilibrium of the vortex by its own rotation. But even in this case, seeing that the moon's orbit is inclined to the ecliptic, the gravitating power of the sun is exerted on the moon, and of necessity she must quit the equatorial plane of the vortex; for the sun can exert no influence on the *matter* of the vortex by his attracting power. The moment, however, the moon has left the equatorial plane of the vortex, the principle of momentum comes into play, and a conical motion of the axis of the vortex is produced, by its seeking to follow the moon in her monthly revolution. This case is, however, very different to the illustration we gave. The vortex is a fluid, through which the moon freely wends her way, passing through the equatorial plane of the vortex twice in each revolution. These points constitutes the moon's nodes on the plane of the vortex, and, from the principles laid down, the force of the moon to disturb the equilibrium of the axis of the vortex, vanishes at these points, and attains a maximum 90° from them. And the effect produced, in passing from her ascending to her descending node, is equal and contrary to the effect produced in passing from her descending to her ascending node,—reckoning these points on the plane of the vortex.

INCLINATION OF THE AXIS.

By whatever means the two planes first became permanently inclined, we see that it is a necessary consequence of the admission of these principles, not only that the axis of the vortex should be drawn aside by the momentum of the earth and moon, ever striving, as it were, to maintain a dynamical balance in the system, in accordance with the simple laws of motion, and ever disturbed by the action of gravitation exerted on the grosser matter of the system; but also, that this axis should follow, the axis of the lunar orbit, at the same mean inclination, during the complete revolution of the node. The mean inclination of the two axes, determined by observation, is 2° 45′, and the monthly equation, at a maximum, is about 15′, being a plus correction in the northern hemisphere, where the moon is between her descending and ascending node, reckoned on the plane of the vortex, and a minus correction, when between her ascending and descending node. And the mean longitude of the node will be the same as the true longitude of the moon's orbit node,—the maximum correction for the true longitude being only about 5° ±.

In the following figure, P is the pole of the earth; E the pole of the ecliptic; L the pole of the lunar orbit; V the mean position of the pole of the vortex at the time; the angle ♈ E L the true longitude of the pole of the lunar orbit, equal to the *true* longitude of the ascending node ± 90°. V L is therefore the mean inclination = 2° 45′; and the little circle, the orbit described by the pole of the vortex *twice* in each sidereal revolution of the moon. The distance of the pole of the vortex from the mean position V, may be approximately estimated, by multiplying the maximum value 15′ by the sine of twice the moon's distance from the node of the vortex, or from its mean position, viz.: the true longitude of the ascending node of the moon on the ecliptic.

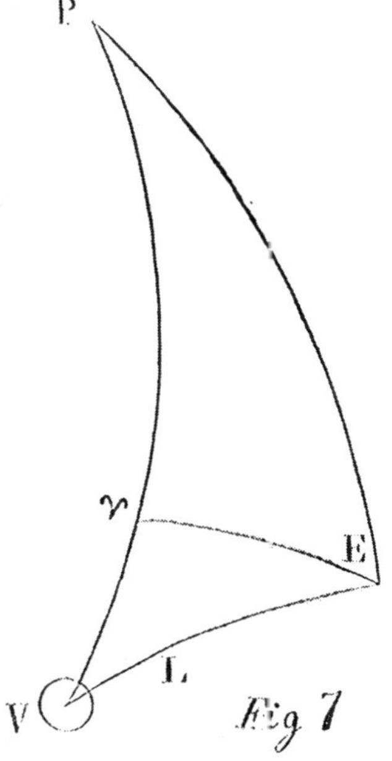

From this we may calculate the true place of the node, the true obliquity, and the true inclination to the lunar orbit. Having indicated the necessity for this correction, and its numerical coefficient, we shall no longer embarrass the computation by such minutiæ, but consider the mean inclination as the true inclination, and the mean place of the node as the true place of the node, and coincident with the ascending node of the moon's orbit on the ecliptic.

POSITION OF THE AXIS OF THE VORTEX.

It is now necessary to prove that the axis of the vortex will still pass through the centre of gravity of the earth and moon.

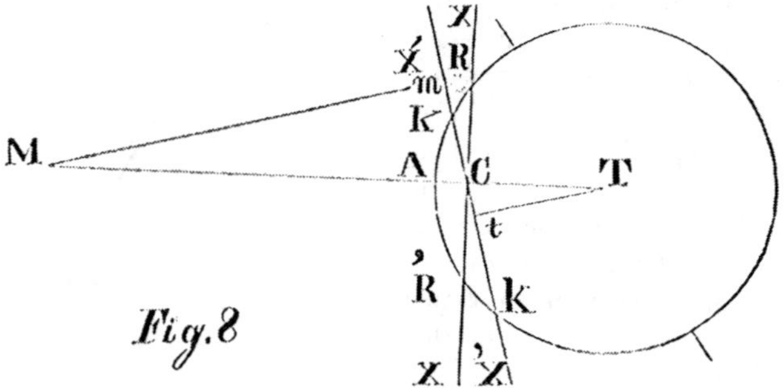

Fig. 8

Let X X now represent the axis of the lunar orbit, and C the centre of gravity of the earth and moon. X′ X′ the axis of the vortex, and K C R the inclination of this axis. Then from

similarity	C t	:	'T t	::	C m	:	M m
but	T t	:	M m	::	Moon's mass	:	Earth's mass.
That is	'T t	:	M m	::	T C	:	M C.

Therefore the system is still balanced; and in no other point but the point C, can the intersection of the axes be made without destroying this balance.

It will be observed by inspecting the figure, that the arc R′ K′ is greater than the arc R K. That the first increases the arc A R, and the second diminishes that arc. The arc R′ K′ is a plus correction therefore, and the smaller arc R K a minus correction. If the moon is between her descending and ascending node, (taking now the node on the ecliptic,) the correction is negative, and we take the smaller arc. If the moon is between her ascending and descending node, the correction is positive, and we take the larger arc. If the moon is 90° from the node, the correction is a maximum. If the moon is at the node, the correction is null. In all other positions it is as the sine of the moon's distance from the nodes. We must now find the maximum value of these arcs of correction corresponding to the mean inclination of 2° 45′.

To do this we may reduce T C to T t in the ratio of radius to cosine of the inclination, and taking T S for radius.

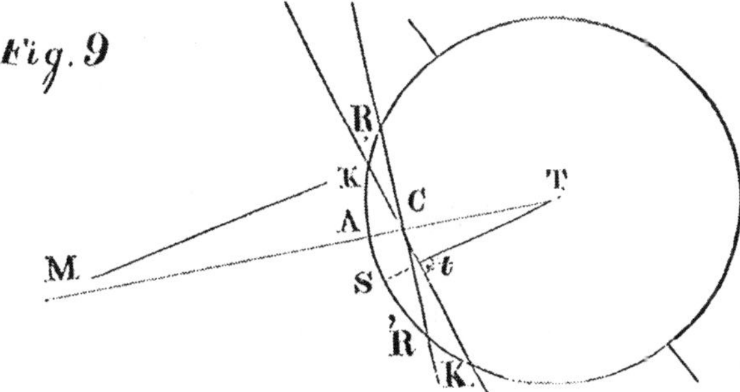

$\frac{\text{T C} \times \text{Cos \&c. (inclination } 2^\circ\ 45')}{\text{R}}$ is equal the cosine of the arc S K′ and S K′ + A S = A K′ and A K′ − A R′ = R′ K′. But from the nature of the circle, arc R K + arc R′ K′ = angle R C K + angle R′ C K′, or equal to double the inclination; and therefore, by subtracting either arc from double the inclination, we may get the other arc.

The maximum value of these arcs can, however, be found by a simple proportion, by saying; as the arc A R, plus the inclination, is to the inclination, so is the inclination to the difference between them; and therefore, the inclination, plus half the difference, is equal the greater arc, and the inclination, minus half the difference, is equal the lesser; the greater being positive, and the lesser negative.

Having found the arc A R, and knowing the moon's distance from either node, we must reduce these values of the arcs R K and R′ K′ just found, in the ratio of radius to the sine of that distance, and apply it to the arc A R or A′ R′, and we shall get the first correction equal to the arc A K or A K′.

Call the arc A R	=	a
" inclination	=	n
" distance from the node	=	d
" arc A K	=	k

and supposing the value of A K be wanted for the northern hemisphere when the moon is between her descending and ascending node, we have

$$k = a - \frac{\left(n - \frac{\frac{n^2}{a + n}}{2}\right) \sin d.}{R}$$

If the moon is between her ascending and descending node, then

$$k = a + \frac{\left(n + \frac{\frac{n^2}{a + n}}{2}\right) \sin d.}{R}$$

The computation will be shorter, however, if we merely reduce the inclination to the sine of the distance from the node for the first correction of the arc A R, if we neglect the semimonthly motion of the axis; for this last correction diminishes the plus corrections, and the first one increases it. If, therefore, one is neglected, it is better to neglect the other also; especially as it might be deemed affectation to notice trifling inequalities in the present state of the elements of the question.

There is one inequality, however, which it will not do to neglect. This arises from the displacement of the axis of the vortex.

DISPLACEMENT OF THE AXIS.

We have represented the axis of the terral vortex as continually passing through the centre of gravity of the earth and moon. Now, by following out the principles of the theory, we shall see that this cannot be the case, except when the moon is in quadrature with the sun. To explain this:

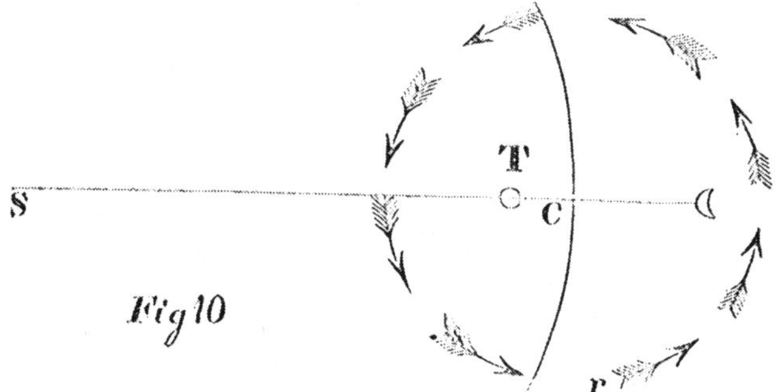

Fig 10

Let the curve passing through C represent a portion of the orbit of the earth, and S the sun. From the principles laid down, the density of the ethereal medium increases outward as the square roots of the distances from the sun. Now, if we consider the circle whose centre is C to represent the whole terral vortex, it must be that the medium composing it varies also in density at different distances from the sun, and at the same time is rotating round the centre. That half of the vortex which is exterior to the orbit of the earth, being most dense, has consequently most inertia, and if we conceive the centre of gravity of the earth and moon to be in the orbit (as it must be) at C, there will not be dynamical balance in the terral system, if the centre of the vortex is also found at C. To preserve the equilibrium the centre of the vortex will necessarily come nearer the sun, and thus be found between T and C, T representing the earth, and ☾ the moon, and C the centre of gravity of the two bodies. If the moon is in opposition, the centre of the vortex will fall between the centre of gravity and the centre of the earth, and have the apparent effect of diminishing the mass of the moon. If, on the other hand, the moon is in conjunction, the centre of the vortex will fall between the centre of gravity and the moon, and have the apparent effect of increasing the mass of the moon. If the moon is in quadrature, the effect will be null. The coefficient of this inequality is 90′, and depends on the sun's distance from the moon. When the moon is more than 90° from the sun, this correction is positive, and when less than 90° from the sun, it is negative. If we call this second correction C, and the moon's distance from her quadratures Q, we have the value of $C = \pm \frac{90' \times \text{Sin } Q}{R}$.

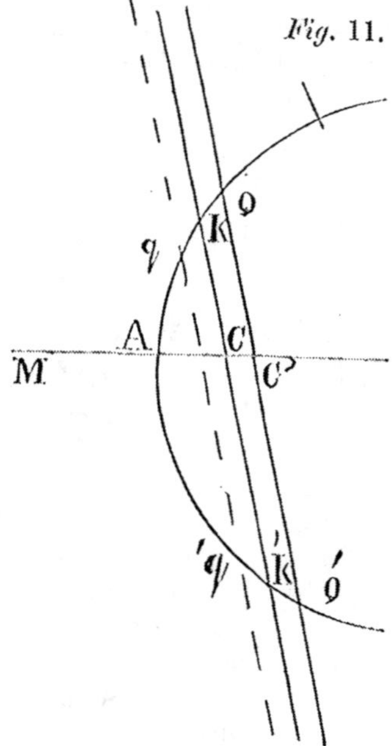

Fig. 11.

This correction, however, does not affect the inclination of the axis of the vortex, as will be understood by the subjoined figure. If the moon is in opposition, the axis of the vortex will not pass through C, but through C′, and Q Q′ will be parallel to K K′. If the moon is in conjunction, the axis will be still parallel to K K′, as represented by the dotted line q q'. The correction, therefore, for displacement, is equal to the arc K Q or K q, and the correct position of the vortex on the surface of the earth at a given time will be at the points Q or q, and Q′ or q', considering the earth as a sphere.

In the spherical triangle A P V, P is the pole of the earth, V the pole of the vortex, A the point of the earth's surface pierced by the radius vector of the moon, A Q is the corrected arc, and P V is the obliquity of the vortex. Now, as the axis of the vortex is parallel to the pole V, and the earth's centre, and the line M A also passes through the earth's centre, consequently

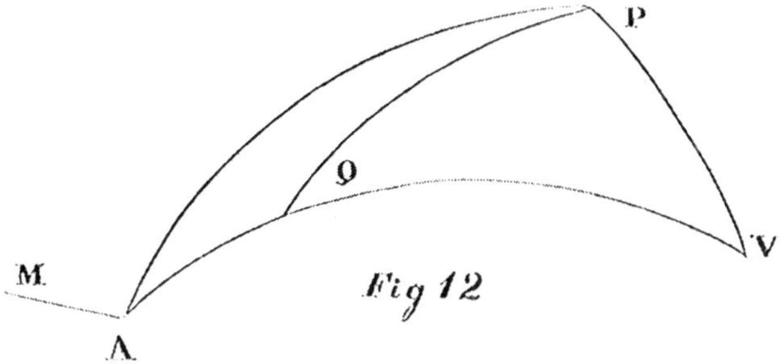

Fig 12

A Q V will all lie in the same great circle, and as P V is known, and P A is equal to the complement of the moon's declination at the time, and the right ascensions of A and V give the angle P, we have two sides and the included angle to find the rest, P Q being the complement of the latitude sought.

We will now give an example of the application of these principles.

*Example.** Required the latitude of the central vortex at the time of its meridian passage in longitude 88° 50′ west, July 2d, 1853.

CENTRAL VORTEX ASCENDING.

Greenwich time of passage	2d. 3h. 1m.
Mean longitude of moon's node	78° 29′
True " "	79 32
Mean inclination of lunar orbit	5 9
True " "	5 13
Obliquity of ecliptic	23 27 32″
Mean inclination of vortex	2 45 0

Then in the spherical triangle P E V.

P E	is equal	23° 27′ 32″
E V	"	7 58 0
E	"	100 28 0
P	"	18 5 7
P V	"	26 2 32

Calling P the polar angle and P V the obliquity of vortex.

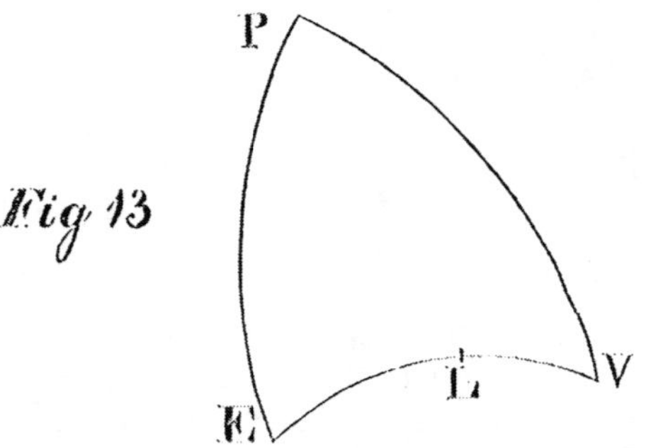

Fig 13

* For convenience to those wishing to verify the calculation of these triangles, we have put down each side and angle as found. Also, as an aid to the navigator.

To find the arc A R.

By combining the two proportions already given, we have by logarithms:

M. R. V. minor	=	3256 Log.	3.512683
M. S. D. of moon	=	940″ "	2.973128
P. S. D. of earth	=	3950 A. C.	6.403403
Radius			10.000000
T. S. D. of moon . . .		885″.5 A. C.	7.052811
Log. Cosine arc A R	=	28° 57′ 3″	9.942025

As the only variable quantity in the above formula is the "True" semi-diameter of the moon at the time, we may add the Constant logarithm 2.889214 to the arithmetical complement of the logarithm of the true semi-diameter, and we have in two lines the log. cosine of the arc A R.

We must now find the arc R K equal at a maximum to 2° 45′. The true longitude of the moon's node being 79° 32′, and the moon's longitude, per Nautical Almanac, being 58° 30′, the distance from the node is 21° 2′, therefore, the correction is

$$-\text{ arc R K} = \frac{-2^\circ 45' \times \sin 21^\circ 2'}{\text{R}} = -59' 13''$$

To find the correction for displacement.

True longitude of sun at date	100° 30′
" of moon "	58 30
Moon's distance from quadrature	48 0

As the moon is less than 90° from the sun this correction is also negative, or

$$\text{Arc K } q = \frac{-90' \times \sin 48^\circ}{\text{R}} = -1^\circ 6' 46''.$$

Arc A R	=	28° 57′ 3″
R K	= −	0 39 13
K q	= −	1 6 46
Sum	=	26 51 4 = corrected arc A Q.

We have now the necessary elements in the Nautical Almanac, which we must reduce for the instant of the vortex passing the meridian in Greenwich time.

July 2d.

Meridian passage, local time, at		. . . . . .	9h. 5m. A. M.
"	in Greenwich time	. . . .	2d. 3h. 1m.
Right ascension . . .	same time	. . .	56° 42′ 45″
Declination north . . .	"	. . .	18 00 1
Obliquity of the vortex .	"	. . .	26 2 32
Polar angle	"	. . .	18 5 7
Arc A Q	"	. . .	26 51 4

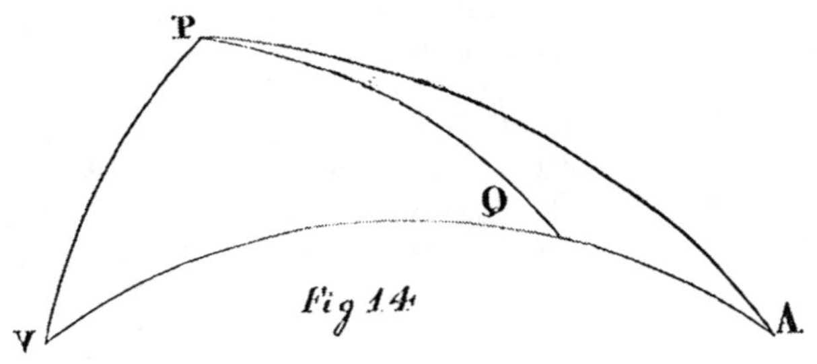

Fig 14

P A = 71° 59′ 59″	P = 128° 37′ 38″
P V = 26 2 32	
V A = 89 3 0	V = 47 59 44
V Q = 62 11 56	A = 20 3 42
P Q = 47 14 22	Q = 26 22 55

Latitude of Q on the sphere = 42° 45′ 38″

CORRECTION FOR PROTUBERANCE.

We have hitherto considered the earth a perfect sphere with a diameter of 7,900 miles. It is convenient to regard it thus, and afterwards make the correction for protuberance. We will now indicate the process for obtaining this correction by the aid of the following diagram.

Let B bisect the chord Z Z′. Then, by geometry, the angle F Q Y is equal to the angle B T F, and the protuberance F Y is equal the sine of that angle, making Q F radius. This angle, made by the axis of the vortex and the surface of the sphere, is commonly between 30° and 40°, according as the moon is near her apogee or perigee; and the correction will be greatest when the angle is least, as at the apogee. At the equator, the whole protuberance of the earth is about 13 miles. Multiply this by the cosine of the angle and divide by the sine, and we shall get the value of the arc Q Y

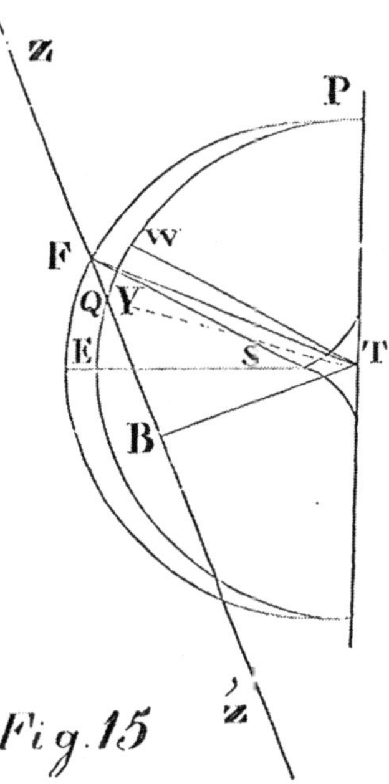

Fig. 15

for the equator. For the smallest angle, when the correction is a maximum, this correction will be about 20′ of latitude at the equator; for other latitudes it is diminished as the squares of the cosines of the latitude. Then add this amount to the latitude E Q, equal the latitude E Y. This, however, is only correct when the axis of the vortex is in the same plane as the axis of the earth; it is, therefore, subject to a minus correction, which can be found by saying, as radius to cosine of obliquity so is the correction to a fourth—the difference of these corrections is the maximum minus correction, and needs reducing in the ratio of radius to the cosine of the angle of the moon's distance from the node; but as it can only amount to about 2′ at a maximum under the most favorable circumstances, it is not necessary to notice it. The correction previously noticed is on the supposition that the earth is like a sphere having T F for radius; as it is a spheroid, we must correct again. From the evolute, draw the line S F, and parallel to it, draw T W; then E W is the latitude of the point F on the surface of the spheroid. This second correction is also a plus correction, subject to the same error as the first on account of the obliquity, its maximum value for an angle of 30° is about 6′, and is greatest in latitude 45°; for other latitudes, it is equal $\frac{6' \times \sin\text{(double the lat.)}}{R}$

The three principal corrections for protuberance may be *estimated* from the following table, calculated for every 15° of latitude for an angle of 30°, or when the correction is greatest.

Latitude.	1st Corr.	2d Corr.	3d Corr.
0	+ 20′	+ 0	— 2
15	+ 19	+ 3	— 1.5
30	+ 15	+ 5	— 1.5
45	+ 10	+ 6	— 1.
60	+ 5	+ 5	— 1
70	+ 1	+ 3	— 0.5

We can now apply this correction to the latitude of the vortex just found:

Latitude on the sphere	42° 45′ 38″ n.
Correction for protuberance	+ 14 22
Correct latitude	43 00 00

MILWAUKIE STORM, JULY 2.

As this example was calculated about ten days before the actual date, we have appended an extract from the Milwaukie papers, which is in the same longitude as Ottawa, in which place the calculation was made. It is needless to remark that the latitude of Milwaukie corresponds to the calculated latitude of the centre of the vortex. It is not intended, however, to convey the idea that the central line is always the most subject to the greatest violence—a storm may have several centres or nuclei of disturbance, which are frequently waning and reviving as the storm progresses. Generally speaking, however, the greatest action is developed along the line previously passed over by the axis of the vortex.

"SUMMIT, Waukesha Co., Wis., July 4, 1853.

"Our town, on Saturday, the 2d, was visited by a terrible storm, which will long be remembered by those who witnessed its effects and suffered from its fury. It arose in the south-west, and came scowling in blackness, sufficient to indicate its anger, for the space of eighty or a hundred rods in *width*, covering our usually quiet village; and for nearly half an hour's duration, the rain fell in torrents, the heavens blazed with the lightning's flashes, trees fell and were uprooted by the fury of the blast, fragments of gates and of buildings, shingles, roof-boards, rafters, circled through the air, the playthings of the wind—and buildings themselves were moved entire from their foundations, and deposited at different distances from their original positions. A barn, fifty-five feet square on the ground, owned by Mr. B. R. Hinckley, is moved from its position some ten feet to the eastward; and a house, some fifteen by eighteen feet on the ground, owned by the same person, fronting the east, was driven by the wind to the opposite side of the street, and now fronts nearly west; and what is most strange, is that the grass, in the route the house must have passed over, stands straight as usual, and gives no evidence that the building was pushed along on the ground. A lady running from a house unroofed by the storm, took an aërial flight over two fences, and finally caught against a tree, which arrested her passage for a moment only, when, giving way, she renewed her journey for a few rods, and was set down unhurt in Mr. O. Reed's wheat field, where, clinging to the growing grain, she remained till the gale went by."*

The weather at this place is briefly recorded in the accompanying abstract from the journal, as well as in an extract from a note to Professor Henry, of the Smithsonian Institution, from a friend of the author's, who has long occupied a high official station in Illinois. But such coincidences are of no value in deciding on the merits of such a theory. It must be tried before the tribunal of the world, and applied to phenomena in other countries with success, before its merits can be fully appreciated. The accompanying record, therefore, is only given to show how these vortices render themselves apparent, and what ought to be observed, and also to exhibit the order of their recurrence and their positions at a given time.

Extract of a note addressed to the Secretary of the Smithsonian Institution, by Hon. John Dean Caton, on this subject.

"As a striking instance of the remarkable coincidences confirmatory of these calculations, I will state, that on Friday, the first of July last, this gentleman† stated that on the next day a storm would pass north of us, being central a little south of Milwaukie, and that he thought, from the state of the atmosphere, the storm would be severe, and that its greatest violence would be felt on the afternoon or night of the next day. At this time the weather was fine, without any indications of a storm, so far as I could judge. At noon on the following day he pointed out the indications of a storm at the north and north-west, consisting of a dark, hazy belt in that direction, extending up a few degrees above the horizon, although so indistinct as to have escaped my observation. At five o'clock a violent storm visited us, which lasted half an hour, although a clear sky was visible at the south the whole time. On Monday morning I learned, from the telegraph office at Chicago, that early on Saturday

* Daily Wisconsin, July 7.

† The author.

afternoon communication with Milwaukie had been interrupted by atmospheric electricity, and that the line had been broken by a storm."

NEW YORK STORM.

After this was written, the author discovered that the vortex was equally violent the day before at New York, July 1st, 1853. An account of this storm follows. The calculation has not been made, but it is easy to perceive that the latitude of the vortex, on July 1st, must be very nearly that of New York—being in latitude 43° next day and ascending.

"At a meeting of the American Association, convened at Cleveland, Professor Loomis presented a long notice of the terrible hail storm in New York on the 1st of July. He traced its course, and minutely examined all the phenomena relating to it, from a mile and a half south-east of Paterson, N. J., to the east side of Long Island, where it appeared nearly to have spent its force. It passed over the village of Aqueenac, striking the Island of New York in the vicinity of the Crystal Palace. It was not much more than half a mile wide. The size of the hail-stones was almost incredibly large, many of them being as large as a hen's egg, and the Professor saw several which he thought as large as his fist. Some of them weighed nearly half a pound. The principal facts in relation to this storm were published at the time, and need not be repeated. The discussions arising among the members as to the origin and the size of these hail-stones, and the phenomena of the storm, were exceedingly interesting. They were participated in by Professors Heustus and Hosford, of Cambridge University, Professor Loomis, and Professors Bache and Redfield. The latter two gentlemen differ somewhat, we should suppose radically, in their meteorological theories, and had some very sharp but very pleasant "shooting" between them."*

* Chicago Democrat.

CENTRAL VORTEX DESCENDING.

We will now make the calculation for the central vortex *descending*, for longitude 88° 50′ west, August 7, 1853,—putting down the necessary elements for the time of the meridian passage in order:

Meridian passage in local time at . . .	2h. 25m. P. M.		
" " in Greenwich time . . .	7d. 8h. 18m.		
Mass of the moon $\frac{1}{72.3}$ M. R. V. minor . .	3,256 miles.		
Obliquity of the vortex, same time . . .	26°	5′	0″
Polar angle of " "	17	41	47
True longitude of moon's node "	78	42	0
" inclination of orbit "	5	5	0
" longitude of the sun "	135	20	0
Moon's longitude "	169	44	0
" distance from node "	91	2	0
" distance from quadrature "	55	36	0
" true semi-diameter "			943
" right ascension "	172	30	0
" declination north "	8	42	20

Constant logarithm . . .	2.889214		
Arith. comp. of log. of 943 .	7.025488		
Log. cos. arc. A R	9.914702	=	34° 44′ 48″
1st. .	correction,	+	2 45 0
2d. ·	correction,	—	1 14 15
Corrected arc A Q		=	36 15 33

P A	=	81°	17′	40″
P V	=	26	5	0
P	=	115	11	47
V	=	63	34	26
A	=	23	28	24
A V	=	92	48	39
Q	=	31	32	18

Complement of lat. = P Q =	48°	49′	41″	
The latitude is therefore for the earth, as a sphere .	41	10	18	
Correction for protuberance +	0	16	0	
True latitude of centre . .	41	26	18	north.
Latitude of Ottowa . . .	41	20	0	"
Vortex passed		6	18	north of Ottowa.

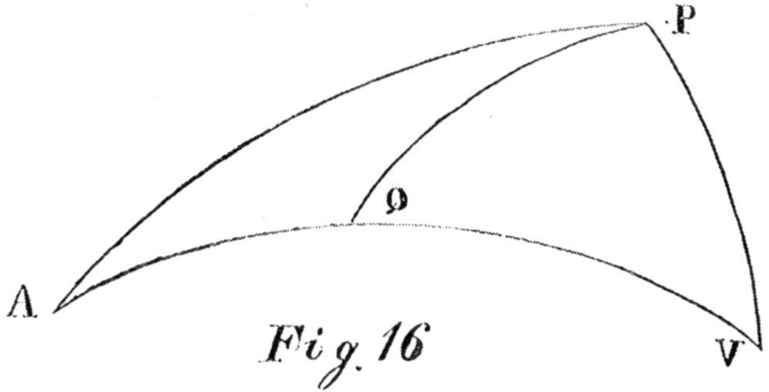

Fig. 16

As this was nearly a central passage, and as the influence was less extensive than usual, on account of great atmospheric pressure with a low dew point, the central disturbance could the more readily be located, and was certainly to the north, and but a few miles. The following is from the record of the weather:

August 6th. Very fine and clear all day; wind from S.-W.; a light breeze; 8 P. M. frequent flashes of lightning in the northern sky; 10 P. M. a *low bank of dense clouds in north*, fringed with cirri, visible during the flash of the lightning; 12 P. M. same continues.

7th. Very fine and clear morning; wind S.-W. moderate; noon, clouds accumulating in the northern half of the sky; wind fresher S.-W.; 3 P. M. a clap of thunder overhead, and black cumuli in west, north, and east; 4 P. M. much thunder, and scattered showers; six miles west rained very heavily; 6 P. M. the heavy clouds passing over to the south; 10 P. M. clear again in north.

August 8th. Clear all day; wind the same (S.-W.); a hazy bank visible all along on *southern horizon*.

This was not a storm, in the ordinary acceptation of the term; but the same cause, under other circumstances, would have produced one; and let it be borne in mind, that although the moon is the chief disturbing cause, and the passages of the vortices are the periods of greatest commotion in both settled and unsettled weather, still the sun is powerful in predisposing the circumstances, whether favorable or unfavorable; and as there is no periodic connection between the passage of a vortex and the concurrence of the great atmospheric waves, it will, of course, happen only occasionally that all the circumstances will conspire to make a storm. There are also other modifying causes, to which we have not yet alluded, which influence the storms at different seasons of the year,—exaggerating their activity in some latitudes, and diminishing it in other latitudes. In this latitude, the months of May, June, and July are marked by more energetic action than August, September, and October. The activity of one vortex also, in one place, seems to modify the activity of another vortex in another place. But the great question to decide is: Do these vortices really exist? Do they follow each other in the *order* indicated by the theory? Do they pass from south to north, and from north to south, at the *times* indicated by the theory? Do they obey, in their monthly revolutions, a mathematical law connecting them with the motions of the moon? We answer emphatically, Yes! And the non-discovery of these facts, is one of the most humiliating features of the present age.

OTTOWA STORM, DECEMBER 22, 1852

To show that the same calculations are applicable for other times, we will make the calculation for the *centre ascending*, for the 22d December, 1852, taking the following elements:

Moon's mer. passage, Dec. 22d . . .	15h. 16m. G. time.
" right ascension, same time . .	51° 57′
" declination north	15 42
" true S. Diameter	886.6″
" distance from node	37
" " " quadrature . .	52
Which gives the arc A R	29 5
1st correction	—1 51
2d "	+1 11
Corrected arc A Q	28 25

And the latitude at the time of the meridian passage = 42° north, or about forty miles north of Ottawa.

Abstract from the record:—

**Dec.* 21st, 1852. Wind N.-E., fine weather.

Dec. 22d. Thick, hazy morning, wind east, much lighter in S.-E. than in N.-W.; 8 A. M., a clear arch in S.-E. getting more to south; noon, very black in W. N.-W.; above, a broken layer of cir. cumulus, the sun visible sometimes through the waves; wind round to S.-E., and fresher; getting thicker all day; 10 P. M., wind south, strong; thunder, lightning, and heavy rain all night, with strong squalls from south.

Dec. 23d. Wind S.-W., moderate, drizzly day; 10 P. M., wind west, and getting clearer.

The next day the vortex passed the latitude of Montreal (the moon being on the meridian about 10 P. M.)

* This was also calculated before the event.

MAGNETIC STORM, DECEMBER 23, 1852.

In the July number of Vol. XVI. of Silliman's Journal, we find certain notices of the weather in 1852, by Charles Smallwood, of St. Martins, nine miles east of Montreal. He mentions "two remarkable electrical storms (which) occurred on the 23d and 31st of December, (in which) sparks $\frac{5}{40}$ of an inch were constantly passing from the conductor to the discharger for several hours each day." At 10 P. M. (23d) the vortex passed over Montreal, and again descending on the 31st North, and was visible at Ottowa on the morning of the 1st of January, with southerly wind setting towards it. On the 29th of December, Mr. Smallwood records "a low auroral arch, sky clear." On the 29th, the vortex was 5° to the northward of Montreal, and the aurora was consequently low—the brightest auroras being when the vortex is immediately north without storm, or one day to the northward, although we have seen it *very low* when the vortex was three days to the north, and no other vortex near.

LIVERPOOL STORM.

On the night of the 24th of December, the same central vortex ascending passed between Cape Clear and Liverpool.

On the 25th, at midnight, the vortex passed to the north of Liverpool: its northerly progress being very slow, being confined for three days between the parallel of Liverpool and its extreme northern limit in latitude about 57°. The accompanying account of the weather will show the result of a long-continued disturbance near the same latitude:

The Baltic, three days out from Liverpool, encountered the vortex on the night of the 23d. On the morning of the 25th, very early, the gale commenced at Liverpool, and did much damage. On the 26th, the vortex attained its northern limit;

but we have not been able to procure any account of its effects to the northward of Liverpool, although there can be but little doubt that it was violent on the coast of Scotland on the 26th; for the next day (27th) the vortex having made the turn, was near the latitude of Liverpool, and caused a *tremendous* storm, thus showing a continued state of activity for several days, or a peculiarly favorable local atmosphere in these parts.

It is very probable, also, that there was a conjunction of the central and inner vortex on the 27th. The inner vortex precedes the central in passing latitude 41°; but as the mean radius of its orbit is less than that of the central, it attains to a higher latitude, and has, consequently, to cross the path of the central, in order again to precede it descending in latitude 41°. As a very trifling change in the elements of the problem will cause great changes in the positions of the vortices on the surface of the earth, it cannot now be asserted that such a conjunction did positively occur at that time; but, it may be suspected, that a double disturbance would produce a greater commotion, or, in other words, a more violent storm.

It is on this account, combined with other auxiliary causes, that the vicinity of Cape Horn is so proverbially stormy, as well as for the low standard of the barometer in that latitude, it is the stationary point of the vortices in ordinary positions of the nodes and perigee of the moon. We have already alluded to the fact, that none of the vortices scarcely ever pass much beyond latitude 80°, and then only under favorable circumstances, so that we ought to infer, that gales in high latitudes should set from the poles towards the storms in lower latitudes. This is, no doubt, the fact, but, nevertheless, a hard southerly blow *may possibly* occur in high northern latitudes, if a storm should be raging very violently in a lower latitude on the opposite side of the pole, the distance across the circle of 80° being only about 1,400 miles. As the different vortices have a different limit in latitude every year, the determination of this turning point is obviously of great practical utility, as the fact may yet be connected with other phenomena, so as to give us the probable character of the polar ice at any assigned time. On this point we have more to say.

PASSAGES OF ALL THE VORTICES.

Our remarks have hitherto been confined to the central vortex. We shall now show from the record, that the other vortices are as effective in deranging the equilibrium of our atmosphere. In the following table we have given the passages of the different vortices, which will serve as their true positions within moderate limits, to calculate from, for all future time.

Passages of the Central and Lateral Vortices, observed in June and July, 1853, in latitude 41° 20′ north.

I signifying inner; O, outer; C, central; A, ascending; D, descending.

Order.	Vortex.	Date.	Meridian Passage.	Passage.	Calculated latitude and Remarks.
1st	I. A.	June 22	7 A. M.	south	Centre. About 40°.
		23	8 A. M.	north	Warsaw. Storm.
2d	O. D.	27	0 moon	north	
		28	1 A. M.	south	See record.
3d	C. A.	July 1	9 A. M.	south	
		2	10 A. M.	north	Lat. 43°. Storm.
4th	I. D.	7	5 P. M.	north	
		8	6 P. M.	south	Lat. New York. Storm.
5th	C. D.	12	5 P. M.	north	Aurora.
		13	6 P. M.	south	Stormy, very.
6th	O. A.	14	10 A. M.	south	
		15	11 A. M.	north	See Record.

The intervals between the ascending and descending passages of the different vortices, are

Between I. A. and I. D. from 11 to 14 days.
" O. A. " O. D. " 10 " 12 "
" C. A. " C. D. " 9 " 11 "

and the effect is greatest when the vortex comes to the meridian before the sun, and least when after the sun; in which case the full effect is not developed, sometimes until the following day.

A brief abstract from a journal of the weather for one sidereal period of the moon, in 1853.

June 21st. Fine clear morning (S. fresh):* noon very warm 88°; 4 P. M. plumous *cirri in south;* ends clear.

22d. Hazy morning (S. very fresh) arch of cirrus in west; 2 P. M., black in W.-N.-W.; 3 P. M., overcast and rainy; 4 P. M., a heavy gust from south; 4.30 P. M., blowing furiously (S. by W.); 5 P. M., tremendous squall, uprooting trees and scattering chimneys; 6 P. M., more moderate (W.)

23d. Clearing up (N.-W.); 8 A. M., quite clear; 11 A. M., bands of mottled cirri pointing N.-E. and S.-W.; ends cold (W.-N.-W.); the cirri seem to rotate from left to right, or with the sun.

24th. Fine clear cool day, begins and ends (N.-W.)

25th. Clear morning (N.-W. light); 2 P. M., (E.) calm; tufts of tangled cirri in north intermixed with radiating streaks, all passing eastward; ends clear.

26th. Hazy morning (S.-E.) cloudy; noon, a heavy windy looking bank in north (S. fresh), with dense cirrus fringe above on its upper edge; clear in S.

27th. Clear, warm, (W.); bank in north; noon bank covered all the northern sky, and fresh breeze; 10 P. M., a few flashes to the northward.

28th. Uniform dense cirro-stratus, (S. fresh); noon showers all round; 2 P. M., a heavy squall of wind, with thunder and rain (S.-W. to N.-W.); 8 P. M., a line of heavy cumuli in south; 8.30 P. M., a very bright and high cumulus in S.-W., protruding through a layer of dark stratus; 8.50 P. M., the cloud bearing E. by S., with three rays of electric light.†

* N. B. The letters in a parenthesis signify the direction of the wind.

† Giving this cloud the average velocity of thirty miles per hour, its

Fig. 17

June 29th. A stationary stratus over all, (S.-W. light); clear at night, but distant lightning in S.

30th. Stratus clouds (N.-E. almost calm); 8 A. M., raining gently; 3 P. M., stratus passing off to S; 8 P. M., clear, pleasant.

July 1st. Fine and clear; 8 A. M., cirrus in sheets, curls, wisps, and gauzy wreathes, with patches beneath of darker shade,

altitude was determined by the sextant at twelve miles, and we think under-estimated. While measuring, the author's attention was drawn to the fact, that although it appeared equally dense above and below, yet its middle part was the brightest, and as there was only a faint glimmer of twilight in the N.-W., he concluded that the cloud was self-luminous; for when the smallest stars were visible, it glowed about as bright as the milky-way in Sagittarius. Occasionally the whole cloud was lit up internally by the lightning, and about this time it sent off three rays: one horizontally, westward, which was the faintest; one about N.-W., towards Jupiter, and the brightest of the three; and another towards the north. These were not cirrus streaks, but veritable streams of electric matter, and had a very decided rotation from left to right, and continued visible about twenty minutes, as represented above..

all nearly motionless; close and warm (N.-E.); a long, low bank of haze in S., with one large cumulus in S.-W., but very distant.

July 2d. At 5 A. M., overcast generally with hazy clouds and fog of prismatic shades, chiefly greenish-yellow; 7 A. M., (S.-S.-E. freshening,) think in W; 8 A. M., (S. fresh) much cirrus, thick and gloomy; 9 A. M., a clap of thunder, and clouds hurrying to N.; a reddish haze all around; at noon the margin of a line of yellowish-red cumuli just visible above a gloomy-looking bank of haze in N.-N.-W., (S. very fresh;) warm, 86°; more cumuli in N.-W.—the whole line of cumuli N. are separated from the clouds south by a clear space. These clouds are borne rapidly past the zenith, but never get into the clear space—they seem to melt or to be turned off N.-E. The cumuli in N. and N.-W., slowly spreading E. and S.; 3 P. M., the bank hidden by small cumuli; 4 P. M., very thick in north, magnificent cumuli visible sometimes through the breaks, and beyond them a dark, watery back-ground, (S. strong); 4.30 P. M., wind round to N.-W. in a severe squall; 5 P. M., heavy rain, with thunder, &c.—all this time there is a bright sky in the south visible through the rain 15° high; 7 P. M., clearing, (S.-W. mod.)

July 3d. Very fine and clear, (N.-W.); noon, a line of large cumuli in N., and dark lines of stratus below, the cumuli moving eastward; 6 P. M., their altitude 2° 40′. Velocity 1° per minute; 9 P. M., much lightning in the bank north.*

July 4th. 6 A. M., a line of small cumulo-stratus, extending

* This day the central vortex passed in about latitude 47° N.—the southern margin cannot be nearer than 250 miles, throwing off the 40′ for the horizontal refraction, would give eight miles of altitude above a tangential plane. Then another seven miles, for curvature, will give an altitude of fifteen miles for the cumuli. The height of these thunder-clouds has been much under-estimated. They seem to rise in unbroken folds to a height of ten and twelve miles frequently; from the data afforded by the theory, we believe they will be found much higher sometimes—even as much as sixteen miles.

east and west, with a clear horizon north and south 10° high. This band* seems to have been thrown off by the central yesterday, as it moves slowly south, preserving its parallelism, although the clouds composing it move eastward. Fine and cool all day—(N.-W. mod.)—Lightning in N.

July 5th. Cloudy (N. almost calm), thick in E., clear in W.; same all day.

6th. Fine and clear (E. light); small cumuli at noon; clear night.

7th. Warm (S. E. light); cirrus bank N. W.; noon (S.) thickening in N.; 6 P. M., hazy but fine; 8 P. M., lightning in N.; 10 P. M., the lightning shows a heavy line of cumuli along the northern horizon; calm and very dark and incessant lightning in N.

8th. Last night after midnight commencing raining, slowly and steadily, but leaving a line of lighter sky south; much lightning all night, but little thunder.

8th. 6 A. M. Very low scud (500 feet high) driving south, still calm below, (N. light); 10 A. M., clearing a little; a bank north with cirrus spreading south; same all day; 9 P. M., wind freshening (N. stormy); heavy cumuli visible in S.; 10.30 P. M., quite clear, but a dense watery haze obscuring the stars; 12 P. M., again overcast: much lightning in S. and N.-W.

* These parallel bands, and bands lying east and west, are frequent in fine weather between two vortices. Sailors consider them a sign of settled weather. After dark there was frequently seen along the northern horizon flashes of lightning in a perfectly clear sky. But they were both faint and low, not reaching more than 4° or 5° above the horizon. After sunset there were very distinct rays proceeding from the sun, but they were shorter than on the evening of the 3d. These are caused by the tops of the great cumuli of the storm, when sunk below the horizon, intercepting the sun's rays, which still shine on the upper atmosphere. The gradation was very marked, and accorded with the different distances of the central vortex on the 3d and 4th—although, on the 4th, the nearest distance must have been over four hundred miles to the southern boundary of the storm.

9th. Last night (2 A. M. of 9th) squall from N.-W. very black; 4 A. M., still raining and blowing hard, the sky a perfect blaze, but very few flashes reach the ground; 7 A. M., raining hard; 8 A. M. (N.-W. strong); a constant roll of thunder; noon (N.-E.); 2 P. M. (N.); 4 P. M. clearing; 8 P. M., a line of heavy cumuli in S., but clear in N.-W., N., and N.-E.*

NEW YORK STORM, JULY 8, 1853.

"At 5 o'clock Friday afternoon, a terrible storm of rain, hail, and lightning, rose suddenly from the north-west, and passed over the upper part of the city and neighborhood. It was quite moderate in the lower part of the town, and probably scarcely felt on Staten Island. The whole affair lasted not more than a quarter of an hour, yet the results were most disastrous, as will be seen by the following accounts from our reporters:

"Happening to be in the neighborhood of the Palace about 5 o'clock Friday evening, we sought shelter under its ample roof from an impending thunder storm, of very threatening appearance, rapidly approaching from the west. We had scarcely passed the northern entrance, and reached the gallery by the nearest flight of steps, when the torrent—it was not rain, but an avalanche of water—struck the building; the gutters were filled on the windward side in a moment, and poured over

* It is worthy of notice here, that New York, which only differs by about 40 miles of latitude and 800 in longitude, had the storm earlier, near the time of the passage, as appears by the appended account of it. This proves, that a storm affects a particular latitude simultaneously, or approximately so. If this had to travel eastward to reach New York, it would have been the 10th instead of the 8th. The principal trouble was, however, in the early part of the evening of the 8th, to the south of Ottawa, where the strong wind was drawn in from the northward. If a vortex passes from north to south, leaving the observer between the passages, there must, nearly always, be a winding up squall from the north to clear away the vapory atmosphere.

an almost unbroken sheet of water, which was driven through the Venetian blind ventilators, into and half way across the north-west gallery, and also through the upper ventilators, falling upon the main floor of the north transept. Workmen hastened to close the blinds, but that did not prevent the deluge. The tinning of the dome being unfinished, the water, of course, came down in showers all over the centre. Many workmen were engaged on the dome when the shower struck it; several of them, in their haste to escape such dangerous proximity to the terrific lightning, came down single ropes, hand over hand. Large number of workmen were engaged all over the exterior, and such a scampering will rarely be witnessed but once in a lifetime. It was found impossible to close a north window, used for ingress and egress of workmen upon the roof, and the water came in, in almost solid columns. For a time the water was nearly two inches deep on the gallery floor, and poured down the stairs in miniature cascades.

"A great number of boxes, bales, and packages of goods lay upon the main floor, among which the water poured down from the edge of the gallery floor in destructive quantities. Fortunately but few goods were opened, and were upon the tables, or the damage would have been irreparable. As it is, we fear some of the goods are injured. In the height of the storm, the centre portion of the fanlight over the western entrance burst in, and several single lights were broken, by staging or otherwise.

"About ten minutes after the storm burst, the most terrific hailstorm we ever saw began to rattle, like discharges of musketry, upon the tin roof and glass sides. Some of the masses of ice were as large as hen's eggs. There were probably a thousand excited workmen in the building, and a good many exhibitors and visitors, among whom there were some twenty ladies, some of whom appeared a good deal alarmed at the awful din. A portion of the frame-work of the addition next to 42d street, went down with a terrible crash, and a part of the brick wall of the engine-house on the opposite side of the street, was blown over, crushing two or three shanties, fortunately without any other injury than driving the occupants out into the storm. But an awful scene occurred on the north side of 43d street, directly opposite the Latting Tower. Here two large unfinished frame buildings were blown, or rather, we should judge from appearances, were crushed down into a mass of ruins, such as may be imagined by supposing a great weight had fallen, with a circular, grinding motion, upon the first fine fabrics. One of them was partly sided, and had the rafters up, but no roof; the other was sided and roofed with tin, and was being plastered. We were told it was three stories high, 50 by 98 feet.

"We reached the ruins among the first, after the burst of the storm subsided a little. The scene was such as we pray God we may never witness again. A small portion of the roof and upper part of the front of the building stood or rather partly hung over the side-walk. The chamber and lower floor of the front rooms lay flat together. The sides were standing. In the rear all were down. In this building, besides the workmen, there were numerous laborers who had taken shelter under its roof when the storm drove them hurriedly from their work. How so many persons escaped death is truly wonderful. It can only be accounted for by supposing that they had a moment's warning, and rushed into the street. The first alarm was from the tearing off a portion of the tin roof, which was carried high over another building, and fell in the street. A horse and cart barely escaped being buried under this. It seems the frame of the other building came down with a deafening crash at the same time, confusing instead of warning those in danger. At any rate, before they could escape, they were buried in a mass of timber, and three of them instantly killed, and four or five dangerously wounded; and others slightly bruised and badly frightened. Several would have perished but for timely assistance to extricate them. In this they were greatly assisted by Jacob Steinant, boss carpenter of the Tower, who with his men rushed to the rescue, notwithstanding the pouring down torrents.

"In Williamsburgh, the storm lasted about fifteen minutes, doing an incalculable amount of damage to dwellings, foliage, &c. Hailstones came down in sizes from that of a hickory-nut to a large apple, some with such force as to drive them through the cloth awnings.

"The storm passed over Brooklyn lightly, in comparison with the effects across the Williamsburgh line. On Flushing avenue, beyond the Naval Hospital, a number of trees were uprooted, and the window-panes of the houses shattered. On the corner of Fulton and Portland avenues, three building were unroofed, and the walls of the houses were sprung to the foundation.

"On Spencer street, a new frame building was levelled with the ground. Along Myrtle, Classon, and other streets and avenues of East Brooklyn, many of the shade trees were uprooted, and the windows smashed. In Jay street, two trees were struck by lightning, but no other damage ensued.

"Several schooners at the foot of Jay street were forced from their moorings, but were soon after secured. A small frame house in Spencer street, just put under roof, was prostrated to the ground.

"We understand that a large barn filled with hay, situated on the road between Bushwick and Flushing, was struck by lightning and destroyed with its contents, embracing several head of live stock."*

July 10th, 3 A. M. Overcast and much lightning in south (N. mod.); 7 A. M., clear except in south; 6 P. M. (E.); 10 P. M., lightning south; 11 P. M., auroral rays long but faint, converging to a point between Epsilon Virginis and Denebola, in west; low down in west thick with haze; on the north the rays con-

* From the *New York Tribune*, July 9, 1853.

verged to a point still lower; lightning still visible in south. This is an aurora in the west.

11th. Fine clear morning (N.-E.); same all day; no lightning visible to-night, but a bank of clouds low down in south, 2° high, and streaks of dark stratus below the upper margin.

12th. Fine and clear (N.-E.); noon, a well defined arch in S.-W., rising slowly; the bank yellowish, with prismatic shades of greenish yellow on its borders. This is the O. A. At 6 P. M., the bank spreading to the northward. At 9 P. M., thick bank of haze in north, with bright auroral margin; one heavy pyramid of light passed through Cassiopœa, travelling *westward* 1½° per minute. This moves to the other side of the pole, but not more inclined towards it than is due to prospective, if the shaft is very long; 11.10 P. M., saw a mass of light more diffuse due east, reaching to *Markab*, then on the prime vertical. It appears evident this is seen in profile, as it inclines downwards at an angle of 10° or 12° from the perpendicular. It does not seem very distant. 12 P. M., the aurora still bright, but the brightest part is now west of the pole, before it was east.

13th, 6 A. M. Clear, east and north; bank of cirrus in N.-W., *i. e.*, from N.-N.-E. to W. by S.; irregular branches of cirrus clouds, reaching almost to south-eastern horizon; wind changed (S.-E. fresh); 8 A. M., the sky a perfect picture; heavy regular shafts of dense cirrus radiating all around, and diverging from a thick nucleus in north-west, the spaces between being of clear blue sky. The shafts are rotating from north to south, the nucleus advancing eastward.

Appearance of the central vortex descending at 8 A. M., July 13th, 1853:

In Fig. 18, the circle represents the whole sky from the zenith to the horizon, yet it can convey but a very faint idea of the regularity and vividness of this display. The reflected image of the sky was received from a vessel of turbid water, which will be found better than a mirror, when the wind will permit.

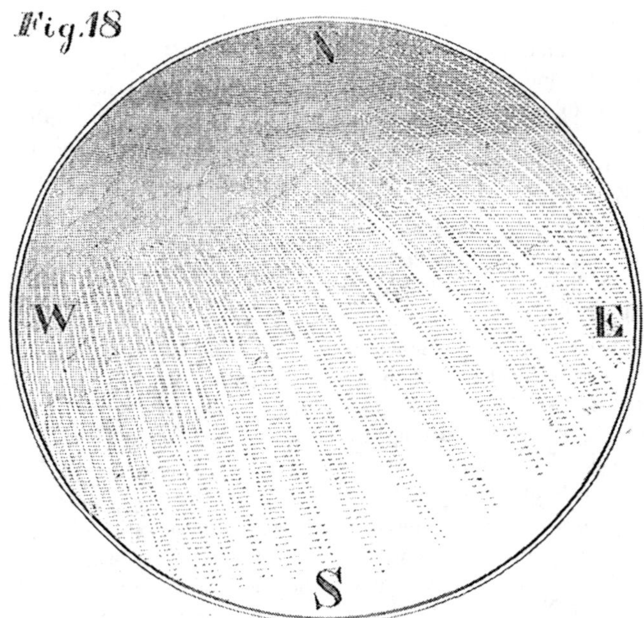

At noon (same day) getting thicker (S.-E. very fresh); 6 P. M., moon on meridian, a prismatic gloom in south, and very thick stratus of all shades; 9 P. M., very gloomy; wind stronger (S.-E.); 10 P. M, very black in south, and overcast generally.

14th. Last night about 12 P. M. commenced raining; 3 A. M., rained steadily; 7 A. M., same weather; 8.20 A. M., a line of low storm-cloud, or scud, showing very sharp and white on the dark back ground all along the southern sky. This line continues until noon about 10° at the highest, showing the northern boundary of the storm to the southward; 8 P. M., same bank visible, although in rapid motion eastward; same time clear overhead, with cirrus fringe pointing north from the bank; much lightning in south (W. fresh); so ends.

15th. Last night a black squall from N.-W. passed south without rain; at 3 A. M. clear above, but very black in south (calm below all the time); 9 A. M., the bank in south again throwing off rays of cirri in a well-defined arch, whose vortex is south: these pass east, but continue to form and preserve their linear direction to the north; no lightning in south to-night.

16th. Clear all day, without a stain, and calm.

17th. Fine and clear (N.-E. light); 6 P. M., calm.

18th. Fair and cloudy (N.-E. light); 6 P. M., calm.

19th. Fine and clear (N. fresh); I. V. visible in S.-W.

20th. 8 A. M., bank in N.-W. with beautiful cirrus radiations; 10 A. M., getting thick with dense plates of cream-colored cirrus visible through the breaks; gloomy looking all day (N.-E. light).*

Appearance of the Inner Vortex at 8 A. M., July 20th, 1853, including the whole sky. (See Fig. 19.)

This was a different passage of the Inner Vortex ascending as compared with the same 28 days before. At that date (June 22) it did great damage in the central parts of Illinois. Still this last passage was very palpable—the clouds were very irregularly assorted—plates of cirrus above and beneath cumulus—various kinds of cirrus clouds, and that peculiar prismatic haze

* These pages are now in the compositors' hands, (Nov. 21st,) and up to the last moment the author has observed carefully in New York the passages of these vortices. October 24th, the inner vortex descending produced a violent storm on the coast, and much damage ensued. November 7th, the same vortex ascending was also severe. And on November 13th, early, the passage of the central vortex ascending, caused a flood in Connecticut of a very disastrous nature. Would it not pay the insurance offices to patronize such investigations in view of such palpable facts as these?

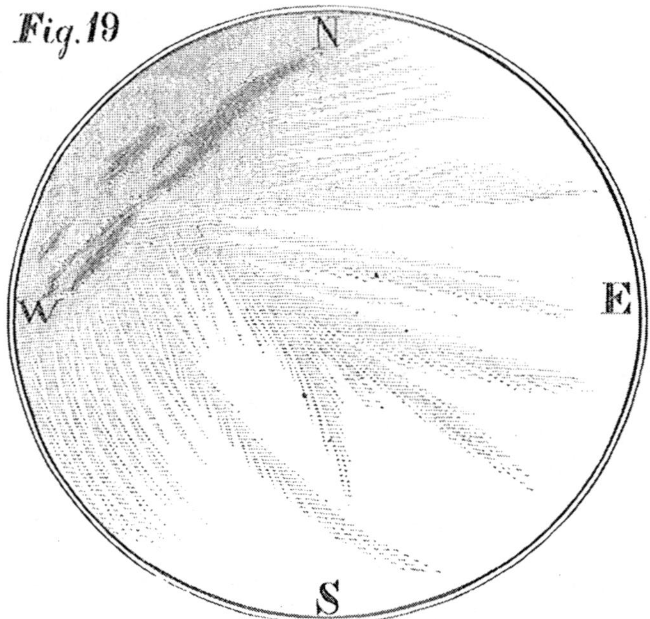

which is a common sign of the passage of a vortex. The appearance depicted above is a very common, although a very evanescent appearance. When the sky appears of a clear blue through the cirri, there will be generally fresh gales without any great electrical derangement; but if the clear spaces are hazy, gradually thickening towards the nucleus, a storm may be expected. Any one who wishes to understand the indications of the clouds, must watch them closely for many years, before he can place much reliance upon them. But we shall again advert to this point.

We have now passed through one sidereal period of the moon. We might continue the record, but it would be tedious.

The passages of these vortices vary in violence at different times, as we might expect; but they never cease to circulate, and never will as long as the moon remains a satellite to the earth; and if we take the passage of any of these vortices, and add thereto the time of one sidereal period of the moon, we get approximately the time of the next passage. When the elements of the lunar orbit tend to accelerate the passages, they may come in 26 days; and when to retard, in 28 days; and these are about the limits of the theory.

Having begun and ended this record of the weather with the passage of the Inner vortex ascending, it may not be amiss to notice one more, (the August passage,) as it offers a peculiarity not often so distinctly marked. We have alluded to the greater force of the storms when the passage of the vortex corresponds to the passage of the line of low barometer or the depression point of a great atmospheric wave, which is also due to the action of the ether. In consequence of these waves passing from west to east, the storm will only be violent when formed a little to the westward. If the storm forms to the eastward, we neither see it nor feel it, as it requires time to develop its strength, and always in this latitude travels eastward; so that storms may generally be said to come from the west, although the exciting cause travels from east to west. In the case now alluded to, the weather indicated a high barometer, and the storm formed immediately to the eastward, even showing a distinct circular outline. We subjoin a description.

August 15th. Clear morning (N.-E.), a bank of cumuli in south: noon quite cloudy in S. and clear in north. (N.-E.)

16th. Clear morning (N.-E.); 3 P. M., getting very black in E. and S.-E., very *clear* to the *westward;* 4 P. M., much thunder and lightning in east, and evidently raining hard; 5 P. M., a violent squall from *east* for 10 minutes; tore up several trees; 6 P. M., the storm passing eastward, clear in west all this time; 6.30 P. M., the storm forming a regular arch, the vertex being in *S.-E.;* 8 P. M., the arch of hazy cirrus and heavy cumulus much lower in S.-E., wind still moderate from east; 10 P. M., clear all around, but lightning in S.-E. and E.

17th. Fine clear morning (W.); noon, scattered cumuli in north; 6 P. M., a beautifully regular arch of dense cumuli and cirrus margin in *N.-E.*, with a constant glimmer of lightning; 7 P. M., very clear to the west, and north-west, and south; along the northern horizon a line of high peaked cumuli terminating in N.-N.-W.; a continued roll of distant thunder in the circular bank in N.-E., and not a moment's cessation to the lightning; the electric excitement advancing westward along the lines of cumuli; the cirrus haze also rising and passing towards S.-W.; 8 P. M., the sky alive with lightning, the cirrus now reaches the zenith; no streaks of lightning coming to the earth; they seem to radiate from the heaviest mass of cumuli, and spread slowly (sufficiently so to follow them) in innumerable fibres over the cloudy cirrus portion of the sky; every flash seems to originate in the same cloud; 8.30 P. M., one branching flash covered the whole north-eastern half of the sky, no leafless tree of the forest could show so many branches; 9.30 P. M., all passed to S.-W. without rain, leaving behind a large cumulus, as if it lagged behind. From this cumulus a straight line of lightning shot up 10° above the cloud into a perfectly clear sky, and terminated abruptly without branching.

We have been thus particular in giving these details, as this was a clear case confirming the principles advanced, that the vortices do not form a continuous line of disturbance, in their daily passage around the earth. It shows also that the barometer, in connection with these principles, will be a far more useful instrument than it has yet proved itself, for practical service as an indicator of the weather.

SECTION THIRD.

OBJECTIONS TO LUNAR INFLUENCE.

We have now presented a theory of the weather, which accounts for many prominent phenomena, a few of which we shall enumerate. It is an observed fact, that in all great storms electrical action is more or less violent, and that without this element it seems impossible to explain the velocity of the wind in the tornado, its limited track, and the formation of large masses of ice or hail in the upper regions of the atmosphere. It is also an observed fact, that the barometer is in continued motion, which can only be legitimately referred to a change in the weight of the atmospheric column. This we have explained as due to atmospheric waves, caused by the greater velocity of rotation of the external ether, as well as to the action of the three great vortices. These causes, however, only partially produce the effect—the greater portion of the daily oscillations is produced by the action of the great radial stream of the solar vortex, as we shall presently explain. It is an observed fact, that, although the storm is frequently violent, according to the depression of the barometer, it is not always so. According to the theory, the storm will be violent, *ceteris paribus*, on a line of low barometer, but may still be violent, when the contrary obtains. Another fact in the disturbance of the magnetic needle during a storm. Storms are also preceded generally by a rise in the thermometer, and succeeded by a fall; also by a fall in the barometer, and succeded by a rise. It is also well known, that hurricanes are unknown at the equator, and probably at the poles also. At all events, they are rare in lat. 80°, and, according to Capt. Scoresby, storms are there frequently raging to the south, while above, there is clear sky and fine weather, with a stiff breeze from the northward. The greater violence of storms in those regions where the magnetic intensity is greater in the same latitude, the probable connection of peculiarities in the electric state of the atmosphere with earthquakes, and the indications of the latter afforded by the magnet; the preponderance of westerly winds at a great elevation in every latitude on the globe visited by man; and the frequent superposition of warm layers of air above cold ones at those elevations, are all facts worthy of note. And the connection of cirrus clouds with storms, as well as with the aurora, indicates that the producing cause is external to the atmosphere, and gradually penetrates below. The theory fully explains this, and is confirmed by the fantastic wreathings and rapid formation of these clouds in straight lines of a hundred miles and upwards. But time would fail us in pointing out a tithe of the phenomena, traceable to the same cause, which keeps our atmosphere in a perpetual state of change, and we shall only advert to one more peculiarity of the theory. It places meteorology on a mathematical basis, and explains why it is that a storm may be raging at one place, while in another, not very remote, the weather may be fine, and yet be dependent on the position of the moon.

That the moon has exerted an influence on the weather has been the popular creed from time immemorial; but, ignorant of the mode in which this influence was exerted, men have often been found who have fostered the popular belief for their own vanity or advantage; and, on the other hand, philosophers have assailed it more by ridicule than by argument, as a relic of a barbarian age. Not so with all; for we believe we are not wrong in stating, that the celebrated Olbers compared the moon's positions with the weather for fifty years, before he gave his verdict against it. He found the average amount of rain at the perigee about equal to the amount at the apogee, as much at the full as at the change, and no difference at the quadratures. But this fact does not throw a feather in the scale by which this theory is weighed. Popular opinions, of remote origin, have almost always some foundation in fact, and it is not much more wise to reject them, than to receive them. The Baron Von Humboldt—a man possessing that rare ingredient of learning, a practical common sense—observes: "That arrogant spirit of incredulity which rejects facts, without attempting to investigate them, is, in some cases, more injurious than an unquestioning credulity."* If a popular belief or prejudice be absurd, its traditional preservation for a thousand years or more may very well account for the absurdity.

The present system of astronomy still retains the motley garniture of the celestial sphere, as handed down from the most remote antiquity; and granting that ages of ignorance and superstition have involved the history of the different constellations in a chaos of contradictory traditions, there is no doubt at the foundation some seeds of truth which may even yet emerge from the rubbish of fable, and bear fruit most precious. That the zodial† signs are significant records of something worthy of being preserved, is prejudice to deny; and we must be allowed to regard the Gorgons and Hydras of the skies as interesting problems yet unsolved, as well as to consider that the belief in lunar influence is a fragment of a true system of natural philosophy which has become more and more debased in postdiluvian times. Amongst those who have not summarily ignored the influence of the moon, is Toaldo, a Spanish physicist, who endeavored to show the connection

* Hum. Cosmos, art. Aerolites.

† We shall in all cases use this abbreviation for the extremely awkward word zodiacal.

between the recurrence of warm and cold seasons, and the semi-revolution of the lunar nodes and apogee, and proposed six of those periods, or about fifty-four years, as the cycle in which the changes of the weather would run through their course. According to the present theory, it is not likely such a cycle will ever be discovered. There are too many secular, as well as periodic influences combining, to produce the effect; and the times are too incommensurable. Lately, Mr. Glaisher has presented a paper to the Royal Society, giving about fourteen years from observation. Others have lately attempted to connect the changes of the seasons with the solar spots, as well as with the variations of the magnetism of the earth, but without any marked result.

It may, however, be urged, that if the sidereal period of the moon be approximately a cycle of change, it would have been detected long ago. One reason why this has been so long concealed, is the high latitude of the observers. Spain, Italy, and Turkey, are better situated than other European countries; but the scientific nations lie further north; and from these the law has gone forth to regulate more southern lands. In the United States, particularly in the great plains of the west, the weather can be better compared; not only on account of the latitude being more favorable, but also on account of the greater magnetic intensity of the western hemisphere.

It must also be remembered that there are in latitude 40°, five or six distinct passages of the disturbing cause in one sidereal period of the moon. If two of these periods are drawn closer together by the change of the elements, the interval between two others must necessarily be increased. Besides, the effect produced is not always the same, for reasons already adverted to. One vortex may be more violent one month, or for a few days in one month, while another may be more active the next. It may also happen that for several successive passages, the passage shall be central in one latitude, while two or three degrees north or south, another place shall be passed by. In different months and in different years, as well as in different seasons of the year, the energy of the ether may be augmented or diminished. But it may be said, that, supposing the theory true, if its indications are so uncertain, it is of little value. By no means. It is true there are many things to be inquired into; but it is a great thing in this science to be able to take the first step in the right direction,—to find even the *key* of the portal. It is a great stride to be able to say, a storm may happen at such a time, but cannot happen at another; that a storm, when raging, will go in this direction, rather than in that; that it will be central here, and less violent yonder; and when we consider its bearing on astronomical and other science, it is difficult to exaggerate its value to the world at large.

Again, it may be said that rain, and cloudy days, and fresh breezes, and even strong winds, sometimes occur, when the vortices do not pass centrally. This is true; yet only indicating that where the vortices are central, an unusual disturbance is taking place. But there is another cause, which was purposely omitted in considering the prominent features of the theory, in order not to encumber the question with secondary influences. By referring to Fig. 3, section 1, we see that the lateral vortices of the globe are continually passing off to the southward, in the northern hemisphere, in a succession of dimples, and continually reforming. We will now represent this mode of action in profile, as it actually occurs in the illustration we have used.

The vortex passing off from O, (Fig. 20,) although it does not actually reach the surface of the atmosphere, affects the equilibrium of the ether, and, for a short distance from the parent vortex, may cause an ascensional movement of the air. If to this is conjoined a northerly wind from the vortex, a band of clouds will be produced, and perhaps rain; but violent storms never occur in the intervals, except as a steady gale, caused by the violence of a distant storm. Thus, it will frequently be noticed that

Fig. 20

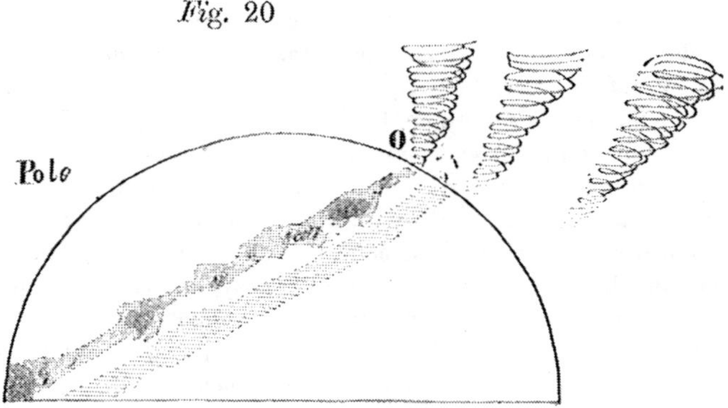

these vortices are flanked by bands of clouds, which pass southward, although the individual clouds may be moving eastward. Hence, instead of disproving the theory, they offer strong evidence of its truth; and could we view the earth from the moon with a telescope, we should no doubt see her beautifully belted.

But it may be again asked, why should not the weather be the same generally, in the same latitude, if this theory be true? If the earth were a globe of level land, or altogether of water, no doubt it would be similar; but it must be remembered, that both land and water are very unequally distributed; that the land is of varying extent and elevation—here a vast plain, far removed from the ocean, and there a mountain chain, interposing a barrier to the free course of the atmospheric currents; sometimes penetrating in full width into the frigid zone, and again dwindling to a few miles under the equator. One very important distinction is also to be remarked, in the superficial area of the different zones, reckoning from the equator, and taking the hemisphere as 100 parts:

Frigid zone	8 parts.
Temperate "	52 "
Torrid "	40 "

For as the time of rotation in every latitude is the same, the area to be disturbed in the same time, is less in high latitudes, and there a greater similarity will obtain, *ceteris paribus.* In lower latitudes, where both land and water stretch away for thousands of miles, it is not wonderful that great differences should exist in the electrical and hygrometric state of the air.

The summer of many countries is always dry—California for instance. In winter, in the same country, the rains are apparently incessant. This of course depends on the power of the sun, in diverting the great annual currents of the atmosphere. As long as the dry north-west trade sets down the coast of California, the circumstances are not favorable for giving full development to the action of the vortices. When the trade wind ceases, and the prevailing winds come from the south, loaded with vapor, the vortices produce storms of any magnitude; but (and we speak from two years' observation) the passages of the vortices are as distinctly marked there in winter time, as they are in the eastern States; and in summer time, also, they are very perceptible. The same remark applies to Mediterranean countries, particularly to Syria and Asia Minor; although the author's opportunity for observing lasted only from April to December, during one season. If we are told it never rains on the coast of Peru, or in Upper Egypt, it does not seriously militate against the theory. The cause is local, and the Samiel and the sand storm of the desert, is but another phase of the question, explicable on the same general principles. From the preceding remarks it will be seen, that in order to foretell the character of particular days, a previous knowledge of the weather at that particular place, and for some considerable time, is requisite; and hence the difficulty of laying down general rules, until the theory is more fully understood.

MODIFYING CAUSES.

We now come to the causes which are auxiliary and interfering. It is natural that we should regard the sun as the first and most influential of these causes, as being the source of that variation in the temperature of the globe, which alternately clothes the colder regions in snow and verdure. The heat of the sun undoubtedly causes the ether of the lower atmosphere to ascend, not by diminution of its specific gravity; for it has no ponderosity; but precisely by increase of tension, due to increase of motion. This aids the ascensional movement of the air, and therefore, when a vortex is in conjunction with the sun, its action is increased—the greatest effect being produced when the vortex comes to the meridian a little before the sun. This has a tendency to make the period of action to appear dependent on the phases of the moon, which being the most palpable of all the moon's variations, has been naturally regarded by mankind as the true *cause* of the changes of the weather. Thus Virgil in his Georgics, speaking of the moon's influence and its signs:

> "Sin ortu in quarto (Namque is certissimus auctor)
> Pura, nec obtusis per cœlum cornibus ibit;
> Totus et ille dies, et qui nascentur ab illo,
> Exactum ad mensem, pluviâ ventisque carebunt."

Hence, also, in the present day we hear sailors speak of the full and change, or the quartering of the moon, in connection with a gale at sea; thus showing, at least, their faith in the influence of the phenomenon. Yet it is actually the case, at certain times, that in about latitude 40° and 41°, the storms appear about a week apart.

There is some reason, also, to suspect, that there is a difference of temperature on opposite sides of the sun. As the synodical rotation is nearly identical with the siderent period of the moon, this would require about forty-four years to run its course, so as to bring the phenomena to exact coincidence again. Since these observations were made, it is understood that Sig. Secchi has determined that the equatorial regions of the sun are hotter than his polar regions. It may be owing to this fact, that we have inferred a necessity for a change, whose period is a multiple of the sun's synodical rotation, but it is worthy of examination by those who possess the necessary conveniences.

Another period which must influence the character of different years, depends on the conjunction of the perigee of the lunar orbit with the node. Taking the mean direct motion of the moon's perigee, and the mean retrograde motion of the node, we find that it takes six years and one day nearly from conjunction to conjunction. Now, from the principles laid down, it follows, that when the perigee of the orbit is due north, and the ascending node in Aries, that the vortices of the earth will attain their greatest north latitude; and when these conditions are reversed, the vortices will reach their highest limit in the lowest latitude. This will materially affect the temperature of the polar regions. In the following table, we have calculated the times of the conjunctions of the apogee and pole of the orbit, taking the mean motions. It may be convenient to refer to by-and-bye, remembering that when the conjunction takes place due south, the vortices reach the highest, but when due north, the vortices in the northern hemisphere have their lowest upper limit:

CONJUNCTION OF APOGEE AND POLE OF ORBIT.*

Year.	Month and Day.	Longitude.
1804, . . .	April 18th, . . .	220°
1810, . . .	" 17th, . . .	104

* It is here assumed, that all the vortices are at their apogee at the same time, and, consequently, they lie in different longitudes; but the central being between, its position is taken for the average position of the three.

Year.	Month and Day.	Longitude.
1816, . . .	April 16th, . . .	348°
1822, . . .	" 15th, . . .	232
1828, . . .	" 14th, . . .	116
1834, . . .	" 12th, . . .	360
1840, . . .	" 11th, . . .	244
1846, . . .	" 10th, . . .	128
1852, . . .	" 9th, . . .	12
1858, . . .	" 8th, . . .	255
1864, . . .	" 7th, . . .	139
1870, . . .	" 6th, . . .	23
1876, . . .	" 5th, . . .	267

By this we see that the vortices have never attained their highest limit during the present century, but that in 1858 their range will be in a tolerable high latitude, and still higher in 1876—neglecting the eccentricity of the orbit.

A very potent influence is also due to the heliocentric longitude of the sun, in determining the character of any given year. Let us explain:

The moon's inertia forces the earth from the mechanical centre of the terral system, but is never able to force her clear from the central axis. With the sun it is different. He possesses many satellites (planets). Jupiter alone, from his great mass and distance, is able to displace the whole body of the sun. If other planets conspire at the same side, the centre of the sun may be displaced a million of miles from the mechanical centre of the solar system. Considering this centre, therefore, as the centre of an imaginary sun, from which heliocentric longitudes are reckoned, the longitude of the real sun will vary with the positions of the great planets of the system. Now, although this *systematic* longitude will not be exactly similar to the heliocentric longitude reckoned from the sun's centre, yet, for the purposes intended, it will correspond sufficiently, and we shall speak of the longitude of the sun as if we reckoned heliocentric longitudes from the mechanical centre of the system. When we come to consider the solar spots, we shall enter into this more fully. In the following diagram we shall be able to perceive a cause for variation of seasons in a given year, as well as for the general character of that year.

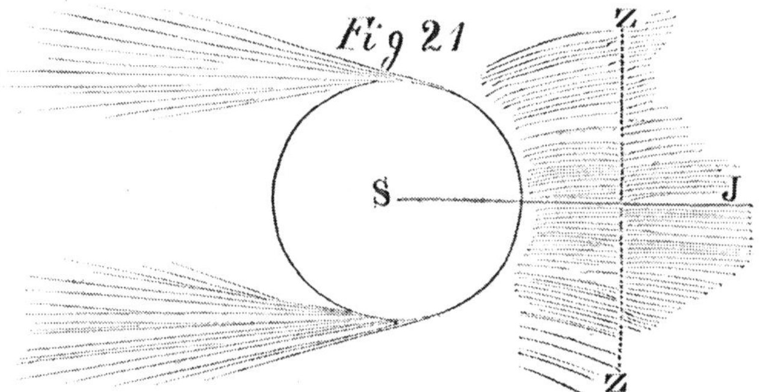

Let S represent the centre of the sun, and the circle a vertical section of the sun, cutting through the centre,—S J being in the equatorial plane of the vortex, of which Z Z′ represents the axis. As the ether descends the poles or axis at Z, it is met by the current down the opposite pole, and is thence deflected in radii along the equatorial plane to J. But on the side S, the ether is opposed by the body of the sun; its direction is consequently changed, and cross currents are produced,—assuming it as a principle, that the ethereal fluid is permeable by other currents of similar matter, and that it tends always to move in right lines. This granted, it is evident that, in passing the sun, the quick moving ether forms a conical shell, (the sun being at the apex,) so that the strongest current of ether is in this conical shell, or at the surface of this conical space. As the plane of the ecliptic is not much inclined to the sun's equator, and this last probably not much inclined to the plane of the vortex, should the earth have the same *heliocentric* longitude at the time, (or nearly the same,) she would be in an eddy, as respects the radial stream, and be protected from its full force by the body of the sun.

Now, the ether comes down the axis with the temperature of space, and may possibly derive a *little* additional temperature in passing over the body of the sun ; so that in this position the earth is protected from the chilling influence of the radial stream, by being protected by the body of the sun. And although, from the immense velocity of the ether, it cannot derive much additional temperature, there may still be an appreciable difference, due to this cause.

It is the chilling influence of the ethereal stream which originated the idea among philosophers, of *frigorific impressions, darted from a clear sky.* In some years the sun will be nearly in the centre of the system ; in other years the axis of the vortex will not come near the sun. And as the sun's longitude may vary through the entire circle, it may happen that the earth's longitude shall coincide in winter or summer, or spring or autumn. When, however, the earth emerges from the protection of the sun, and enters the conical shell, considered as a space of considerable depth, she will again be exposed to the full force of the radial stream, rendered more active by the previous deflection, and by the numerous cross currents pervading it ; so that a mild and calm winter may be succeeded by a cold and stormy spring. The present season, (1853,) the earth's longitude coincided with the sun's longitude in about 135°, and consequently was in the conical space spoken of, during February and March ; but the radius rector of the sun's centre, being then less than 300,000 miles, the protection was not as complete as it is sometimes. Still, the general fineness of these months was remarkable ; yet in April and May, when the earth became again exposed to the action of the solar stream, the effect was to retard the spring, and disappoint the prognostications of the weather-wise. In applying these principles, we must consider the effect in those latitudes which are more readily affected,—that is, in the temperate zone, midway between the two extreme zones of heat and cold.

In 1837 and 1838, the longitude of the sun's centre corresponded with the earth's, in August and September, when there was neither rain nor electrical excitement; and consequently those seasons were sickly over the whole country. Now, there is another cause which renders the months of August, September, and October, deficient in electrical energy, and consequently more prone to be sickly. If, therefore, the two causes unite their influence, the autumnal months will be more sickly at those times. This last cause, however, only affects the *northern latitudes* in autumn, and consequently, *ceteris paribus*, the autumnal months should not be so proverbially sickly in the southern hemisphere. This is, however, only suggestive.

Again, in 1843, the winter was very mild in January and February; but in March it turned cold and stormy, and continued through April. In this year the longitude of the sun was nearly the same as in 1853,—the two longitudes of the earth and sun corresponding about the last of January; but in March, the earth forsook the comparative calm produced by the sun's position, and hence the greater cold.*

Thus it appears at every step we take, that the different members of the solar system do indeed belong to the same family, whose least motions have their influence on the rest. Who could have anticipated that the position of Jupiter in his orbit had anything to do with the health of this remote planet, or with the mildness of its seasons? In this we have a clue to the origin of that astrological jargon about planetary aspects being propitious or malign. Philosophers are even yet too prone to wrap themselves in their mantle of academic lore, and despise the knowledge of the ancients, while there is reason to

* It is far from improbable that the effect produced in one zone of climate, may be reversed in another, from the nature of the cause.

believe that the world once possessed a true insight into the structure of the solar system. As war became the occupation of mankind, under the despotic rule of ambition, so truth retired, and ignorance seizing upon her treasures, has so mutilated and defaced them, that their original beauty no longer appears. Let us hope that the dawn of a better day is approaching.

There is yet another cause (just alluded to) which modifies the action of the vortices.

We have shown that, if the periodic times of the planets are approximately equal to the periodic times of the contiguous parts of the solar vortex, the density of the ether is directly as the square roots of the distances from the centre. As the earth is at her perihelion about the first of January, the density of the surrounding ether is then less than in other parts of the orbit; consequently, if we suppose that there is a continual tendency to equilibrium, the ether of space must press inwards, during the time between the perihelion and aphelion, (*i. e.*, from January to July,) lowering the temperature and increasing the electrical action of those months. As the distance from the sun is most rapidly augmenting about the first of April, and the effective power of the sun's radiation is most rapidly increasing in May; by combining the two we shall find, that about the first of May we shall have considerable electrical action, and cold weather. This explains also, in part, the prevalent tradition of certain days in May being very cold.* When the earth leaves the aphelion, a reaction takes place, being most rapid in September. There is then an *escape* of ether from the earth, which keeps up the temperature, and causes these months to be sickly, from the negative electrical state of the atmosphere. In the southern hemisphere, the effects in the same season will

* That the 11th, 12th, and 13th of May should recede 2° in temperature as determined by Mædler from observations of 86 years, at a time when the power of the sun so rapidly augments, is strongly confirmatory of the theory. See *Cosmos*, p. 121.

be reversed, which may partly account for the greater degree of cold in that hemisphere, and for accelerating the approach of both summer and winter, while in the north they were both retarded.

We must now advert to another cause, which of all others is probably the most important, at least to the other members of the solar system.

In every part of the solar vortex the ether is continually pressing outwards. We are not now speaking of the radial stream, but of the slower spiral motion of the ether around the axis of the vortex, whose centrifugal force is bearing the whole body of the ether outwards, thus rarefying the central parts, and thus giving rise to the polar influx, from which arises the radial stream. This may be made more intelligible, by reflecting that the polar current is comparatively dense ether, and that the length of the axis of the vortex prevents this influx current coming in sufficient quantities to restore an equilibrium in the density of the medium. Yet, what does come down the poles, is distributed rapidly along the equatorial plane, leaving the space still rarefied. Now we perceive, that in order for the radial stream to continue in action, requires the whole medium of the vortex to be also moving outward; it is therefore continually condensed as it proceeds. This condensation necessarily converts much of the specific heat of the ether into sensible heat; so that the *temperature* of the medium is continually increasing, as the distance from the sun increases.

When we contemplate the solar system as the emanation of one Great Mind, we naturally seek for evidence of the wisdom of a supreme intelligence in *all* the arrangements of that system. But, however humbly and reverently we may speak of these arrangements, we can scarcely avoid the wish, that the planetary distances had been differently arranged, if Newton's doctrine be true, that space is a vacuum, and that the heat of a planet, is inversely as the squares of the distances from the sun.

For, to speak of the temperature of space, except as dependent on this law, is one of those many incomprehensible inconsistencies with which philosophers are chargeable. If the Newtonian philosophy is literally true, space has *no temperature*, and the surface heat of the planet Neptune is nearly 1,000 times less than on our own globe. Again, on Mercury it is seven times greater, which heat would scorch and consume every organic substance on the earth, and speedily envelope the boiling ocean in a shroud of impermeable vapor. Granting even that space may not be a vacuum, and yet the law of gravitation be true, we may still be allowed to consider both Saturn and Uranus and Neptune, as inhospitable abodes for intelligent creatures; and, seeing the immensity of room in the system, there is no reason why these planets might not have been permitted to revolve nearer the great source of light and life and cheering emanations. To suggest the resources of Omnipotence is no argument. He has surrounded us with analogies which are seen, by which we may attain a knowledge of those which are not seen; and we have every reason to suppose that the great Author of nature is not indifferent to the aspects under which his works reveal him unto his creatures. Yet there is (on the above hypothesis) an apparent want of harmony in the planetary distances; and if frail mortality may be permitted to speak out, an explanation is needed to obviate this seeming anomaly in the economy of the world. The more we learn of the physical arrangements of the universe, the more do they correspond with our experience of the nice adaptation of the means to the end which obtains in our own globe, and we can only judge of other planets by the analogies around us. Here, there, are extremes of temperature it is true: it is necessary there should be, and we can see and understand the necessity in all such cases, and how they conduce to the general average of good. But, astronomers can give no reason why it is necessary that some planets of our system should be placed so remote that the sun is frittered down to a star, whose heatless light is but a mockery to those frigid realms.

Now, according to this theory, the temperature of Neptune may be far more uniform and conducive to life than that of our own globe. The chilling influence of the solar stream at that planet being nearly null, and the temperature of the surrounding space far greater. So also Mercury, instead of being the burning planet of the schools, may suffer the most from cold.

The planet Mars is generally considered, of all the members of the system, most nearly to resemble our own world. The telescope not only reveals seas and continents, but the snowy circles round his poles, which appear to increase and diminish, as his winter is beginning or ending. This planet's ecliptic is similar to our own in inclination or obliquity, his distance, also, is far greater, and his winter longer; yet, for all this, his snow zones are less than on our own globe. This anomalous fact has, we believe, never been noticed before; but it is explicable on the theory, and therefore confirms it. Mars has no satellite, and therefore his centre will be coincident with the centre of the marsial vortex. There will be no *lateral vortices* to derange his atmosphere, and if the axis of his vortex coincides also with the axis of the planet, the central vortex will be continually over the poles, *and there will be no storms on the planet Mars.* A capital fact connected with this, is the want of belts, as in Jupiter and Saturn; for these planets have satellites, and if *they* are not massive enough, the belts may be produced by an obliquity in the axis of the Jovial and Saturnial vortices. If Mars had an aurora like the earth, it is fair to presume the telescope would ere this have shown it. He is, therefore, in equilibrium. In applying this reasoning to the earth, we perceive that a certain influence is due to the difference of temperature of the ethereal medium surrounding the earth, at perihelion and aphelion, being least at the former, and greatest at the latter.

As a modifying and interfering cause in the action of the vortices, we must mention the great natural currents of the atmosphere, due to the earth's rotation.

It is considered that the sun is the principal cause of these great currents. By elevating the surface atmosphere of the equator, a lateral current is induced from the north and south; but on account of the enlarging circles of latitude, their direction tends more from the north-east and south-east. These currents are usually called the trades. Without disputing the correctness of this, it may be doubted whether the whole effect is due to the sun. As this principle affects the ocean likewise, it is necessary to look into it; and in order to simplify the question, we will first suppose our globe covered entirely by the ocean, without any protuberant land.

Let us assign a uniform depth of ten miles to this ocean. In the Fig. following, the two circles will represent the surface and bottom of the ocean respectively. The axis of rotation

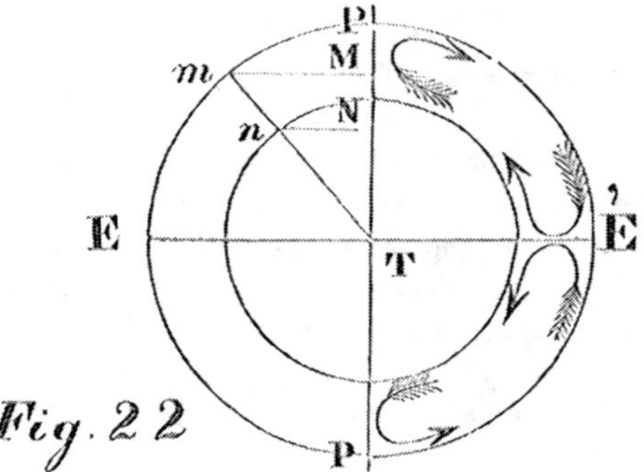

Fig. 22

is thus represented by the line P P′. Let us consider two particles of water at m and n, as feeling the influence of this rotation; they will, of course, be both urged towards the equator by the axifugal force. Now, every particle in the ocean being also urged by the same force, it might be supposed that after a protuberant mass of water had accumulated at the equator E E′, the whole ocean would be in equilibrium. This would not follow. The particle at *m* is urged by a greater force than *n*; consequently the particle at *n* is overborne by the pressure at *m*. Considering both in the same direction, yet the particle at *n* must give way, and move in the opposite direction. Just as the heaviest scale of the balance bears up the lightest, although both gravitate towards the same point. This is so self-evident that it would seem unnecessary to dwell upon it, had not the scientific world decided that the rotation of the earth can cause no currents either in the atmosphere or in the ocean.

The axifugal forces of the two particles *m* and *n* are directly as the lines M *m* and N *n*, and if the gravitating forces were also as the radii T *m* and T *n*, no motion would be produced. Admitting even the Newtonian law to be rigidly exact, the earth cannot be considered a homogeneous globe, but, on the contrary, the density of the central parts must be nearly thirty times greater than the density of the surface of the ocean. The ratio of the gravitating forces of these two particles is, therefore, less than the ratio of their respective radii, and the axifugal tendency of the particle at *n* is more than proportionally restrained by the central gravitation; and hence *m* will move towards the equator, and *n* towards the poles, as represented in the Fig.

It is on account of the overwhelming momentum of the surface waters of the South Pacific over the North, that the Pacific, at Panama, stands six or seven feet higher than the Atlantic. We shall again allude to this interesting fact.

According to newspaper reports of a lecture, delivered in New York, by Lieut. Maury, U. S. N., this gentleman endeavors to explain the currents of the ocean, by referring them to evaporation in the tropics. The vapor leaves the salt of the water behind, and thus, by continual accumulation, the specific gravity of the tropical waters is greater than that of the superficial waters nearer the poles; the lighter water, therefore, passes towards the equator, and the heavier water below, towards the poles. If this be a correct statement of that gentleman's theory, fidelity to our standards compels us to question the soundness of the conclusion. The mere fact of the surface water of the ocean being lighter than that of the bottom, cannot on any known principles of science cause any movement of the surface waters towards the equator. When such an acute and practical physicist is driven, by the palpability of the fact that the polar waters are continually tending towards the equator, to seek the cause in the tropical evaporation, it shows that the dogma, which teaches that rotation can produce no motion, is unsound.

Sir John Herschel, in speaking of the solar spots, says: "We may also observe that the tranquillity of the sun's polar, as compared with his equatorial regions (if his spots be really atmospheric), cannot be accounted for by its rotation on its axis only, but must arise from some cause external to the sun, as we see the belts of Jupiter and Saturn and our trade winds arise from a cause external to these planets combining itself with their rotations, which *alone* (and he lays an emphasis on the word) can produce no motions when once the form of equilibrium is attained."

With respect to the origin of the solar spots, we have no disposition to question the conclusion; but, as regards the *principle* laid down, that rotation can produce no motions when once the form of equilibrium is attained, we must unequivocally dispute it. If our atmosphere were of uniform density, the rotation of the earth would cause no current such as we have described; with our atmosphere as it is, the result will be different. The momenta of two portions of matter are the products of their inertiæ by their motions, and, in the present case, we must take the inertiæ of equal spaces. A cubic inch of air at the surface, and at three miles above the surface, is as 2 to 1; but their centrifugal velocity varies only as the radii of the respective spheres, or as 1320 to 1321. In the polar regions, therefore, the momentum of the surface air preponderates, and, in this case, the *surface* current is towards the equator, and the upper current towards the poles. When, however, the centrifugal velocity is considerably increased in a lower latitude, and the curvature of the surface becomes more and more inclined to the direction of that resolved part of the centrifugal force, which is always *from* the axis, the surface layers will evince a tendency to leave the surface, and an intermingling will then take place in the space between latitude 70° and 50°, or in latitude 60°. As this layer is continually urged on in the same direction by the surface layer of latitudes above 60°, the upper layer now becomes a current setting *towards* the equator, and, consequently, the back current occupies the surface. Now, considering that the rarefying action of the sun is elevating the air under the equator, there must necessarily be an upper current from the equator to the poles; so that if we conceive the two currents to meet about latitude 30°, there will be a second intermingling, and the current from the poles will again occupy the surface. Thus, we regard a part of the effect of the trades to the rotation of the earth, which is the chief impelling power at the poles, as the sun is at the equator; and the latitudes 60° and 30° will be marked by some especial phenomena of temperature, and other meteorological features which do actually obtain. These would be much more marked if the irregular configuration of land and sea, the existence of mountain chains, and the different heating power of different latitudes, owing to the unequal distribution of the land, did not interfere; and the currents of the air (disregarding the deflection east and west) might then be represented by a treble link or loop, whose nodes would vary but little from latitudes 30° and 60°. As it is, it has, no doubt, its influence, although unimportant, when compared with the disturbing action of the ethereal vortices.

There is another phenomenon due to the action of the radia stream, which has given much trouble to the physicist, and which has yet never been explained. This is the horary oscillations of the atmospheric pressure which, in some countries, are so regular that the time of day may be ascertained by the height of the barometer. According to Humboldt, the regularity of the ebb and flow in the torrid regions of America, is undisturbed by storms or earthquake. It is supposed that the maxima occur at 9 A. M. and 10½ P. M., and the minuima at 4 A. M. and 4¼ P. M. From the morning minimum to the morning maximum is, therefore, five hours; from the evening minimum to the evening maximum is 6¼ hours; from the evening maximum to the morning minimum is 5½ hours, and from the morning maximum to the evening minimum is 7¼ hours. Again, these oscillations are greatest at the equator, and diminish with the increase of latitude.

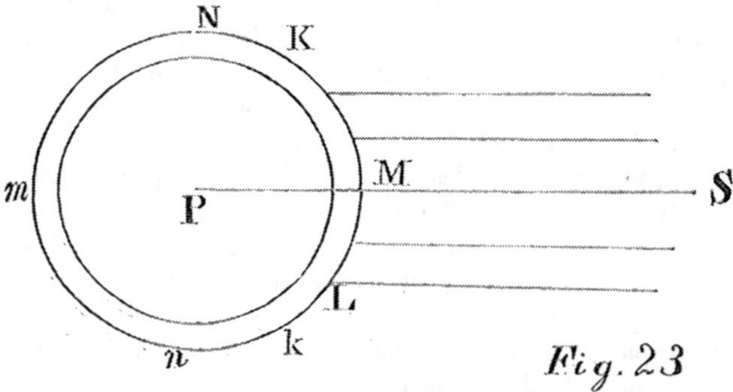

Fig. 23

If we suppose the earth's axis perpendicular to the plane of the vortex, and P the pole in the above figure, and S P the line joining the centre of the earth and sun, M and *m* will represent the points in the earth's equator where it is midday and midnight respectively. The solar stream penetrates the terral vortex, and strikes the earth's atmosphere along the lines parallel to S P. The direct effect would be to pile up the atmosphere at N and *n*; and therefore, were the earth at rest, the maximum would be at 6 A. M. and 6 P. M., and the minimum at midday and midnight; but the earth rotating from N towards M, carries along the accumulated atmosphere, being more sluggish in its motions than the producing cause, which cause is still exercised to force it back to N. From this cause the maximum is now found at K. For a like reason the minimum at M would be found at L, but on account of the motion of the earth being now in the same direction as the solar stream, the minimum is found still more in advance at *k*; so that, according to the theory, the interval between the morning maximum and the evening maximum, should be greater than the interval between the evening maximum and the morning maximum; and so it is, the first being 13½ hours and the last 10½ hours. The morning minimum should also be less marked than the evening minimum, and this also is a fact. The effect also should be greater in the tropics than in high latitudes, which again also obtains; being 1.32 French lines at the equator, and only 0.18 at latitude 70°. Had the earth no obliquity, the effect would be as the squares of the cosines of the latitude; but the ratio is diminished by the inclination of the axis. But there are other variations of the barometer of longer period, apparently depending on the phases of the moon, but which cannot be reconciled to the attracting power of the moon as an atmospheric tide; and Arago concluded that they were due to some *special cause*, of which the nature and mode of action are unknown. Perhaps this theory will obviate the difficulty, as although the central vortex comes to the meridian at the same time as the moon, its effect will be different on the inferior meridian to what it is on the superior one; whereas the moon's attraction should be the same on both. That the passage of a vortex over or near a particular place should affect the barometer, is too obvious to need explanation, and therefore we may say that the theory will explain all those varieties, both small and great, which have caused so much speculation for the last fifty years.

TERRESTRIAL MAGNETISM.

In applying the theory to the magnetism of the earth, we must bear in mind that the earth is probably magnetic by induction, and not in virtue of its own specific action. The rotation of the surrounding ether, and the consequent production of a radial stream, calls the ether into motion within the earth's interior, as well as on the surface; but it does not follow that the ether shall also enter the earth at its poles and escape at its equator, for the obliquity of the vortex would interfere with this result. It is sufficient that this does occur in the terral vortex immediately surrounding the earth. From late experiments it is pretty well established that the axial direction of the needle, (and of other bodies also,) is due to peculiar internal arrangement in laminæ or layers, the existence of which is favorable to the passage of the magnetic current.

According to the experiments* of Dr. Tyndal, it is found that the magnetism of a body is strongest along the line of greatest density. As, therefore, the laminæ of bodies may be considered planes of pressure, when these planes are suspended horizontally, the directive force is greatest, and the longest diameter of the body sets axial. On the other hand, when the body was suspended so that the laminæ were vertical, the longest diameter set equatorial. Now, we know that the crust of the earth is composed of laminæ, just as the piece of shale in Doctor Tyndal's experiments, and that these layers are disposed horizontally. And whatever force originally arranged the land and water on our globe, it is evident that the continents are longest

* Plucker first discovered that a plate of tourmaline suspended with its axis vertical, set axial.

from north to south, and therefore correspond to the natural direction of the magnetic force.

In consequence of the intrinsic difficulties of this question, and the mystery yet attaching to it, we may be permitted to enter a little more minutely into it, and jointly consider other questions of interest, that will enable us to refer the principal phenomena of terrestrial magnetism to our theory.

We have before adverted to the discrepancies in the earth's compression, as determined by the pendulum, and also to the uncertainty of the moon's mass, as deduced from the nutation of the earth's axis. It is also suspected that the southern hemisphere is more compressed than the northern; and other phenomena also point out the inadequacy of the law of gravitation, to account for the figure of the earth.

From the invariability of the axis of rotation, we must conclude that whatever form is the true form, it is one of equilibrium. In casting our eyes over the map of the world, we perceive that the surface is very unequally divided into land and sea; and that the land is very unequally arranged, both north and south, and east and west. If we compare the northern and southern hemisphere, we find the land to the water about 3 to 1. If we take the Pacific portion, and consider the north end of New Zealand as a centre, we can describe a great circle taking in one half the globe, which shall not include one-tenth of the whole land. Yet the average height of the remaining nine-tenths, above the level of the sea, is nearly 1,000 feet. Call this nine-tenths nearly equal to one-fourth of the whole surface, and the protuberant land in the hemisphere, opposite the South Pacific, amounts to $\frac{1}{50,000}$ part of the whole mass of the earth, or about $\frac{1}{700}$ of the mass of the moon. Again, the mean density of the earth is about $5\frac{1}{2}$,—water being unity,—and the mean density of the surface land is only about half this; but three-fourths of the whole surface is water. Hence, we see that the materials of the interior of the earth must be either metallic or very compressible. To assign a metallic nucleus to the earth, is repugnant to analogy; and it is not rendered even probable by facts, as we find volcanic emissions to contain no heavier elements than the sedimentary layers. Besides, there are indications of a gradual increase of density downwards, such as would arise from the compressibility of the layers. Seeing, therefore, the equilibrium of the whole mass, and the consequent hydrostatic balance of the land in the sea,—seeing also the small compressibility of the solid portions, and the great compressibility of the fluid, the inference is legitimate that the whole is hydrostatically balanced, and that our globe is a globe of water, with an intermediate shell of land, specifically lighter than the fluid in which it is suspended. Where this shell is of great thickness, it penetrates to greater depths, and attains to greater elevations above the surface of the aqueous globe; where it is less thick, it is found below the surface, and forms the bottom of the upper ocean. Recent soundings give much greater depths to some parts of the ocean, than the most elevated land upon the globe. Captain Denham, of H. B. M. ship Herald, lately sounded in 37° south and 37° west, and found bottom at 7,706 fathoms, or about nine English miles.

As the interior portions of our globe are totally unknown, and the compressibility of water is well established, it is just as sane to consider water the most abundant element of nature, as solid land. The great question to ask is, whether there may not be other phenomena incompatible with this supposition? It is plain that the permanency of terrestrial latitudes and longitudes would be unaffected by the conditions we have supposed. Would the precession of the equinoxes be also unaffected? Mr. Hopkins has entered into such an investigation, and concludes: "Upon the whole, then, we may venture to assert that the minimum thickness of the crust of the globe, which can be deemed consistent with the observed amount of precession, cannot be less than one-fourth or one-fifth of the radius of the earth." These investigations were made on the hypothesis of the interior fluidity being caused by the fusion of the central portions of a solid globe; but it is evident that the analytical result would be the same if these central parts were water, inclosed by an irregularly-spherical shell of land. Nor would the result be affected, if we considered certain portions of the interior of this solid shell to be in a state of fusion, as no doubt is the case.

May not the uncertainty of the mass of the moon, be owing to the fact that this shell is not so rigidly compacted but that it may yield a little to external force, and thus also account for the tides in the Pacific groups, rather obeying the centrifugal force due to the orbit velocity of the earth, than the attraction of the moon?

Since the days of Hipparchus the sidereal day has not diminished by the hundreth part of a second; and, consequently, seeing that the contraction of the mass must be limited by the time of rotation, it is inferred that the earth has not lost $\frac{1}{300}$th of one degree of heat since that time. This conclusion, sound as it is, is scarcely credible, when we reflect on the constant radiation into a space 60° below zero. Admit that the globe is a globe of water, whose average temperature is the temperature it receives from the sun, and the difficulty vanishes at once. Its diameter will be invariable, and the only effect of the cooling of the solid parts will be to immerse them deeper in the water, to change the *relative* level of the sea without changing its volume. This is no puerile argument when rightly considered; but there is another phenomenon which, if fairly weighed, will also conduct us to the same views.

It is now a fact uncontroverted, that the sea does actually change its level, or rather, that the elevation of continents is not only apparent but real. The whole coast of Sweden and Finland is rising at the present day at the rate of four feet in a century, while on the south a contrary effect is produced. Various hypotheses have been formed concerning this interesting fact. Yet from the indications of geology, it must have been an universal phenomenon in the early ages of the world, in order to account for the emersion of sedimentary deposits from the fluid which deposited them. May not internal fires be yet spreading, and the continents expanding instead of contracting? And may there not be an inequality in this process, so as necessarily to immerse in one direction nearly as much as to elevate in another? One fact is certain, the elements are scattering the materials of the land along its Oceanic coasts, which of itself must produce a very minute effect in disturbing the hydrostatic balance; but a more efficient agent is the earthquake and volcano.

The upheaving of tracts of land by earthquakes, as on the coast of Chili, would thus be satisfactorily explained, by attributing a certain resistance due to cohesion or friction preventing a *gradual* change of level, but producing it suddenly by the jar of the earthquakes. May we not inquire also, whether the facility with which the earth seems moved by this destructive agent, does not point to the same solution as the irregularity of the figure of the earth?

This is a subject on which it is allowable to speculate, especially if any light can be thereby thrown on the still more mysterious source of terrestrial magnetism. It is for such a purpose that we have permitted ourselves to digress from that subject. In this connection we also may acknowledge our indebtedness to the sacred volume for the first germ of this theory of the weather.

Believing in the authenticity of the Mosaic history of the deluge, the author found it difficult to refer that event to other than natural causes, called into action by the operation of other causes, and all simultaneous with the going forth of the fiat of Omnipotence. Thus reasoning, he was led to regard the deluge as a physical phenomenon inviting solution, and as a promising exponent to the climatology of the early world. He looked upon the bow of promise, as the autograph of the Creator, the signature to a solemn bond, upon which the eye of man had never before rested. But if there was no rainbow before the deluge, there was no rain; and following up this clue, he was not only enabled to solve the problem, but also led to the true cause, which produces the principal commotions in our atmosphere.

Science boasts of being the handmaid of religion; yet there are names of note in her ranks who have labored rather to invest this phenomenon with the mantle of fable, and to force it into collision with the records graven on the rocky pages of geognosy. But the world is ever prone to be captivated by the brilliancy of misapplied talents, instead of weighing merit by its zeal in reconciling the teachings of those things which are seen, with those which are revealed.

If our globe be constituted as we suppose, the land might experience repeated submersions, without involving the necessity of any great departure from established laws. And we might refer to the historical record of one of these, with all the minute particulars as positive data, imposing on us the necessity of admitting that the solid parts of the globe are hydrostatically balanced in the sea. But, modern science is not always correctly defined when called the pursuit of truth, nor human learning the means of discovering it.

If we could divest ourselves of this prejudice, we should have a ready solution of the difficulty presented by the earth having two north magnetic poles, and probably two also in the south. For, by regarding the old and new continents as two distinct masses of land whose bases are separated by 6,000 miles of water, we recognize two great magnets, dependent, however, for their magnetism, on the rotation of the terral vortex.

This is no place to enter into a lengthy discussion of such a difficult subject as magnetism, but we may be allowed to enter a protest against the current theory of electro-magnetism, viz.: that a force is generated by a galvanic current at right angles to the producing cause, which is contrary to the fundamental principles of mechanics. We may conceive that a current is induced from or to the surrounding space by the rarefaction or condensation attending the transmission of such a current along a wire, and that rotation should follow, just as a bent pipe full of small holes at the lower end, and immersed in water as a syphon, will generate a vorticose motion in the water; but mere juxtaposition, without participation and communication with the general current, is irrational, and, therefore, not true.

We have always regarded a magnetic needle as a part of the great natural magnet, the earth; that its north pole actually points to the north, and its south pole to the south; and, being free to move, it is affected by the circular motion of the surrounding ether, and by every motion by which the ether is directed. If there was any attraction between the earth and the needle, opposite poles would be presented, but it is not so—the force is merely directive.

MAGNETIC VARIATIONS.

Let us now see whether we cannot assign an adequate cause for the secular and periodic variations in the inclination and declination of the needle. These have been generally referred to changes of temperature, as in fact, also, the magnetism of the earth is sometimes ascribed to galvanic or electric currents, called forth by a daily change of temperature. Our theory gives a totally different explanation of these variations.

In the northern hemisphere, the north point of the needle moves from east to west in the morning from about 8½ A. M. to 1½ P. M., and returns to its mean position about 10 P. M. It then passes over to the east, and again returns to its mean position about 8 or 9 A. M. The analogy of this motion, with the horary changes in the barometer, indicate a common origin. Humboldt, in the instructions he drew up for the Antartic Expedition under Sir James Ross, says: "The phenomena of periodical variations depend manifestly on the action of *solar heat*, operating probably through the medium of thermo electric currents induced on the earth's surface. Beyond this rude guess, however, *nothing is yet known of their physical cause.* It is even still a matter of speculation whether the solar influence be a principal or only a subordinate cause." That the sun may exert a modifying influence on the phenomenon is not unlikely, but that he cannot be the principal cause, is evident from the following considerations. These horary variations of the magnetic needle are as great at the bottom of deep mines far removed from solar influence, as on the surface. They are as great, *ceteris paribus*, on a small island in the midst of the ocean, as in the interior of continents, where the heating power of the surface is vastly greater. They are extremely regular, so that between the tropics, according to the sagacious Humboldt, "the time of the day may be known by the direction of the needle, as well as by the height of the barometer."

But what is the cause of these variations? This question is the most difficult of all physical problems, and we shall only aim at indicating the causes which are yet perhaps too intricately involved to afford a positive numerical determination. Admitting the existence of two principal solid masses whose general direction is from south to north, and that these masses are more susceptible of permeation by the ethereal fluid than the waters in which they are suspended, we have a general solution of the position of the magnetic poles, and of the isogonic, isoclinic, and isodynamic lines. Considering, too, that the southern poles of these masses are the points of ingress, and the northern poles the points of egress, it is easily understood that the ethereal medium having the temperature of space, will cause the southern hemisphere to be colder than the northern, and also that the magnetic poles will be the poles of maximum cold, and the centres respected by the isothermal and isogeothermal lines.

The general direction of the magnetism of the earth may be considered as the controlling influence, therefore, in determining the position of the magnetic needle; but there are other causes which, to some extent, will modify the result. That half of the globe turned away from the sun will partake of the density of the ether at that distance, which is greater than on the side next the sun; the magnetic intensity ought, therefore, to be greater in the night than in the day. The poles of the great terrestrial magnets, or even the position of a magnetic needle on the surface, are continually placed by the earth's rotation in a different relation to the axes of the terral vortex, and the tangential current, which is continually circulating around the globe, has its inclination to a given meridian in a perpetual state of change. If we conceive that there is a tendency to force the needle at right angles to this current, we shall have an influence which varies during the day, during the year, and during the time occupied by a complete revolution of the node. The principal effect, however, of the horary variation of the needle is due to the radial stream of the sun, which not only penetrates the atmosphere, but also the solid crust of the earth. Its principal influence is, however, an indirect influence, as we shall endeavor to explain.

No fact in the science of electro-magnetism is, perhaps, better established than the disposition of an ethereal current to place itself at right angles to the magnetic meridian, and conversely, when the current is not free to move, to place the needle at right angles to the current. Now, the terrestrial magnet or magnets, may be considered to be surrounded by a body of ether in rotation, which, in the earth, on its surface, and for some distance from the surface, is made to conform to the general rule, that is, to circulate at right angles to the magnetic meridian. Outside this again, the ether more and more conforms to the position of the axis of the vortex, and this position varying, it must exert *some* influence on the surface currents, and, therefore, change in some degree the position of the magnetic meridian. The radial stream comes from the sun in parallel lines, and strikes the globe and its superficial ethereal envelope just as we have shown its action on the atmosphere; but in this last case the magnetic equator is not a great circle, neither can we suppose its effects to be an accumulation of a fluid which is imponderable at points 90° from the plane passing through the centre of the earth and sun, and coincident with the plane of the central meridian, and a depressing effect on that meridian. Its precise influence must be, from the nature of the cause, to deflect the circular current towards the poles, in places less than 90° from the meridian, and a contrary effect must be produced in places greater than 90° from the meridian. Let us assume, for argument's sake, that the magnetic poles of the earth correspond to the poles of rotation, the parallels of latitude will, therefore, represent the ethereal currents circulating around the globe. Now, at sunrise, the radial stream of the solar vortex is tangential to the surface, and, therefore, can produce no change in these currents. As the sun ascends say about 8 or 9 A. M., the radial stream striking only the surface of the earth perpendicularly in that place where the sun is vertical (which we will suppose at the equator), streams off on every side, as the meridians do from the pole, and the circles of latitude (that is the ethereal currents) being parallel to the equator, they are met by the radial stream obliquely, and deflected towards either pole. By this deflection they are no longer at right angles to the meridians. But, from the principle of reaction above noticed, the magnetic meridians will place themselves at right angles to the current, or, in other words, the magnetic pole will change its position on the surface of the earth with respect to that particular place. But, in other parts of the world, the meridians are in opposite phases at the same instant of absolute time; therefore, the magnetic poles are not points, but wide areas enclosing the magnetic poles of all the countries under the sun. As this conforms to observation, it is worthy our especial attention, and may be understood by the subjoined figure, in which the oblique curves represent the course of the tangential current in the different positions of the sun, the parallel lines representing the solar radial stream.

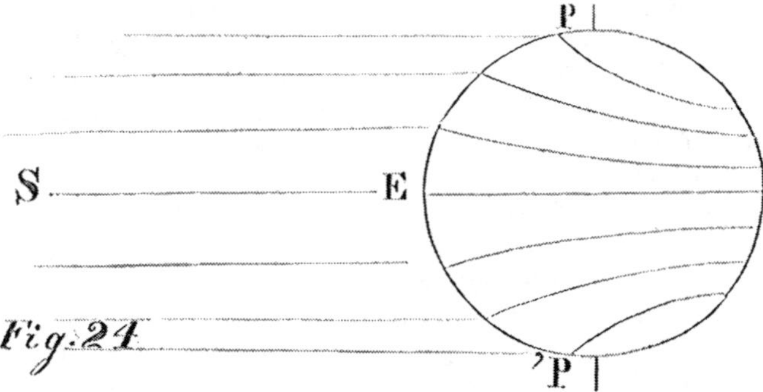

Fig. 24

As the sun gains altitude the action of the radial stream is at a greater and greater angle to the circular currents, and attains its maximum at noon, still acting, however, after noon; but seeing that the circular current possesses a force of re-action, that is, that the magnetism of the earth is ever striving to bring these currents to their natural direction, an hour or two after noon, the currents tend again to the equator, and the maximum deflection is passed, and finally ceases a few hours after sunset. Now let us attend to what is going on on the opposite side of the world. The radial stream passing over the polar regions, now produces a contrary effect: the ethereal atmosphere of the great magnet is accumulated on the farthest side from the sun, by the action of the radial stream passing over the polar region, the parallel currents are now bent towards the equator, being at a maximum in places where it is an hour or two past midnight. Before they were concave to the equator, and now they are convex; the magnetic meridian is therefore deflected the contrary way to what it was in the day time, by the same principle of reaction. After the maximum, say at 4 A. M., the deflection gradually ceases, and the magnetic meridian returns to its mean position at 8 or 9 A. M. These times, however, of maximum and minimum, must vary with the time of the year, or with the declination of the sun, with the position of the moon in her orbit, with the perigee of the orbit, and with the place of the ascending node; there are also minor influences which have an effect, which present instrumental means cannot render appreciable.

What says observation? The needle declines from its mean position in the whole northern hemisphere to the westward, from about 8.30 A. M., until 1.30 P. M.; it then gradually returns to its mean position by 10 P. M. After 10 P. M., it passes over to the eastward, and attains its maximum deflection about three or four hours after midnight, and is found again at its mean position about 9 A. M. Now, this is precisely the direction of the deviation of the magnetic meridian, the needle therefore only follows the meridian, or still continues to point to the temporary magnetic pole. And although we have assumed, for the sake of simplicity, that the mean magnetic pole corresponds to the pole of rotation; in truth there are two magnetic poles, neither of which correspond; yet still the general effect will be the same, although the numerical verification will be rendered more difficult.

In the southern hemisphere the effect is the reverse, (this southern hemisphere, however, must be considered separated from the northern by the magnetic equator, and not by the geographical one,) the needle declines to the eastward in the morning, and goes through the same changes, substituting east for west, and west for east. Does observation decide this to be to be a fact also? Most decidedly it does; and this alone may be considered a positive demonstration, that the theory which explains it is true. The contrary deflection of the needle in the northern and southern hemisphere may be formally proclaimed as utterly beyond the reach of the common theory of magnetism to explain. This difficulty arises from considering the needle as the disturbed body instead of the earth; and also from the fact that the effect of solar heat must be common to needles in both hemispheres, and act upon similar poles, and consequently the deflection must be in the same direction.

But a still more capital feature is presented by the discovery of Colonel Sabine, that the deflection is in contrary directions at the Cape of Good Hope, at the epoch of the two equinoxes. This arises from the great angle made by the magnetic meridian at this place, with the terrestrial meridian—the variation being by Barlow's tables, 30° to the westward. The sun varies in declinatiôn 47° throughout the year. At the southern solstice, therefore the radial stream strikes the circular current on the southern side, and deflects it towards the equator, rendering the declination to the westward in the morning; but at the northern solstice the radial stream strikes the current on its northern side, and the deflection is eastward in the morning. And the vicinity of the Cape of Good Hope is, perhaps, the only part of the world where this anomaly will obtain; as it is necessary not only that the declination shall be considerable, but also that the latitude shall not be very great.

Observation also determines that the amount of the horary variation increases with the latitude. Near the equator, according to Humboldt, it scarcely amounts to three or four minutes, whilst it is from thirteen to fourteen minutes in the middle of Europe. The theory explains this also; for as the circles recede from the equator, the angles made by their planes with the direction of the radial stream increases, and hence the force of deflection is greater, and the effect is proportioned to the cause. We have also a satisfactory explanation of the fact that there has not yet been discovered a line of *no variation of horary declination* as we might reasonably anticipate from the fact that the declinations are in *contrary directions* in the northern and southern hemisphere. This is owing to the ever-varying declination of the sun. There would be such a line, no doubt, if the axis of the earth were perpendicular to the plane of the orbit, and the magnetic pole coincided with the pole of rotation: for then the equator would be such a line.

MAGNETIC STORMS.

But there are also irregular fluctuations in the direction of the magnetic needle. These depend on the moon, and are caused by the passage of the vortices over or near to the place of observation. The action of these vortices is proved to be of variable force, whether arising from atmospheric conditions, or due to an increased activity of the ethereal medium throughout the whole system, is at present immaterial. They do vary, and sometimes the passage of a vortex will deflect the needle a whole degree. At other times, there are magnetic storms extending over a great part of the earth's surface; but there is reason to suppose, that the extent of these storms has been over estimated. Thus, on the 25th of September, 1841, a magnetic storm was observed in Toronto, and at the same time there was one felt at the Cape of Good Hope. There is no great mystery in this. If we suppose the axis of the central vortex, for instance, to have passed Toronto in latitude 43° 33′ north, in ordinary positions of the moon, in her orbit, the southern portion of the axis would be in 33° or 34° south latitude, and consequently would have passed near the Cape of Good Hope on the same night. Now, we certainly could not expect the northern portion of the vortex to be intensely active, without the southern portion being in the same state of activity. That this is the true explanation is proved by magnetic storms in the same hemisphere being comparatively limited in extent; as, according to Gauss and Weber, magnetic storms which were simultaneously felt from Sicily to Upsala, did not extend from Upsala to Alten. Still it would not be wonderful if they were felt over a vast area of thousands of miles as a consequence of *great* disturbance in the elasticity of the ether in the terral vortex; as the solid earth must be permeable to all its motions, and thus be explicable on the general principles we have advanced.

But besides these variations which we have mentioned, there are changes steadily going on, by which the isodynamic, isogonic and isoclinic lines are permanently displaced on the surface of our planet. These must be attributed to changes of temperature in the interior of the globe, and to the direction in the progress of subterranean fires, which it may also be expected will change the isogeothermal lines. But there are changes, which although of long period, are yet periodic, one of which is obviously due to the revolution of the lunar nodes in eighteen and a half years, and the revolution of the apogee in nine years. The first is continually changing the obliquity of the axis of the vortex, and they both tend to limit the vortices in their extreme latitudes; but the planet Jupiter has an indirect influence, which is probably equal, if not greater, than the action of the moon, in changing the magnetic declination.

From the investigations of Lamont, it would appear, that the period of the variations of magnetic declination is about $10\frac{1}{3}$ years, while, more recently, R. Wolfe has suggested the connection between this variation and the solar spots, and assigns a period of 11.11 years, and remarks, that it "corresponds more exactly with the variations in magnetic declination than the period of $10\frac{1}{3}$ years established by Lamont. The magnetic variations accompany the solar spots, not only in their regular changes, but even in their minor irregularities: this latter fact is itself sufficient to prove definitely the important relations between them."*

As the planet Jupiter exerts the greatest influence on the sun, in forcing the centre from the mechanical centre of the system, the longitude of the sun will in a great measure depend on the position of this planet; and, in consequence, the sun will generally revolve around this centre in a period nearly equal to the period of Jupiter. The sidereal period of Jupiter is about twelve years, but the action of the other planets tend to shorten this period (at least, that has been the effect for the last twenty or thirty years), and bring it nearly to the period assigned by M. Wolfe to the variations in the magnetic declinations. As this has its influence on the radial stream, and the radial stream on the declination, we see at once the connection between them. When we come to a consideration of the solar spots, we shall exhibit this influence more fully.

AURORA BOREALIS.

Let us now examine another phenomenon. The Aurora Borealis has been generally considered to be in some way connected with the magnetism of the earth, and with the position of the magnetic pole. It is certain that the appearance of this meteor does affect the needle in a way not to be mistaken, and (although not invariably) the vertex of the luminous arch will usually conform to the magnetic meridian. Yet (and this is worthy of attention), the observations made in the North Polar Expeditions† "appear to prove, that in the immediate vicinity of the magnetic pole the development of light is not in the least degree more intense or frequent than at some distance from it." In fact, as the American magnetic pole is, as stated, in latitude 73°, the central vortex will seldom reach so high,

* Silliman's Journal for March and April, 1853.

† Humboldt, *Cosmos*, p. 193, London ed.

and, consequently, the aurora ought at such times to be more frequent in a lower latitude. In a late work by M. de la Rive, this gentleman expresses the opinion, that the cause of the aurora is not due to a radiation of polar magnetism, but to a purely electrical action.* His explanation, however, is not so satisfactory as his opinion. Now, we have examined numerous cases of auroral displays, and never yet found one which could not be legitimately referred to the action of ethereal vortices. Generally, the aurora will not be visible, when the upper surface of the atmosphere of that latitude in which the vortex is known to be (reckoning in the direction of the magnetic meridian) is below the horizon, which shows that the brightest portion is in the atmosphere. In latitude 41° even, it may show itself when the vortex is three days north, more frequently when one or two days north; but when the vortex passes centrally, or south, it rarely is seen, and this is the only difficulty in explaining it by the theory. But, when we reflect that the ether shoots out in straight lines, and at an angle corresponding to the magnetic dip, we are at no loss to perceive the reason of this. If each minute line composing the light were seen endwise, it would be invisible; if there were millions such in the same position, they could add nothing to the general effect; but, when viewed sideways, the case would be different, there would be a continued reduplication of ray upon ray, until in the range of some hundreds of miles an effect might be produced amounting to any degree of intensity on record. Now, this is the case when the aurora is immediately overhead, it will be invisible to those below, but may be seen by persons a hundred miles south; so, also, when it is to the south, it is too oblique to the line of vision to be seen, especially as all the rays to the northward of the observer can contribute nothing to increase the effect. That it is of the nature of rays very much diffused, can hardly be doubted; and, therefore, if only

* See Silliman's Journal for September, 1853.

of a few miles in depth, its impressions are too faint to be sensible. By referring to the record of the weather in the second section of this work, an auroral display will be found on July 12th, the central vortex having passed a little to the northward the same evening, and the next day passing south *descending*. On that occasion the author saw an inclined column, in profile, due east, and between himself and a line of bluffs and timber, about eight miles distant; and, he has not any doubt, that the mass of rays began where he stood. As in a shower, every drop, passing through a conical surface, whose axis passes through the sun and through the eye, contributes to form the apparently distant rainbow.

The altitude of this meteor has been much exaggerated, especially of those rings or luminous arches, which are often detached completely from the luminous bank. On the 24th of May, a bright aurora was visible at Ottawa, but the author's attention was engrossed by the most brilliant arch of light he had ever seen. It was all the time south of the zenith, and had no visible connection with the aurora north. At 9 hours, 59 minutes, 30 seconds mean solar time, Arcturus was in the exact centre of the band, at which time it was very bright, and full 7° wide. At the same time, Prof. G. W. Wheeler observed the aurora in Perryville, in the State of Missouri, only 1° of longitude to the westward, but did not see the arch.* The difference of latitude between the two places being 3° 30′, and the weather, as he states, clear and still, there is only one reason why he did not see the arch: it must have been too *low*, and had become merged in the bank of light. At the time mentioned, the altitude of Arcturus was 68° 30′, and, as Prof. Wheeler assigns only 10° as the altitude of the bank, the maximum elevation of the arch, on the supposition of its composing a part of the bank, was 43 miles. At Perryville, the bank and streamers had disappeared at 10 o'clock. At Ottawa,

* See Silliman's Journal for September, 1853.

the arch or bow disappeared at 10 h. 5 m., differing only the fraction of a minute from the time at Perryville; but, the bank was still visible, but low and faint, the greatest altitude having been over 30°. To show the rapid fluctuations in width and position of this bow, we will add a few of the minutes taken at the time with great care, in hopes some other observer had been equally precise. When first seen, there were three luminous patches, or elongated clouds of light: one in Leo, one in Bootes, and another in Ophinchus, all in line. This was about 9 h. 15 m. The times following are correct to 30 seconds:

9h.	42m.	30s.	Bow complete; south edge 2° north of Arcturus.
9	45	30	Northern edge diffuse south; edge bright, and well defined; 10° wide in zenith; north edge on Alphacca.
9	47	30	South edge 5° north of Arcturus; north edge close to Cor. Caroli.
9	53	30	Eastern half composed of four detached bands *shingling* over each other.
9	58	30	Arcturus on south; bow narrower.
9	59	30	Arcturus in the middle of the band; very bright and regular in outline, and widest at the zenith.
10	0	30	Arcturus on northern edge; north side better defined than the southern.
10	2	0	Arcturus 1° north; very bright.
10	2	30	Glamma and Delta Leonis, northern edge.
10	3	0	Regulus on southern age; getting faint.
10	5	0	Fast fading away.
10	5	30	Scarcely visible; bank in north faint.

This aurora was due to the *inner vortex ascending*, whose period was at this time 28 days.

There are several circumstances to be observed in this case. The bow brightened and faded simultaneously with the aurora, and respected the vertex of the auroral bank, being apparently concentric with it. The bow, therefore, depends on the same cause, but differs from the aurora in being limited to the *surface* of the atmosphere in which the vortex has produced a wave to the southward of its central path, as may be understood by inspecting Fig. 2, Sec. 1,—the figure representing the polar current of the central vortex. On the 29th of May, 1840,* the author saw a similar phenomenon, at the same time of night, and passing over the same stars southward until it reached within 5° of Jupiter and Saturn, to which it was parallel. This atmospheric wave offers a greater resistance to the passage of the ether: hence the light. On this account it is, also, that when the passage of a vortex is attended by an auroral display there will be no thunder-storm. There may be an increase of wind; but the atmosphere at such times is too dry to make a violent storm, and there is a silent restoration of the equilibrium, by the ether passing through the dry atmosphere, without meeting any condensable vapor, and becoming luminous on account of the greater resistance of the air when unmixed with vapor. We thus see also the connection between the aurora and the linear cirri, and we have a triumphant explanation of the fact, that when the observer is north of the northern limit of the vortices, he sees the aurora to the south and not to the north; for, to see it to the northward, he would have to see it in the same latitude as it appears in the south, and, consequently, have to see across twice the complement of the latitude. We thus see, also, why the temperature falls after an aurora; for, the passage of electricity in any shape, must have this effect on account of the great specific caloric of this fluid. We see, also, why the aurora should be more frequent where the magnetic intensity is great-

* This was the central vortex ascending.

est, and be consequently invisible at the equator, and why the magnetic needle is so sensibly affected at the time of its occurrence. We may, perhaps, here be allowed to allude to another phenomenon connected with terrestrial magnetism and electricity.

EARTHQUAKES.

The awful and destructive concussions which sometimes are produced at great depths beneath the surface of the soil, would seem to indicate that no force but that of electricity is adequate to account for the almost instantaneous desolation of wide tracts of the earth's surface. But we do not mean to say that the action of the terral vortices, combined with the internal conditions of our planet, is the only cause; although it is far from improbable that the same activity of the ether, which generates through these vortices, the full fury of the hurricane in the tropics, may be simultaneously accompanied by a *subterranean* storm. And physicists are too rash to reject the evidence on which the connection of the phenomena rests.

In the extract given by Colonel Reid, in his "Law of Storms," from Sir George Rodney's official report of the great hurricane of 1780, it is stated, that, "Nothing but an earthquake could have occasioned the *foundations* of the strongest buildings to be rent; and I am convinced that the violence of the wind must have prevented the inhabitants from feeling the earthquake which certainly attended the storm."* Again, in the Savannah-la-Mar hurricane, which occurred the same year and month, the Annual Register, published at Jamaica, states, that at the same time, "a smart shock of an earthquake was felt." The general serenity of equatorial regions is due to the fact that they are beyond the limit of the vortices, as in Peru, where neither rain nor lightning nor storm is ever seen. Thunder and rain, without storms, however, are common in other tropical countries,

* Reid's Law of Storms, p. 350.

also out of the reach of the vortices. But even in those parts, (as the Antilles,) lying in the track of these vortices, the weather is not as *frequently* disturbed as in higher latitudes. The storms of the Antilles, when they do occur, however, are fearful beyond any conception, showing the presence of some cause, auxiliary to the ordinary disturbing action of the vortices, which, when simultaneously occurring, adds tremendously to their force.

That earthquakes are preceded *sometimes* by a peculiar haziness and oppressiveness, similar to that which sometimes precedes a storm, is a current opinion in volcanic countries. And Humboldt, who doubts the connection, has to confess that sudden changes of weather have *succeeded* violent earthquakes, and that "during the great earthquake of Cumana, he found the inclination of the needle was diminished 48′." He also mentions the simultaneous occurrence of shocks, from earthquakes, and a clap of thunder, and the agitation of the electrometer during the earthquake, which lasted from the 2d of April to the 17th of May, 1808; but concluding that "these indications presented by clouds, by modifications of atmospheric electricity, or by calms, cannot be regarded as *generally* or *necessarily* connected with earthquakes, since in Peru, Canada, and Italy, earthquakes are observed, along with the purest and clearest skies, and with the freshest land and sea breezes. But if no meteorological phenomena indicates the coming earthquake, either on the morning of the shock or a few days previously, the influence of certain periods of the year, (the vernal and autumnal equinoxes,) the commencement of the rainy season in the tropics, after long drought, cannot be overlooked, even though the genetic connection of meteorological processes, with those going on in the interior of our globe, is still enveloped in obscurity."*

It is at the equinoxes that the earth changes her distances from the sun most rapidly, and whether she is passing from her

* Humboldt, *Cosmos*, p. 203.

perihelion or from her aphelion, the density of the ether externally is changing in the subduplicate ratio of these distances, and consequently at these times there will be the greatest disturbance of the electric equilibrium. How far our views of the internal structure of our globe, (considered along a diameter as a solid crust, then a fused mass separated from the lower ocean by another solid crust, and separated from a similar arrangement on the opposite side by an interposed mass of water, perhaps also possessing a solid nucleus,) may affect this question, is difficult to say; but that the agent is electric, appears highly probable; and very recently it has been discovered, by M. Ratio Menton, that a piece of iron, suspended by attraction to a magnet, will fall on the approach of an earthquake; thus indicating that the power of the magnet is temporarily weakened by the action of some disturbing force.

SECTION FOURTH.

THE SOLAR SPOTS.

WE have yet many phenomena to investigate by the aid of the theory, and we will develop them in that order which will best exhibit their mutual dependence. The solar spots have long troubled astronomers, and to this day no satisfactory solution of the question has been proposed; but we shall not examine theories. It is sufficient that we can explain them on the same general principles that we have applied to terrestrial phenomena. There can be but little doubt about the existence of a solar atmosphere, and, reasoning from analogy, the constituent elements of the sun must partake of the nature of other planetary matter. That there are bodies in our system possessing the same elements as our earth, is proved by the composition of meteoric masses, which, whether they are independent bodies of the system, or fragments of an exploded planet, or projected from lunar volcanoes, is of little consequence; they show that the same elements are distributed to other bodies of the system, although not necessarily in the same proportions. The gaseous matter of the sun's atmosphere may, therefore, be safely considered as vapors condensable by cold, and the formation of vortices over the surface of this atmosphere, brings down the ether, and causes it to intermingle with this atmosphere. But, from the immensely rapid motion of the polar current of the solar vortex, this ether may be considered to enter the atmosphere of the sun with the temperature of space.

Sir John Herschel, in commenting on the theory of Mr. Redfield before the British Association, convened at Newcastle in 1838,* suggested an analogy to terrestrial hurricanes, from a suspected rotation and progressive motion in these spots. From their rapid formation, change of shape, and diameter, this view is allowable, and, taken in conjunction with the action of the ethereal currents, will account for all the phenomena. The nucleus of the spot is dense, like the nucleus of a storm on the earth, and surrounded by a penumbon precisely as our storms are fringed with lighter clouds, permitting the light of the sun to penetrate. And, it has been observed, that these spots seem to follow one another in lines on the same parallel of solar latitude (or nearly the same), exactly as we have determined the action of the vortices on the surface of the earth from observation. These spots are never found in very high latitudes—not much above 30° from the solar equator. If we consider this equator to be but slightly inclined to the plane of the vortex, this latitude would be the general position of the lateral solar vortices, and, in fact, be confined principally to a belt on each side of the equator, between 15° and 30° of solar latitude, rather than at the equator itself. This, it is needless to say, is actually the case. But, a more capital feature still has been more recently brought to light by observation, although previously familiar to the author, who, in endeavoring to verify the theory, seriously injured his sight, by observing with inadequate instrumental means. This is the periodicity of the spots.

We have already observed, that there is reason to suppose that the action of the inner vortex of the earth is probably greater than that of the outer vortex, on account of the conflicting currents by which it is caused. And the full development of this vortex requires, that the central vortex or

* Silliman's Journal, vol. xxxv., page 283.

mechanical axis of the system shall be nearly tangential to the surface. In this position, the action of the central vortex is itself at a maximum; and, when the planets of the system are so arranged as to produce this result, we may expect the greatest number of spots. If the axis or central vortex approaches to coincidence with the axis of the sun, the lateral vortices disappear, and the central vortex being then perpendicular to the surface, is rendered ineffective. Under these circumstances, there will be no spots on the sun's disc. When, on the other hand, all the planets conspire at the same side to force the sun out from the mechanical centre of the system, the surface is too distant to be acted on by the central vortex, and the lateral vortices are also thrown clear of the sun's surface, on account of the greater velocity of the parts of the vortex, in sweeping past the body of the sun. In this case, there will be but few spots. The case in which the axis of the vortex coincides with the axis of the sun, is much more transient than the first position, and hence, although the interval between the maxima will be tolerably uniform, there will be an irregularity between a particular maximum, and the preceding and subsequent minimum.

The following table exhibits the solar spots, as determined by Schwabe, of Dessau:

Year of observation.	Groups of spots observed.	Number of days.
1826	118	277
1827	161	273
1828	225	282
1829	199	244
1830	190	217
1831	149	239
1832	84	270
1833	33	267
1834	51	273
1835	173	244

Year of observation.	Groups of spots observed.	Number of days.
1836	272	200
1837	333	168
1338	282	202
1839	162	205
1840	152	263
1841	102	283
1842	68	307
1843	34	324

Previous to the publication of this table, the author had inferred the necessity of admitting the existence of another planet in the solar system, from the phenomenon of which we are speaking. He found a sufficient correspondence between the minima of spots to confirm the explanation given by the theory, and this was still more confirmed by the more exact determination of Schwabe; yet there was a little discrepancy in the synchronous values of the ordinates, when the theory was graphically compared with the table. Previous to the discovery of Neptune, the theory corresponded much better than afterwards, and as no doubt could be entertained that the anomalous movements of Uranus were caused by an exterior planet, he adopted the notion that there were two planets exterior to Uranus, whose positions at the time were such, that their mechanical effects on the system were about equal and contrary. Consequently, when Neptune became known, the existence of another planet seemed a conclusion necessary to adopt. Accordingly, he calculated the heliocentric longitudes and true anomalies, and the values of radius vector, for all the planets during the present century, but not having any planetary tables, he contented himself with computing for the nearest degree of true anomaly, and the nearest thousand miles of distance. Then by a composition and resolution of all the forces, he deduced the radius vector of the sun, and the longitude of his centre, for each past year of the century. It was in view of a little outstanding discrepancy in the times of the minima, as determined by theory and observation, that he was induced to consider as almost certain the existence of a theoretical planet, whose longitude, in 1828, was about 90°, and whose period is from the theory about double that of Neptune. And for convenience of computation and reference, he has been in the habit of symbolizing it by a volcano. The following table of the radii vectores of the sun, and the longitude of his centre, for the years designated in Schwabe's table, is calculated from the following data for each planet:

Planets.	Masses.	Mean distances.	Eccentricities.	Long. of Perihelion.
♃	$\frac{1}{1048}$	494.800.000	0.0481	11°
♄	$\frac{1}{3510}$	907.162.000	0.0561	89
♅	$\frac{1}{23000}$	1824.290.000	0.0166	167
♆	$\frac{1}{20000}$	2854.000.000	0.0088	0
Δ	$\frac{1}{28000}$	4464.000.000		

Dates.	Rad. vector.	Sun's long.	Ordinates.		No. of spots in Schwabe's table.	
Jan. 1, 1826	528,000	320°	+ 84		118	
" 1827	480,000	339	+ 36		161	
" 1828	432,000	352	— 12	Max.	225	Max.
" 1829	397,000	38	— 47		199	
" 1830	358,000	71	— 86		190	
" 1831	324,000	104	— 120		149	
" 1832	311,000	144	— 133		84	
" 1833	300,000	183	— 144	Min.	33	Min.
" 1834	307,000	220	— 137		51	
" 1835	338,000	263	— 106		173	
" 1836	389,000	302	— 55		272	
" 1837	419,000	337	+ 25	Max.	333	Max.
" 1838	488,000	3	+ 44		282	
" 1839	551,000	29	+ 107		162	
" 1840	632,000	51	+ 188		152	
" 1841	680,000	80	+ 236		102	
" 1842	730,000	105	+ 286		68	
" 1843	766,000	128	+ 322		34	Min.
" 1844	783,000	152	+ 339	Min	52	

Dates.	Rad. vector.	Sun's long.	Ordinates.		No. of spots in Schwabe's table.
Jan. 1, 1845	772,000	174	+ 328		114
" 1846	728,000	196	+ 284		157
" 1847	660,000	218	+ 216		
" 1848	563,000	240	+ 119		Observed. Max.
" 1849	447,000	261	+ 3	Max.	
" 1850	309,000	283	— 135		
" 1851	170,000	323	— 274		
" 1852	53,000	41	— 391	Min.	
" 1853	167,000	133	— 277		
" 1854	315,000	160	— 129		
" 1855	475,000	183	+ 31	Max.	
" 1856	611,000	203	+ 167		
" 1857	720,000	225	+ 276		

It is necessary to observe here, that the values of the numbers in Schwabe's table are the numbers for the whole year, and, therefore, the 1st of July would have been a better date for the comparison; but, as the table was calculated before the author was cognizant of the fact, and being somewhat tedious to calculate, he has left it as it was, viz., for January 1st of each year. Hence, the minimum for 1843 appears as pertaining to 1844. The number of spots ought to be inversely as the ordinates approximately—these last being derived from the Radii Vectores minus, the semi-diameter of the sun = 444,000 miles.

In passing judgment on this relation, it must also be borne in mind, that the recognized masses of the planets cannot be the true masses, if the theory be true. Both sun and planets are under-estimated, yet, as they are, probably, all to a certain degree proportionally undervalued, it will not vitiate the above calculation much.

The spots being considered as solar storms, they ought also to vary in number at different times of the year, according to the longitude of the earth and sun, and from their transient character, and the slow rotation of the sun, they ought, *ceteris paribus*, to be more numerous when the producing vortex is over a visible portion of the sun's surface.

The difficulty of reconciling the solar spots, and their periodicity to any known principle of physics, ought to produce a more tolerant spirit amongst the scientific for speculations even which may afford the slightest promise of a solution, although emanating from the humblest inquirer after truth. The hypothesis of an undiscovered planet, exterior to Neptune, is of a nature to startle the cautious timidity of many; but, if the general theory be true, this hypothesis becomes extremely probable. We may not have located it exactly. There may be even two such planets, whose joint effect shall be equivalent to one in the position we have assigned. There may even be a comet of great mass, capable of producing an effect on the position of the sun's centre (although it follows from the theory that comets have very little mass). Yet, in view of all these suppositions, there can be but little doubt that the solar spots are caused by the solar vortices, and these last made effective on the sun by the positions of the great planets, and, therefore, we have indicated a new method of determining the existence and position of all the planets exterior to Neptune. On the supposition that there is only one more in the system, from its deduced distance and mass, it will appear only as a star of the eleventh magnitude, and, consequently, will only be recognizable by its motion, which, at the greatest, will only be ten or eleven seconds per day.

MASSES OF THE SUN AND PLANETS.

We have alluded to the fact of the radial stream of the sun necessarily diminishing the sun's power, and, consequently, diminishing his apparent mass. The radial stream of all the planets will do the same, so that each planet whose mass is derived from the periodic times of the satellites, will also appear too small. But, there is also a great probability that some modification must be made in the wording of the Newtonian law. The experiments of Newton on the pendulum, with every variety of substance, was sufficient justification to entitle him to infer, that inertia was as the weight of matter universally. But, there was one condition which could not be observed in experimenting on these substances, viz., the difference of temperature existing between the interior and surface of a planet.

We have already expressed the idea, that the cause of gravity has no such mysterious origin as to transcend the power of man to determine it. But that, on the contrary, we are taught by every analogy around us, as well as by divine precept, to use the visible things of creation as stepping stones to the attainment of what is not so apparent. That we have the volume of nature spread out in tempting characters, inviting us to read, and, assuredly, it is not so spread in mockery of man's limited powers. As science advances, strange things, it is true, are brought to light, but the more *rational* the queries we propound, in every case the more satisfactory are the answers. It is only when man consults the oracle in irrational terms that the response is ambiguous. Alchemy, with its unnatural transmutations, has long since vanished before the increasing light. Why should not attraction also? Experience and experiment, if men would only follow their indications, are consistently enforcing the necessity of erasing these antiquated chimeras from the book of knowledge; and inculcating the great truth, that the physical universe owes all its endless variety to differences in the form, size, and density of planetary atoms in motion, according to simple mechanical principles. These, combined with the existence of an all-pervading medium filling space, between which and planetary matter no bond of union subsists, other than that which arises from a continual interchange of motion, are the materials from which the gems of nature are elaborated. But, simplicity of means is what philosophy has ever been reluctant to admit, preferring rather the occult and obscure.

If action be equal to reaction, and all nature be vibrating with motion, these motions must necessarily interfere, and some effect should be produced. A body radiating its motion on every side into a physical medium, produces waves. These waves are a mechanical effect, and the body parts with some of its motion in producing them; but, should another body be placed in juxtaposition, having the same motion, the opposing waves neutralize each other, and the bodies lose no motion from their contiguous sides, and, therefore, the reaction from the opposite sides acts as a propelling power, and the bodies approach, or tend to approach each other. If one body be of double the inertia, it moves only half as far as the first; then, seeing that this atomic motion is radiated, the law of force must be directly as the mass, and inversely as the squares of the distances. There may be other atomic vibrations besides those which we call light, heat, and chemical action, yet the joint effect of all is infinitesimally small, when we disregard the united *attraction* of all the atoms of which the earth is composed. The *attraction* of the whole earth at the surface causes bodies to fall 16 feet the first second of time; but, if two spheres of ice of one foot diameter, were placed in an infinite space, uninfluenced by other matter, and only 16 feet apart, they would require nearly 10,000 years to fall together by virtue of their mutual attraction. Our conceptions, or, rather, our misconceptions, concerning the force of gravity, arises from our forgetting that every pound of matter on the earth contributes its share of the force which, in the aggregate, is so powerful. Hence, the cause we have suggested, is fully adequate to account for the phenomena. Whether the harmony of vibrations between two bodies may not have an influence in determining the amount of interference, and, consequently, produce *some* difference between the gravitating mass and its inertia, is a question which, no doubt, will ultimately be solved; but this harmony of vibrations must depend, in some degree, on the atomic weight, temperature, and intensity of atomic motion.

That a part of the mass of the earth is *latent*, may be inferred from certain considerations: 1st, from the discrepancies existing in the results obtained for the earth's compression by the pendulum and by actual measurement; and, 2d, from the irregularity of that compression in particular latitudes and longitudes. The same may also be deduced from the different values of the moon's mass as derived from different phenomena, dependent on the law of gravitation. Astronomers have hitherto covered themselves with the very convenient shield of errors of observation; but, the perfection of modern instruments now demand a better account of all outstanding discrepancies. The world requires it of them.

The mass of the moon comes out much greater by our theory than nutation gives. The mass deduced from the theory is only dependent on the relative inertiæ of the earth and moon. That given by nutation depends on gravity. If, then, a part of the mass be latent, nutation will give too small a value. But, in addition to this, we are justified in doubting the strict wording of the Newtonian law, deriving our authority from the very foundation stone of the Newtonian theory.

It is well known that Newton suspected that the moon was retained in her orbit by the same force which is usually called weight upon the surface, sixteen years before the fact was confirmed, by finding a correspondence in the fall of the moon and the fall of bodies on the earth. Usually, in all elementary works, this problem is considered accurately solved. Having formed a different idea of the mechanism of nature, this fact presented itself as a barrier beyond which it was impossible to pass, until suspicions, derived from other sources, induced the author to inquire: Whether the phenomenon did exactly accord with the theory? We are aware that it is easy to place the moon at such a distance, that the result shall strictly correspond with the fact; but, from the parallax, as derived from observation (and if this cannot be depended on certainly, no magnitudes in astronomy can), we find, *that the moon does not fall from the tangent of her orbit, as much as the theory requires.* As this is of vital importance to the integrity of the theory we are advocating, we have made the computation on Newton's own data, except such as were necessarily inaccurate at the time he wrote; and we have done it arithmetically, without logarithmic tables, that, if possible, no error should creep in to vitiate the result. We take the moon's elements from no less an authority than Sir John Herschel, as well as the value of the earth's diameter.

Mass of the moon	$\frac{1}{80}$
Mean distance in equatorial radii .	59.96435
Sidereal period in seconds . . .	2360591

The vibrations of the pendulum give the force of gravity at the surface of the earth, and it is found to vary in different latitudes. The intensity in any place being as the squares of the number of vibrations in a given time. This inequality depends on the centrifugal force of rotation, and on the spheroidal figure of the earth due to that rotation. At the equator the fall of a heavy body is found to be 16.045223 feet, per second, and in that latitude the squares of whose sine is $\frac{1}{3}$, it is 16.0697 feet. The effect in this last-named latitude is the same as if the earth were a perfect sphere. This does not, however, express the whole force of gravity, as the rotation of the earth causes a centrifugal tendency which is a maximum at the equator, and there amounts to $\frac{1}{289}$ of the whole gravitating force. In other latitudes it is diminished in the ratio of the squares of the cosines of the latitude; it therefore becomes $\frac{1}{434}$ in that latitude the square of whose sine is $\frac{1}{3}$. Hence the fall per second becomes 16.1067 feet for the true gravitating force of the earth, or for that force which retains the moon in her orbit.

The moon's mean distance is 59.96435 equatorial radii of the earth, which radius is, according to Sir John Herschell, 20.923.713 feet. Her mean distance as derived from the parrallax is not to be considered the radius vector of the orbit, inasmuch as the earth also describes a small orbit around the common centre of gravity of the earth and moon; neither is radius vector to be considered as her distance from this common centre; for the attracting power is in the centre of the earth. But the mean distance of the moon moving around a movable centre, is to the same mean distance when the centre of attraction is fixed, as the sum of the masses of the two bodies, to the first of two mean proportionals between this sum and the largest of the two bodies inversely. (Vid Prin. Prop. 60 Lib. Prim.) The ratio of the masses being as above 80 to 1 the mean proportional sought is 80.666 and in this ratio must the moon's mean distance be diminished to get the force of gravity at the moon. Therefore as 81 is to 80.666, so is 59.96435 to 59.71657 for the moon's distance in equatorial radii of the earth. Multiply this last by 20.923,713 to bring the semi-diameter of the lunar orbit into feet=1.249.492.373, and this by 6.283185, the ratio of the circumference to the radius, gives 7.850.791.736 feet, for the mean circumference of the lunar orbit.

Further, the mean sidereal period of the moon is 2360591 seconds and the $\frac{1}{2360591}$th part of 7.850.791.736 is the arc the moon describes in one second = 3325.77381 feet, the square of which divided by the diameter of the orbit, gives the fall of the moon from the tangent or versed size of that arc.

$$= \frac{11067771.36876644}{2498984746} = 0.004426106 \text{ feet.}$$

This fraction is, however, too small, as the ablatitious action of the sun diminishes the attraction of the earth on the moon, in the ratio of $178\frac{29}{40}$ to $177\frac{29}{40}$. So that we must increase the fall of the moon in the ratio of 711 to 715, and hence the true fall of the moon from the tangent of her orbit becomes 0.00451 feet per second.

We have found the fall of a body at the surface of the earth, considered as a sphere, 16.1067 feet per second, and the force of gravity diminishes as the squares of the distances increases. The polar diameter of the earth is set down as 7899.170 miles, and the equatorial diameter 7925.648 miles; therefore, the mean diameter is 7916.189 miles.* So that, reckoning in mean radii of the earth, the moon's distance is 59.787925, which squared, is equal to 3574.595975805625. At one mean radius distance, that is, at the surface, the force of gravity, or fall per second, is as above, 16.1067 feet. Divide this by the square of the distance, it is $\frac{16.1067}{3574.595975805625} = 0.0045058$ feet for the force of gravity at the moon. But, from the preceding calculation, it appears, that the moon only falls 0.0044510 feet in a second, showing a deficiency of $\frac{1}{82}$d part of the principal force that retains the moon in her orbit, being more than double the whole disturbing power of the sun, which is only $\frac{1}{178}$th of the earth's gravity at the moon: yet, on this $\frac{1}{178}$th depends the revolution of the lunar apogee and nodes, and all those variations which clothe the lunar theory with such formidable difficulties. The moon's mass cannot be less than $\frac{1}{86}$, and if we consider it greater, as it no doubt is, the results obtained will be still more discrepant. Much of this discrepancy is owing to the expulsive power of the radial stream of the terral vortex; yet, it may be suspected that the effect is too great to be attributed to this, and, for this

* The real diameter of the earth in that latitude, whose sine is one-third, is a little greater than this; but the true mean is more favorable for the Newtonian law.

reason, we have suggested that the fused matter of the moon's centre may not gravitate with the same force as the exterior parts, and thus contribute to increase the discrepancy.

As there must be a similar effect produced by the radial stream of every vortex, the masses of all the planets will appear too small, as derived from their gravitating force; and the inertia of the sun will also be greater than his apparent mass; and if, in addition to this, there be a portion of these masses latent, we shall have an ample explanation of the connection between the planetary densities and distances. We must therefore inquire what is the particular law of force which governs the radial stream of the solar vortex. It will be necessary to enter into this question a little more in detail than our limits will justify; but it is the resisting influence of the ether, and its consequences, which will appear to present a vulnerable point in the present theory, and to be incompatible with the perfection of astronomical science.

LAW OF DENSITY IN SOLAR VORTEX.

Reverting to the dynamical principle, that the product of every particle of matter in a fluid vortex, moving around a given axis, by its distance from the centre and angular velocity, must ever be a constant quantity, it follows that if the ethereal medium be uniformly dense, the periodic times of the parts of the vortex will be directly as the distances from the centre or axis; but the angular velocities being inversely as the times, the absolute velocities will be equal at all distances from the centre.

Newton, in examining the doctrine of the Cartesian vortices, supposes the case of a globe in motion, gradually communicating that motion to the surrounding fluid, and finds that the periodic times will be in the duplicate ratio of the distances from the centre of the globe. He and his successors have always assumed that it was impossible for the principle of gravity to be true, and a Cartesian plenum also; consequently, the question has not been fairly treated. It is true that Descartes sought to explain the motions of the planets, by the mechanical action of a fluid vortex *solely;* and to Newton belongs the glorious honor of determining the existence of a centripetal force, competent to explain these motions mathematically, (but not physically,) and rashly rejected an intelligible principle for a miraculous virtue. If our theory be true, the visible creation depends on the existence of both working together in harmony, and that a physical medium is absolutely necessary to the existence of gravitation.

If space be filled with a fluid medium, anology would teach us that it is in motion, and that there must be inequalities in the direction and velocity of that motion, and consequently there must be vortices. And if we ascend into the history of the past, we shall find ample testimony that the planetary matter now composing the members of the solar system, was once one vast nebulous cloud of atoms, partaking of the verticose motion of the fluid involving them. Whether the gradual accumulation of these atoms round a central nucleus from the surrounding space, and thus having their tangential motion of translation converted into vorticose motion, first produced the vortex in the ether; or whether the vortex had previously existed, in consequence of conflicting currents in the ether, and the scattered atoms of space were drawn into the vortex by the polar current, thus forming a nucleus at the centre, as a necessary result of the eddy which would obtain there, is of little consequence. The ultimate result would be the same. A nucleus, once formed, would give rise to a central force, tending more and more to counteract the centripulsive power of the radial stream; and in consequence of this continually increasing central power, the heaviest atoms would be best enabled to withstand the radial stream, while the lighter atoms might be carried away to the outer boundaries of the vortex, to congregate at leisure, and, after the lapse of a thousand years, to again face the radial stream in a more condensed mass, and to force a passage to the very centre of the vortex, in an almost parabolic curve. That space is filled with isolated atoms or planetary dust, is rendered very probable by a fact discovered by Struve, that there is a gradual extinction in the light of the stars, amounting to a loss of $\frac{1}{107}$ of the whole, in the distance which separates Sirius from the sun. According to Struve, this can be accounted for, "by admitting as very probable that space is filled with an *ether*, capable of intercepting in some degree the light." Is it not as probable that this extinction is due to planetary dust, scattered through the pure ether, whose vibrations convey the light,—the material atoms of future worlds,—the debris of dilapidated comets? Does not the Scripture teach the same thing, in asserting that the heavens are not clean?

The theory of vortices has had many staunch supporters amongst those deeply versed in the science of the schools. The Bernoullis proposed several ingenious hypothesis, to free the Cartesian system from the objections urged against it, viz.: that the velocities of the planets, in accordance with the three great laws of Kepler, cannot be made to correspond with the motion of a fluid vortex; but they, and all others, gave the vantage ground to the defenders of the Newtonian philosophy, by seeking to refer the principle of gravitation to conditions dependent on the density and vorticose motion of the ether. When we admit that the ether is imponderable and yet material, and planetary matter subject to the law of gravitation, the objections urged against the theory of vortices become comparatively trivial, and we shall not stop to refute them, but proceed with the investigation, and consider that the ether is the original source of the planetary motions and arrangements.

On the supposition that the ether is uniformly dense, we have shown that the periodic times will be directly as the distances from the axis. If the density be inversely as the distances, the periodic times will be equal. If the density be inversely as the square roots of the distances, the times will be directly in the same ratio. The celebrated J. Bernoulli assumed this last ratio; but seeking the source of motion in the rotating central globe, he was led into a hypothesis at variance with anology. The ellipticity of the orbit, according to this view, was caused by the planet oscillating about a mean position,—sinking first into the dense ether,—then, on account of superior buoyancy, rising into too light a medium. Even if no other objection could be urged to this view, the difficulty of explaining why the ether should be denser near the sun, would still remain. We might make other suppositions; for whatever ratio of the distances we assume for the density of the medium, the periodic times will be compounded of those distances and the assumed ratio. Seeing, therefore, that the periodic times of the planets observe the direct ses-plicate ratio of the distances, and that it is consonant to all analogy to suppose the contiguous parts of the vortex to have the same ratio, we find that the density of the ethereal medium in the solar vortex, is directly as the square roots of the distances from the axis.

Against this view, it may be urged that if the inertia of the medium is so small, as is supposed, and its elasticity so great, there can be no condensation by centrifugal force of rotation. It is true that when we say the ether is condensed by this force, we speak incorrectly. If in an infinite space of imponderable fluid a vortex is generated, the central parts are rarefied, and the exterior parts are unchanged. But in all finite vortices there must be a limit, outside of which the motion is null, or perhaps contrary. In this case there may be a cylindrical ring, where the medium will be somewhat denser than outside. Just as in water, every little vortex is surrounded by a circular wave, visible by reflection. As the density of the planet Neptune appears, from present indications, to be a little denser than Uranus, and Uranus is denser than Saturn, we may conceive that there is such a wave in the solar vortex, near which rides this last magnificent planet, whose ring would thus be an appropriate emblem of the peculiar position occupied by Saturn. This may be the case, although the probability is, that the density of Saturn is much greater than it appears, as we shall presently explain.

In order to show that there is nothing extravagant in the supposition of the density of the ether being directly as the square roots of the distances from the axis, we will take a fluid whose law of density is known, and calculate the effect of the centrifugal force, considered as a compressing power. Let us assume our atmosphere to be 47 miles high, and the compressing power of the earth's gravity to be 289 times greater than the centrifugal force of the equator, and the periodic time of rotation necessary to give a centrifugal force at the equator equal to the gravitating force to be 83 minutes. Now, considering the gravitating force to be uniform, from the surface of the earth upwards, and knowing from observation that at 18,000 feet above the surface, the density of the air is only $\frac{1}{2}$, it follows, (in accordance with the principle that the density is as the compressing force,) that at $43\frac{1}{2}$ miles high, or 18,000 feet *below* the surface of the atmosphere, the density is only $\frac{1}{8000}$ part of the density at the surface of the earth. Let us take this density as being near the limit of expansion, and conceive a hollow tube, reaching from the sun to the orbit of Neptune, and that this end of the tube is closed, and the end at the sun communicates with an inexhaustible reservoir of such an attenuated gas as composes the upper-layer of our atmosphere; and further, that the tube is infinitely strong to resist pressure, without offering resistance to the passage of the air within the tube; then we say, that, if the air within the tube be continually acted on by a force equal to the mean centrifugal force of the solar vortex, reckoning from the sun to the orbit of Neptune, the density of the air at that extremity of the tube, would be greater than the density of a fluid formed by the compression of the ocean into one single drop. For the centrifugal force of the vortex at 2,300,000 miles from the centre of the sun, is equal to gravity at the surface of the earth, and taking the mean centrifugal force of the whole vortex as one-millionth of this last force; so that at 3,500,000 miles from the surface of the sun, the density of the air in the tube (supposing it obstructed at that distance) would be double the density of the attenuated air in the reservoir. And the air at the extremity of the tube reaching to the orbit of Neptune, would be as much denser than the air we breathe, as a number expressed by 273 with 239 ciphers annexed, is greater than unity. This is on the supposition of infinite compressibility. Now, in the solar vortex there is no physical barrier to oppose the passage of the ether from the centre to the circumference, and the density of the ethereal ocean must be considered uniform, except in the interior of the stellar vortices, where it will be rarefied; and the rarefaction will depend on the centrifugal force and the length of the axis of the vortex. If this axis be very long, and the centrifugal velocity very great, the polar influx will not be sufficient, and the central parts will be rarefied. We see, therefore, no reason why the density of the ether may not be three times greater at Saturn than at the earth, or as the square roots of the distances directly.

BODES' LAW OF PLANETARY DISTANCES.

Thus, in the solar vortex, there will be two polar currents meeting at the sun, and thence being deflected at right angles, in planes parallel to the central plane of the vortex, and strongest in that central plane. The velocity of expansion must, therefore, diminish from the divergence of the radii, as the distances increase; but in advancing along these planes, the ether of the vortex is continually getting more dense, which operates by absorption or condensation on the radial stream; so that the velocity is still more diminished, and this in the ratio of the square roots of the distances directly. By combining these two ratios, we find that the velocity of the radial stream will be in the ses-plicate ratio of the distances inversely. But the force of this stream is not as the velocity, but as the square of the velocity. The *force* of the radial stream is consequently as the cubes of the distances inversely, from the axis of the vortex, reckoned in the same plane. If the ether, however, loses in velocity by the increasing density of the medium, it becomes also more dense; therefore the true force of the radial stream will be as its density and the square of its velocity, or directly as the square roots of the distances, and inversely as the cubes of the distances, or as the 2.5 power of the distances inversely.

If we consider the central plane of the vortex as coincident with the plane of the ecliptic, and the planetary orbits, also, in the same plane; and had the force of the radial stream been inversely as the square of the distances, there could be no disturbance produced by the action of the radial stream. It would only counteract the gravitation of the central body by a certain amount, and would be exactly proportioned at all distances. As it is, there is an outstanding force as a disturbing force, which is in the inverse ratio of the square roots of the distances from the sun; and to this is, no doubt, owing, in part, the fact, that the planetary distances are arranged in the inverse order of their densities.

Suppose two planets to have the same diameter to be placed in the same orbit, they will only be in equilibrium when their densities are equal. If their densities are unequal, the lighter planet will continually enlarge its orbit, until the force of the radial stream becomes proportional to the planets resisting energy. This, however, is on the hypothesis that the planets are not permeable by the radial stream, which, perhaps, is more consistent with analogy than with the reality. And it is more probable that the mean atomic weight of a planet's elements tends more to fix the position of equilibrium for each. Under the law of gravity, a planet may revolve at any distance from the sun, but if we superadd a centripulsive force, whose law is not that of gravity, but yet in some inverse ratio of the distances, and this force acts only superficially, it would be possible to make up in volume what is wanted in density, and a lighter planet might thus be found occupying the position of a dense planet. So the planet Jupiter, respecting only his resisting surface, is better able to withstand the force of the radial stream at the earth than the earth itself. To understand this, it is necessary to bear in mind, that, as far as planetary matter is concerned, the earth could revolve in Jupiter's orbit in the same periodic time as Jupiter, under the law of gravity; but that, in reality, the whole of the gravitating force is not effective, and that the equilibrium of a planet is due to a nice balance of interfering forces arising from the planet's physical peculiarities. As in a refracting body, the density of the ether may be considered inversely as the refraction, and this as the atomic weight of the refracting material, so, also, in a planet, the density of the ether will be inversely in the same ratio of the density of the matter approximately. Hence, the density of the ether within the planet Jupiter is greater than that within the earth; and, on this ethereal matter, the sun has no power to restrain it in its orbit, so that the centrifugal momentum of Jupiter would be relatively greater than the centrifugal momentum of the earth, were it also in Jupiter's orbit with the same periodic time. Hence, to make an equilibrium, the earth should revolve in a medium of less density, that there may be the same proportion between the external ether, and the ether within the earth, as there is between the ether around Jupiter and the ether within; so that the centrifugal tendency of the dense ether at Jupiter shall counteract the greater momentum of the dense ether within Jupiter; or, that the lack of centrifugal momentum in the earth should be rendered equal to the centrifugal momentum of Jupiter, by the deficiency of the centrifugal momentum of the ether at the distance of the earth.

If, then, the diameters of all the planets were the same (supposing the ether to act only superficially), the densities would be as the distances inversely;* for the force due to the radial stream is as the square roots of the distance inversely, and the force due to the momentum, if the density of the ether within a planet be inversely as the square root of a planet's distance, will also be inversely as the square roots of the distances approximately. We offer these views, however, only as suggestions to others more competent to grapple with the question, as promising a satisfactory solution of Bode's empirical formula.

If there be a wave of denser ether cylindrically disposed around the vortex at the distance of Saturn, or between Saturn and Uranus, we see why the law of densities and distances is not continuous. For, if the law of density changes, it must be owing to such a ring or wave. Inside this wave, the two forces will be inverse; but outside, one will be inverse, and the other direct: hence, there should also be a change in the law of distances. As this change does not take place until we pass Uranus, it may be suspected that the great disparity in the density of Saturn may be more apparent than real. The density of a planet is the relation between its mass and volume or extension, no matter what the form of the body may be. From certain observations of Sir Wm. Herschel—the Titan of practical astronomers—the figure of Saturn was suspected to be that of a square figure, with the corners rounded off, so as to leave both the equatorial and polar zones flatter than pertained to a true spheroidal figure. The existence of an unbroken ring around Saturn, certainly attaches a peculiarity to this planet which prepares us to meet other departures from the usual

* This is, perhaps, the nearest ratio of the densities and distances.

order. And when we reflect on the small density, and rapid rotation, the formation of this ring, and the figure suspected by Sir Wm. Herschel, it is neither impossible nor improbable, that there may be a cylindrical vacant space surrounding the axis of Saturn, or at least, that his solid parts may be cylindrical, and his globular form be due to elastic gases and vapors, which effectually conceal his polar openings. And also, by dilating and contracting at the poles, in consequence of inclination to the radial stream, (just as the earth's atmosphere is bulged out sufficiently to affect the barometer at certain hours every day,) give that peculiarity of form in certain positions of the planet in its orbit. Justice to Sir Wm. Herschell requires that *his* observations shall not be attributed to optical illusions. This view, however, which may be true in the case of Saturn, would be absurd when applied to the earth, as has been done within the present century. From these considerations, it is at least possible, that the density of Saturn may be very little less, or even greater than the density of Uranus, and be in harmony with the law of distances.

It is now apparently satisfactorily determined, that Neptune is denser than Uranus, and the law being changed, we must look for transneptunean planets at distances corresponding with the new law of arrangement. But there are other modifying causes which have an influence in fixing the precise position of equilibrium of a planet. Each planet of the system possessing rotation, is surrounded by an ethereal vortex, and each vortex has its own radial stream, the force of which in opposing the radial stream of the sun, depends on the diameter and density of the planet, on the velocity of rotation, on the inclination of its axis, and on the density of the ether at each particular vortex; but the numerical verification of the position of each planet with the forces we have mentioned, cannot be made in the present state of the question. There is one fact worthy of note, as bearing on the theory of vortices in connection with the rotation of the planets, viz.: that observation has determined that the axial rotation and sidereal revolution of the secondaries, are identical; thus showing that they are without vortices, and are motionless relative to the ether of the vortex to which they belong. We may also advert to the theory of Doctor Olbers, that the asterodial group, are the fragments of a larger planet which once filled the vacancy between Mars and Jupiter. Although this idea is not generally received, it is gathering strength every year by the discovery of other *fragments*, whose number now amounts to twenty-six. If the idea be just, our theory offers an explanation of the great differences observable in the mean distances of these bodies, and which would otherwise form a strong objection against the hypothesis. For if these little planets be fragments, there will be differences of density according as they belonged to the central or superficial parts of the quondam planet, and their mean distances must consequently vary also.

There are some other peculiarities connecting the distances and densities, to which we shall devote a few words. In the primordial state of the system, when the nebulous masses agglomerated into spheres, the diameter of these nebulous spheres would be determined by the relation existing between the rotation of the mass, and the gravitating force at the centre; for as long as the centrifugal force at the equator exceeded the gravitating force, there would be a continual throwing off of matter from the equator, as fast as it was brought from the poles, until a balance was produced. It is also extremely probable, (especially if the elementary components of water are as abundant in other planets as we have reason to suppose them to be on the earth,) that the condensation of the gaseous planets into liquids and solids, was effected in a *brief period of time*,* leaving the lighter and more elastic substances as a nebulous

* This is an important consideration, as bearing on the geology of the earth.

atmosphere around globes of semi-fluid matter, whose diameters have never been much increased by the subsequent condensation of their gaseous envelopes. The extent of these atmospheres being (in the way pointed out) determined by the rotation, their subsequent condensation has not therefore changed the original rotation of the central globe by any appreciable quantity. The present rotation of the planets, is therefore competent to determine the former diameters of the nebulous planets, i. e., the limit where the present central force would be balanced by the centrifugal force of rotation. If we make the calculation for the planets, and take for the unit of each planet its present diameter, we shall find that they have condensed from their original nebulous state, by a quantity dependent on the distance from the centre of the system; and therefore on the original temperature of the nebulous mass at that particular distance. Let us make the calculation for Jupiter and the earth, and call the original nebulous planets the nucleus of the vortex. We find the

Equatorial diameter of Jupiter's nucleus in equatorial diameters of Jupiter = 2.21, and the equatorial diameter of the earth's nucleus, in equatorial diameters of the earth = 6.59. Now, if we take the original temperature of the nebulous planets to be inversely, as the squares of the distances from the sun, and their volumes directly as the cubes of the diameters in the unit of each, we find that these cubes are to each other, in the inverse ratio of the squares of the planet's distances; for,

$$2.21^3 : 6.59^3 :: 1^2 : 5.2^2,$$

showing that both planets have condensed equally, allowing for the difference of temperature at the beginning. And we shall find, beginning at the sun, that the diameters of the nebulous planets, *ceteris paribus*, diminish outwards, giving for the nebulous sun a diameter of 16,000,000 miles,* thus indicating his original great temperature.

* It is not as likely that the condensation of the sun was so sudden

That the original nebulous planets did rotate in the same time as they do at present, is proved by Saturn's ring; for if we make the calculation, we find that the nucleus of the Saturnian vortex was just about twice the diameter of Saturn. Now, the diameter of the planet is about 80,000 miles, which will also be the semi-diameter of the nebulous planet; and the middle of the outer ring has also a semi-diameter of 80,000 miles; therefore, the ring is the equatorial portion of the original nebulous planet, and ought, on this theory, to rotate in the same time as Saturn. According to Sir John Herschel, Saturn rotates in 10 hours, 29 minutes, and 17 seconds, and the ring rotates in 10 hours, 29 minutes, and 17 seconds: yet this is not the periodic time of a satellite, at the distance of the middle of the ring; neither ought the rings to rotate in the same time; yet as far as observation can be trusted, both the inner and outer ring do actually rotate in the same time. The truth is, the ring rotates too fast, if we derive its centrifugal force from the analogy of its satellites; but it is, no doubt, in equilibrium; and the effective mass of Saturn on the satellites is less than the true mass, in consequence of his radial stream being immensely increased by the additional force impressed on the ether, by the centrifugal velocity of the ring. If this be so, the mass of Saturn, derived from one of the inner satellites, will be less than the same mass derived from the great satellite, whose orbit is considerably inclined. The analogy we have mentioned, between the diameters of the nebulous planets and their distances, does not hold good in the case of Saturn, for the reason already assigned, viz.: that the nebulous planet was probably not a globe, but a cylindrical ring, vacant around the axis, as there is reason to suppose is the case at present.

And now we have to ask the question, Did the ether involved in the nebulous planets rotate in the same time? This does not

as that of the planets, and therefore in this case this distance is only approximate.

necessarily follow. The ether will undoubtedly tend to move with increasing velocity to the very centre of motion, obeying the great dynamical principle when unresisted. If resisted, the law will perhaps be modified; but in this case, its motion of translation will be converted into atomic motion or heat, according to the motion lost by the resistance of atomic matter. This question has a bearing on many geological phenomena. As regards the general effect, however, the present velocity of the ether circulating round the planets, may be considered much greater than the velocities of the planets themselves.

PERTURBATIONS DUE TO THE ETHER.

In these investigations it is necessary to bear in mind that the whole resisting power of the ether, in disturbing the planetary movements, is but small, in comparison with gravitation. We will, however, show that, in the case of the planets, there is a compensation continually made by this resistance, which leaves but a very small outstanding balance as a disturbing power. If we suppose all the planets to move in the central plane of the vortex in circular orbits, and the force of the radial stream, (or that portion which is not in accordance with the law of gravitation,) to be inversely as the square roots of the distances from the sun, it is evident, from what has been advanced, that an equilibrium could still obtain, by variations in the densities, distances and diameters of the planets. Supposing, again, that the planets still move in the same plane, but in elliptical orbits, and that they are in equilibrium at their mean distances, under the influence or action of the tangential current, the radial stream, and the density of the ether; we see that the force of the radial stream is too great at the perihelion, and too small at the aphelion. At the perihelion the planet is urged from the sun and at the aphelion towards the sun. The density and consequent momentum is also relatively too great at the perihelion, which also urges the planet from the sun, and at the aphelion, relatively too small, which urges the planet towards the sun; and the law is the same in both cases, being null at the mean distance of the planet, and at a maximum at the apsides; it is, consequently, as the cosine of the planets eccentric anomaly at other distances, and is positive or negative, according as the planet's distance is above or below the mean.

At the planet's mean distance, the circular velocity of the vortex is equal to the circular velocity of the planet, and, at different distances, is inversely in the sub-duplicate ratio of those distances. But the circular velocity of a planet in the same orbit, is in the simple ratio of the distances inversely. At the perihelion, the planet therefore moves faster than the ether of the vortex, and at the aphelion, slower; and the difference is as the square roots of the distances; but the force of resistance is as the square of the velocity, and is therefore in the simple ratio of the distances, as we have already found for the effect of the radial stream, and centrifugal momentum of the internal ether. At the perihelion this excess of tangential velocity creates a resistance, which urges the planet towards the sun, and at the aphelion, the deficiency of tangential velocity urges the planet from the sun,—the maximum effect being at the apsides of the orbit, and null at the mean distances. In other positions it is, therefore, as the cosines of the eccentric anomaly, as in the former case; but in this last case it is an addititious force at the perihelion, and an ablatitious force at the aphelion, whereas the first disturbing force was an ablatitious force at the perihelion, and an addititious force at the aphelion; therefore, as we must suppose the planet to be in equilibrium at its mean distance, it is in equilibrium at all distances. Hence, a planet moving in the central plane of the vortex, experiences no disturbance from the resistance of the ether.

As the eccentricities of the planetary orbits are continually changing under the influence of the law of gravitation, we must inquire whether, under these circumstances, such a change would not produce a permanent derangement by a change in the mean force of the radial stream, so as to increase or diminish the mean distance of the planet from the sun. The law of force deduced from the theory for the radial stream is as the 2.5 power of the distances inversely. But, by dividing this ratio, we may make the investigation easier; for it is equivalent to two forces, one being as the squares of the distances, and another as the square roots of the distances. For the former force, we find that in orbits having the same major axis the mean effect will be as the minor axis of the ellipse *inversely*, so that two planets moving in different orbits, but at the same mean distance, experience a less or greater amount of centripulsive force from this radial stream, according as their orbits are of less or greater eccentricity, and this in the ratio of the minor axis. On the other hand, under the influence of a force acting centripulsively in the inverse ratio of the square roots of the distances, we find the mean effect to be as the minor axis of the ellipse *directly*, so that two planets in orbits of different eccentricity, but having the same major axis, experience a different amount from the action of this radial stream, the least eccentric orbit being that which receives the greatest mean effect. By combining these two results, we get a ratio of equality; and, consequently, the action of the radial stream will be the same for the same orbit, whatever change may take place in the eccentricity, and the mean distance of the planet will be unchanged. A little consideration will also show that the effect of the centrifugal momentum due to the density of ether will also be the same by change of eccentricity; for the positive will always balance the negative effect at the greatest and least distances of the planet. The same remark applies to the effect of the tangential current, so that no change can be produced in the major axes of the planetary orbits by change of eccentricity, as an effect of the resistance of the ether.

We will now suppose a planet's orbit to be inclined to the central plane of the vortex, and in this case, also, we find, that the action of the radial stream tends to increase the inclination in one quadrant as much as it diminishes it in the next quadrant, so that no change of inclination will result. But, if the inclination of the orbit be changed by planetary perturbations, the mean effect of the radial stream will also be changed, and this will tell on the major axis of the orbit, enlarging the orbit when the inclination diminishes, and contracting it when it increases. The change of inclination, however, must be referred to the central plane of the vortex. Notwithstanding the perfection of modern analysis, it is confessed that the recession of the moon's nodes does yet differ from the theory by its 350th part, and a similar discrepancy is found for the advance of the perigee.* This theory is yet far too imperfect to say that the action of the ethereal medium will account for these discrepancies; but it certainly wears a promising aspect, worthy the notice of astronomers. There are other minute discordancies between theory and observation in many astronomical phenomena, which theory *is* competent to remove. Some of these we shall notice presently; and, it may be remarked, that it is in those minute quantities which, in astronomy, are usually attributed to errors of observation, that this theory will eventually find the surest evidence of its truth.

KEPLER'S THIRD LAW ONLY APPROXIMATELY TRUE.

But it may be asked: If there be a modifying force in astronomy derived from another source than that of gravitation, why is it that the elements of the various members of the system derived solely from gravitation should be so perfect? To this it may be answered, that although astronomers have endeavored to derive every movement in the heavens from that

* Mechanique Celeste. Theory of the Moon.

great principle, they have but partially succeeded. Let us not surrender our right of examining Nature to the authority of a great name, nor call any man master, either in moral or physical science. It is well known that Kepler's law of the planetary distances and periods, is a direct consequence of the Newtonian law of gravitation, and that the squares of the periodic times ought to be proportional to the cubes of the mean distances. These times are given accurately by the planets themselves, by the interval elapsing between two consecutive passages of the node, and as in the case of the ancient planets we have observations for more than two thousand years past, these times are known to the fraction of the second. The determination of the distances however, depends on the astronomer, and a tyro in the science might suppose that these distances were actually measured; and so they are roughly; but the astronomer does not depend on his instruments, he trusts to *analogy*, and the mathematical perfection of a law, which in the abstract is true; but which he does not know is rigidly exact when applied to physical phenomena. From the immense distance of the planets and the smallness of the earth, man is unable to command a base line sufficiently long, to make the horizontal parallax a sensible angle for the more distant planets; and there are difficulties of no small magnitude to contend with, with those that are the nearest. In the occasional transit of Venus across the sun, however, he is presented with a means of measuring on an enlarged scale, from which the distance of the sun is determined; and by *analogy* the distance of all the planets. Even the parallax of the sun itself is only correct, by supposing that the square of the periodic time of Venus is in the same proportion to the square of the periodic time of the earth as the cube of her distance is to the cube of the earth's distance. Our next nearest planet is Mars, and observations on this planet at its opposition to the sun, invariably give a larger parallax for the sun—Venus giving 8.5776″ while Mars gives about 10″. It is true that the first is obtained under more favorable circumstances; but this does not prove the last to be incorrect. It is well known that the British Nautical Almanac contains a list of stars lying in the path of the planet Mars about opposition, (for the very purpose of obtaining a correct parallax,) that minute differences of declination may be detected by simultaneous observations in places having great differences of latitude. Yet strange to say, the result is discredited when not conformable to the parallax given by Venus. If then, we cannot trust the parallax of Mars, *à fortiori*, how can we trust the parallax of Jupiter, and say that his mean distance exactly corresponds to his periodic time? Let us suppose, for instance, that the radius vector of Jupiter fell short of that indicated by analogy by 10,000 miles, we say that it would be extremely difficult, nay, utterly impossible, to detect it by instrumental means. Let not astronomers, therefore, be too sure that there is not a modifying cause, independent of gravitation, which they will yet have to recognize. The moon's distance is about one-fourth of a million of miles, and Neptune's 2854 millions, or in the ratio of 10,000 to 1; yet even the moon's parallax is not trusted in determining her mass, how then shall we determine the parallax of Neptune? It is therefore *possible* that the effective action of the sun is in some small degree different, on the different planets, whether due to the action of the ether, to the similarity or dissimilarity of material elements, to the temperature of the different bodies, or to all combined, is a question yet to be considered.

As another evidence of the necessity of modifying the strict wording of the Newtonian law, it is found that the disturbing action of Jupiter on different bodies, gives different values for the mass of Jupiter. The mass deduced from Jupiter's action on his satellites, is different from that derived from the perturbations of Saturn, and this last does not correspond with that given by Juno: Vesta also gives a different mass from the comet of Encke, and both vary from the preceding values.*

In the analytical investigation of planetary disturbances, the disturbing force is usually divided into a radial and tangential force; the first changing the law of gravitation, to which law the elliptic form of the orbit is due. The radial disturbing force, therefore, being directed to or from the centre, can have no influence over the first law of Kepler, which teaches that the radius vector of each planet having the sun as the centre, describes equal areas in equal times. If the radial disturbing force be exterior to the disturbed body, it will diminish the central force, and cause a progressive motion in the aphelion point of the orbit. In the case of the moon this motion is very rapid, the apogee making an entire revolution in 3232 days. Does this, however, correspond with the law of gravitation? Sir Isaac Newton, in calculating the effect of the sun's disturbing force on the motion of the moon's apogee, candidly concludes thus: "Idoque apsis summa singulis revolutionibus progrediendo conficit 1° 31′ 28″. Apsis lunæ est duplo velocior circiter." As there was a necessity for reconciling this stubborn fact with the theory, his followers have made up the deficiency by resorting to the tangential force, or, as Clairant proposed, by continuing the approximations to terms of a higher order, or to the square of the disturbing force.

Now, in a circular orbit, this tangential force will alternately increase and diminish the velocity of the disturbed body, without producing any permanent derangement, the same result would obtain in an elliptical orbit, if the position of the major axis were stationary. In the case of the moon, the apogee is caused to advance by the disturbing power of the radial force, and, consequently, an exact compensation is not effected: there remains a small excess of velocity which geometers have considered equivalent to a doubling of the radial force, and have

*Mechanique Celeste. Masses of the planets.

thus obviated the difficulty. To those not imbued with the profound penetration of the modern analyst, there must ever appear a little inconsistency in this result. The major axis of a planet's orbit depends solely on the velocity of the planet at a given distance from the sun, and the tangential portion of the disturbance due to the sun, and impressed upon the moon, must necessarily increase and diminish alternately the velocity of the moon, and interfere with the equable description of the areas. If, then, there be left outstanding a small excess of velocity over and above the elliptical velocity of the moon, at the end of each synodical revolution, in consequence of the motion impressed on the moon's apogee by the radial force, the *legitimate* effect would be a small enlargement of the lunar orbit every revolution in a rapidly-increasing ratio, until the moon would at last be taken entirely away. In the great inequality of Jupiter and Saturn, this tangential force is not compensated at each revolution, in consequence of continual changes in the configuration of the two planets at their heliocentric conjunctions, with respect to the perihelion of their orbits, and the near commensurability of their periods; and the effect of the tangential force is, in this case, legitimately impressed on the major axes of the orbits. But why (we may ask) should not this also be expended on the motion of the aphelion as well as in the case of the moon? Astronomy can make no distinctions between the orbit of a planet and the orbit of a satellite. And, we might also ask, why the tangential resistance to the comet of Encke should not also produce a retrograde motion in the apsides of the orbit, instead of diminishing its period? To the honor of Newton, be it remembered, that he never resorted to an explanation of this phenomenon, which would vitiate that fundamental proposition of his theory, in which the major axis of the orbit is shown to depend on the velocity at any given distance from the focus.

Some cause, however, exists to double the motion of the

apogee, and that there is an outstanding excess of orbital velocity due to the tangential force, is also true. This excess may tell in the way proposed, provided some other arrangement exists to *prevent* a permanent dilation of the lunar orbit; and this provision may be found in the increasing density of the ether, which prevents the moon overstepping the bounds prescribed by her own density, and the force of the radial stream of the terral vortex. In the case of Jupiter and Saturn, their mutual action is much less interfered with by change of density in the ether in the enlarged or contracted orbit, and, consequently, the effect is natural. Thus, we have in the law of density of the ethereal medium a better safeguard to the stability of the dynamical balance of the system, than in the profound and beautiful Theorems of La Grange. It will, of course, occur to every one, that we are not to look for the same law in every vortex, and it will, therefore, appear as if the satellites of Jupiter, whose theory is so well known, should render apparent any deviation between their periodic times and the periodic times of the contiguous parts of the vortex, which would obtain, if the density of the ether in the Jovian vortex were not as the square roots of the distances directly. But, we have shown how there can be a balance preserved, if the tangential resistance of the vortex shall be equal and contrary at the different distances at which the satellites are placed; that is, if these two forces shall follow the same law. These are matters, however, for future investigation.

LIGHT AND HEAT.

But will not the admission of a verticose motion of the ethereal medium, affect the aberration of light? It is well known that the question has been mooted, whether the velocity of reflected light is the same as that of direct light. The value of aberration having been considered 20″.25, from the eclipses of Jupiter's satellites, while later determinations, from observations on Polaris, give 20″.45. It cannot be doubted that light, in traversing the central parts of the solar vortex, that is, having to cross the whole orbit of the earth, should pass this distance in a portion of time somewhat different to a similar distance outside the earth's orbit, where the density is greater, and consequently induce an error in the aberration, determined by the eclipses of Jupiter's satellites. In the case of Polaris, the circumstances are more equal; still, a difference ought to be detected between the deduced aberration in summer and in winter, as, in the first case, the light passes near the axis of the solar vortex, where (according to the theory) a change of density occurs. This is an important practical question, and the suggestion is worthy attention. Now, the questions occurs, will light pass through the rarefied space with greater velocity than through the denser ether beyond? From recent experiments, first instituted by Arago, it is determined that light passes with less velocity through water than through air; and one result of these experiments is the confirmation they give to the theory of Fresnel, that the medium which conveys the action of light partly partakes of the motion of the refracting body. This of itself is a strong confirmation of this theory of an ethereal medium. It may also be remarked, that every test applied to the phenomenon of light, adds additional strength to the undulatory theory, at the expense of the Newtonian theory of emission. As light occupies time in traversing space, it must follow from the theory that it does not come from the radiant point exactly in straight lines, inasmuch as the ether itself is in motion tangentially,—the velocity being in the sub-duplicate ratio of the distances from the sun inversely

May not that singular phenomenon,—the projection of a star on the moon's disc, at the time of an occultation,—be due to this curvature of the path of a ray of light, by considering that the rays from the moon have less intensity, but more mechanical momentum, and consequently more power to keep a straight direction? Let us explain: we have urged that light, as well as heat, is a mechanical effect of atomic motion, propagated through an elastic medium; that, *ceteris paribus*, the product of matter by its motion is ever a constant quantity for equal spaces throughout the universe,—in a word, that it is, and must necessarily be, a fundamental law of nature. All departures from this law are consequences of accidental arrangements, which can only be considered of temporary duration. Our knowledge of planetary matter requires the admission of differences in the density, form, and size of ultimate atoms, and, according to the above law, when the atoms are of uniform temperature or motion, the product of the matter of each by its motion, when reduced to the same space, will be constant. The momentum of two different atoms, therefore, we will consider equal, for the sake of illustration; yet this momentum is made up of two different elements,—matter and motion. Let us exaggerate the difference, and assign a ratio of 1000 to 1. Suppose a ball of iron of 1000 lbs., resting upon a horizontal plane, should be struck by another ball of 1 lb., having a motion of 1000 feet in a second, and, in a second case, should be struck by a ball of 1000 lbs., having a velocity of 1 foot per second, the momentum of each ball is similar; but experience proves that the motion impressed on the ball at rest is not similar; the ponderous weight and slow motion is far more effective in displacing this ball, for the reason that time is essential to the distribution of the motion. If the body to be struck be small as, for instance, a nail, a greater motion and less matter is more effective than much matter and little motion. Hence, we have a *distinction* applicable to the difference of momentum of luminous and calorific rays. The velocity of a wave of sound through the atmosphere, is the same for the deep-toned thunder and the shrillest whistle,—being dependent on the density of the medium, and not on the source from which it emanates. So it is in the ethereal medium.

This view is in accordance with the experiments of M. Delaroche and Melloni, on the transmission of light and heat through diaphanous bodies—the more calorific rays feeling more and more the influence of thickness, showing that more motion was imparted to the particles of the diaphanous substance by the rays possessing more material momentum, and still more when the temperature of the radiating body was low, evidently analogous to the illustration we have cited. Light may therefore be regarded as the effect of the vibration of atoms having little mass, and as this mass increases, the rays become more calorific, and finally the calorific effect is the only evidence of their existence; as towards the extreme red end of the spectrum they cease to be visible, owing to their inability to impart their vibrations to the optic nerve. This may also influence the law of gravitation. In this we have also an explanation of the dispersion of light. The rays proceeding from atoms of small mass having less material momentum, are the most refrangible, and those possessing greater material momentum, are the least refrangible; so that instead of presenting a difficulty in the undulatory theory of light, this dispersion is a necessary consequence of its first principles.

It is inferred from the experiments cited, and the facts ascertained by them, viz.: that the velocity of light in water is less than its velocity in air; that the density of the ether is greater in the first case; but this by no means follows. We have advocated the idea, that the ethereal medium is less dense within a refracting body than without. We regard it as a fundamental principle. Taking the free ether of heaven; the vibrations in the denser ether will no doubt be slowest; but within a refracting body we must consider there is motion lost, or *light absorbed*, and the time of the transmission is thus increased.

There has been a phenomenon observed in transits of Mercury and Venus across the sun, of which no explanation has been rendered by astronomers. When these planets are visible on the solar disc, they are seen surrounded by rings, as if the light was intercepted and increased alternately. This is no doubt due to a small effect of interference, caused by change of velocity in passing through the rarefied nucleus of these planetary vortices, near the body of the planet, and through the denser ether beyond, acting first as a concave, and secondly as a convex refracting body; always considering that the ray will deviate *towards* the side of least resistence, and thus interfere.

That heat is simply atomic motion, and altogether mechanical, is a doctrine which ought never to have been questioned. The interest excited by the bold experiments of Ericson, has caused the scientific to *suspect*, that heat can be converted into motion, and motion into heat—a fact which the author has considered too palpable to deny for the last twenty years. He has ever regarded matter and motion as the two great principles of nature, ever inseparable, yet variously combined; and that without these two elements, we could have no conception of anything existing.

It may be thought by some, who are afraid to follow truth up the rugged precipices of the hill of knowledge, that this theory of an interplanetary plenum leads to materialism; forgetting, that He who made the world, formed it of matter, and pronounced it "very good." We may consider ethereal matter, in one sense, *purer* than planetary matter, because unaffected by chemical laws. Whether still purer matter exists, it is not for us to aver or deny. The Scriptures teach us that "there is a natural body and there is a spiritual body." Beyond this we know nothing. We, however, believe that the *invisible* world of matter, can only be comprehended by the indications of that which is visible; yet while humbly endeavoring to connect by one common tie, the various phenomena of matter and motion, we protest against those doctrines which teach the eternal duration of the present order of things, as being incompatible with the analogies of the past, as well as with the revelations of the future.

SECTION FIFTH.

COMETARY PHENOMENA.

THE planetary arrangements of the solar system are all *à priori* indications of the theory of vortices, not only by the uniform direction of the motions, the circular orbits in which these motions are performed, the near coincidence of the planes of these orbits, and the uniform direction of the rotation of the planets themselves; but, also, by the law of densities and distances, which we have already attempted to explain. In the motions of comets we find no such agreement. These bodies move in planes at all possible inclinations in orbits extremely eccentrical and without any general direction—as many moving contrary to the direction of the planets as in the opposite direction; and when we consider their great volume, and their want of mass, it appears, at first sight, that comets do present a serious objection to the theory. We shall point out, however, a number of *facts* which tend to invalidate this objection, and which will ultimately give the preponderance to the opposite argument.

Every fact indicative of the nature of comets proves that the nuclei are masses of material gases, similar, perhaps (at least in the case of the short-period comets), to the elementary gases of our own planet, and, consequently, these masses must be but small. In the nascent state of the system, the radial stream of the vortex would operate as a fan, purging the planetary materials of the least ponderable atoms, and, as it were, separating the wheat from the chaff. It is thus we conceive that the average atomic density of each planet has been first determined by the radial stream, and, subsequently, that the solidification of the nebulous planets has, by their atomic density, assigned to each its position in the system, from the consequent relation which it established between the density of the ether within the planet, and the density of the ether external to it, so that, according to this view, a single isolated atom of the same density as the mean atomic density of the earth could (*ceteris paribus*) revolve in an orbit at the distance of the earth, and in the same periodic time. This, however, is only advanced by way of illustration.

The expulsive force of the radial stream would thus drive off this cometary dust to distances in some inverse ratio of the density of the atoms; but, a limit would ultimately be reached, when gravitation would be relatively the strongest—the last force diminishing only as the squares of the distances, and the first diminishing in the compound ratio of the squares and the square roots of the distances. At the extreme verge of the system, this cometary matter would accumulate, and, by accumulation, would still further gather up the scattered atoms—the sweepings of the inner space—and, in this condensed form, would again visit the sun in an extremely elongated ellipse. It does not, however, follow, that all comets are composed of such unsubstantial materials. There may be comets moving in parabolas, or even in hyperbolas—bodies which may have been accumulating for ages in the unknown regions of space, far removed from the sun and stars, drifting on the mighty currents of the great ethereal ocean, and thus brought within the sphere of the sun's attraction; and these bodies may have no analogy to the periodical comets of our system, which last are those with which we are more immediately concerned.

The periodical comets known are clearly arranged into two distinct classes—one having a mean distance between Saturn and Uranus, with a period of about seventy-five years, and another class, whose mean distance assigns their position between the smaller planets and Jupiter, having periods of about six years. These last may be considered the siftings of the smaller planets, and the first the refuse of the Saturnian system. In this light we may look for comets having a mean distance corresponding to the intervals of the planets, rather than to the distances of the planets themselves. One remarkable fact, however, to be observed in these bodies is, that all their motions are in the same direction as the planets, and, with one exception, there is no periodical comet positively known whose motion is retrograde.

The exception we have mentioned is the celebrated comet of Halley, whose period is also about seventy-five years. In reasoning on the resistance of the ether, we must consider that the case can have very little analogy with the theory of projectiles in air; nor can we estimate the inertia of an infinitely divisible fluid, from its resisting influence on atomic matter, by a comparison of the resistance of an atomic fluid on an atomic solid. Analogy will only justify comparisons of like with like. The tangent of a comet's orbit, also, can only be tangential to the circular motion of the ether at and near perihelion, which is a very small portion of its period of revolution. As far as the tangential resistance is concerned, therefore, it matters little whether its motion be direct or retrograde. If a retrograde comet, of short period and small eccentricity, were discovered moving also near the central plane of the vortex, it would present a very serious objection, as being indicative of contrary motions in the nascent state of the system. There is no such case known. So, also, with the inclinations of the orbits; if these be great, it matters little whether the comet moves in one way or the other, as far as the tangential current of the vortex is concerned. Yet, when we consider the average inclination of the orbit, and not of its plane, we find that the major axes of nearly all known cometary orbits are very little inclined to the plane of the ecliptic.

In the following table of all the periodical comets known, the inclination of the major axis of the orbit is calculated to the nearest degree; but all cometary orbits with very few exceptions, will be found to respect the ecliptic, and never to deviate far from that plane:

Designations of the Comets.		Periodic times.	Inclination of Major Axes.	Motion in Orbit.	Planetary Intervals.
Encke	1818	3 years.	1°	Direct	Mars & Ceres.
De Vico	1844		2	Direct	
Faye	1843		4	Direct	Ceres
De Avrest	1851	From	1	Direct	
Brorsen	1846	five	7	Direct	and
Messier	1766	to	0	Direct	
Clausen	1743	six	0	Direct	Jupiter.
Pigott	1783	or	4	Direct	
Pons	1819	seven	3	Direct	
Biela	1826	years.	9	Direct	
Blaupain	1819		2	Direct	
Lexell	1770		1	Direct	
Pons	1812		17	Direct	
Olbers	1815	about	40	Direct	Saturn
De Vico	1846	75	13	Direct	and
Brorsen	1847	years.	12	Direct	Uranus.
Westphal	1852		21	Direct	
Halley	1682		16	Retrograde	

From which it appears, that the objection arising from the great inclination of the *planes* of these orbits is much less important than at first it appears to be.

Regarding then, that a comet's mean distance depends on its mean atomic density, as in the case of the planets, the undue enlargement of their orbits by planetary perturbations is inadmissible. In 1770 Messier discovered a comet which approached nearer the earth than any comet known, and it was found to move in a small ellipse with a period of five and a half years; but although repeatedly sought for, it was the opinion of many, that it has never been since seen. The cause of this seeming anomaly is found by astronomers in the disturbing power of Jupiter—near which planet the comet must have passed in 1779, but the comet was not seen in 1776 before it passed near Jupiter, although a very close search was kept up about this time. Now there are two suppositions in reference to this body: the comet either moved in a larger orbit previous to 1767, and was then caused by Jupiter to diminish its velocity sufficiently to give it a period of five and a half years, and that after perihelion it recovered a portion of its velocity in endeavoring to get back into its natural orbit; or if moving in the natural orbit in 1770, and by passing near Jupiter in 1779 this orbit was deranged, the comet will ultimately return to that mean distance although not necesarily having elements even approximating those of 1770. In 1844, September 15th, the author discovered a comet in the constellation Cetus, (the same previously discovered by De Vico at Rome,) and from positions *estimated with the naked eye*, approximately determined the form of its orbit and its periodic time to be very similar to the lost comet of 1770. These conclusions were published in a western paper in October 1844, on which occasion he expressed the conviction, that this was no other than the comet of 1770. As the question bore strongly on his theory he paid the greater attention to it, and had, previously to this time, often searched in hopes of finding that very comet. Since then, M. Le Verrier has examined the question of identity and given his decision against it; but the author is still sanguine that the comet of 1844 is the same as that of 1770, once more settled at its natural distance from the sun. This comet returns to its perihelion on the 6th of August, 1855, according to Dr. Brünnow, when, it is hoped, the question of identity will be reconsidered with reference to the author's principles; and, that when astronomers become satisfied of this, they will do him the justice of acknowledging that he was the first who gave publicity to the fact, that the "Lost Comet" was found.

That comets do experience a resistance, is undeniable; but not in the way astronomers suppose, if these views be correct. The investigations of Professor Encke, of Berlin, on the comet which bears his name, has determined the necessity of a correction, which has been applied for several returns with apparent success. But there is this peculiarity about it, which adds strength to our theory: "The Constant of Resistance" requires a change after perihelion. The necessity for this change shows the action of the radial stream. From the law of this force, (reckoning on the central plane of the vortex,) there is an outstanding portion, acting as a disturbing power, in the subduplicate ratio of the distances inversely. If we only consider the mean or average effect in orbits nearly circular, this force may be considered as an ablatitious force at all distances below the mean, counterbalanced by an opposite effect at all distances above the mean. But when the orbits become very eccentrical, we must consider this force as momentarily affecting a comet's velocity,—diminishing it as it approaches the perihelion, and increasing it when leaving the perihelion. A resolution of this force is also requisite for the comet's distance above the central plane of the vortex, and a correction, likewise, for the intensity of the force estimated in that plane. There is also a correction necessary for the perihelion distance, and another for the tangential current; but we are only considering here the general effect. By diminishing the comet's proper velocity in its orbit, if we consider the attraction of the sun to remain the same, the general effect *may* be (for this depends on the tangential portion of the resolved force preponderating) that the absolute velocity will be increased, and the periodic time shortened; but after passing the perihelion, with the velocity of a smaller orbit, there is also superadded to this already undue velocity, the expulsive power of the radial stream, adding additional velocity to the comet; the orbit is therefore enlarged, and the periodic time increased. Hence the necessity of changing the "Constant of Resistance" after perihelion, and this will generally be found necessary in all cometary orbits, if this theory be true. But this question is one which may be emphatically called the most difficult of dynamical problems, and it may be long before it is fully understood.

According to the calculations of Professor Encke, the comet's period is accelerated about 2 hours, 30 minutes, at each return, which he considers due to a resisting medium. May it not rather be owing to *the change of inclination of the major axis of the orbit, to the central plane of the vortex?* Suppose the inclination of the *plane* of the orbit to remain unchanged, and the eccentricity of the orbit also, if the longitude of the perihelion coincides with that of either node, the major axis of the orbit lies in the ecliptic, and the comet then experiences the greatest mean effect from the radial stream; its mean distance is then, *ceteris paribus*, the greatest. When the angle between the perihelion and the nearest node increases, the mean force of the radial stream is diminished, and the mean distance is diminished also. When the angle is 90°, the effect is least, and the mean distance least. This is supposing the ecliptic the central plane of the vortex. When Encke's formula was applied to Biela's comet, it was inadequate to account for a tenth part of the acceleration; and although Biela moves in a much denser medium, and is of less dense materials, even this taken into account will not satisfy the observations,—making no other change in Encke's formula. We must therefore attribute it to changes in the elements of the orbits of these comets. Now, the effect of resistance should also have been noticed, as an acceleration of Halley's comet in 1835, yet the period was prolonged. To show that our theory of the *cause* of these anomalies corresponds with facts, we subjoin the elements in the following tables, taken from Mr. Hind's catalogue:

THE ELEMENTS OF ENCKE'S COMET.

Date of Perihelion.	Longitude of Perihelion.	Longitude of nearest Node,	Difference of Longitude.
1822	157° 11′ 44″	154° 25′ 9″	2° 46′ 35″
1825	157 14 31	154 27 30	2 47 1
1829	157 17 53	154 29 32	2 48 21
1832*	157 21 1	154 32 9	2 41 52
1835	157 23 29	154 34 59	2 48 30
1838	157 27 4	154 36 41	2 50 23
1842	157 29 27	154 39 10	2 50 17
1845	157 44 21	154 19 33	3 24 48
1848	157 47 8	154 22 12	3 24 56
1852	157 51 2	154 23 21	3 27 41

In this we see a regular increase of the angle, which ought to be attended with a small acceleration of the comet; but the change of inclination of the orbit ought also to be taken into consideration, to get the mean distance of the comet above the plane of the vortex, and, by this, the mean force of the radial stream.

In the following table, the same comparison is made for Biela's comet:—

ELEMENTS OF BIELA'S COMET.

Date of Perihelion.	Longitude of the Perihelion.	Longitude of the nearest Node.	Difference of Longitude.
1772	110° 14′ 54″	74° 0′ 1″	36° 14′ 53″
1806	109 32 23	71 15 15	38 17 8
1826	109 45 50	71 28 12	38 17 38†
1832	110 55 55	68 15 36	41 45 19
1846	109 2 20	65 54 39	43 7 41

Between 1832 and 1846, the increase of the angle is twice as great for Biela as for Encke, and the angle itself throws the major axis of Biela 10° above the ecliptic, whereas the angle made by Encke's major axis, is only about 1°; the cosine of the

* The orbit this year was determined under very unfavorable circumstances.

† According to other tables, this angle would be much greater than is given in Mr. Hind's catalogue.

first angle, diminishes much faster therefore, and consequently the same difference of longitude between the perihelion and node, will cause a greater acceleration of Biela; and according to Prof. Encke's theory, Biela would require a resisting medium twenty-five times greater than the comet of Encke to reconcile observation with the theory. Halley's comet can scarcely be considered to have had an orbit with perfect elements before 1835. If they were known accurately for 1759, we should no doubt find, that the angle between the node and perihelion *diminished* in the interval between 1759 and 1835, as according to the calculations of M. Rosenberg, the comet was six days behind its time—a fact fatal to the common ideas of a resisting medium; but this amount of error must be received as only approximate.

No comet that has revisited the sun, has given astronomers more trouble than the great comet of 1843. Various orbits have been tried, elliptical, parabolic and hyperbolic; yet none will accord with all the observations. The day before this comet was seen in Europe and the United States, it was seen close to the body of the sun at Conception, in South America; yet this observation, combined with those following, would give an orbital velocity due to a very moderate mean distance. Subsequent observations best accorded with a hyperbolic orbit; and it was in view of this anomaly, that the late Sears C. Walker considered that the comet came into collision with the sun in an elliptical orbit, and its *debris* passed off again in a hyperbola. That a concussion would not add to its velocity is certain, and the departure in a hyperbolic orbit would be contrary to the law of gravitation. This principle is thus stated by Newton:—"In parabola velocitas ubique equalis est velocitati corporis revolventis in circulo ad dimidiam distantiam; in ellipsi minor est in hyperbola major." (Vid. Prin. Lib. 1. Prop. 6 Cor. 7.)

But as regards the *fact*, it is probable that Mr. Walker's

views are correct, so far as the change from an ellipse to an hyperbola is considered. The Conception observation cannot be summarily set aside, and Professor Peirce acknowledges, that "If it was made with anything of the accuracy which might be expected from Captain Ray, it exhibits a decided anomaly in the nature of the forces to which the comet was subjected during its perihelion passage." The comet came up to the sun almost in a straight line against the full force of the radial stream; its velocity must therefore necessarily have been diminished. After its perihelion, its path was directly *from* the sun, and an undue velocity would be kept up by the auxiliary force impressed upon it by the same radial stream; and hence, the later observations give orbits much larger than the early ones, and there can be no chance of identifying this comet with any of its former appearances, even should its orbit be elliptical. This unexpected confirmation of the theory by the observation of Capt. Ray, cannot easily be surmounted.

We must now endeavor to explain the physical peculiarities of comets, in accordance with the principles laid down. The most prominent phenomenon of this class is the change of diameter of the visible nebulosity. It is a most singular circumstance, but well established as a fact, that a comet contracts in its dimensions on approaching the sun, and expands on leaving it. In 1829, accurate measures were taken on different days, of the diameter of Encke's comet, and again in 1838. The comet of 1618 was also observed by Kepler with this very object, and also the comet of 1807; but without multiplying instances, it may be asserted that it is one of those facts in cometary phenomena, to which there are no exceptions. According to all analogy, the very reverse of this ought to obtain. If a comet is chiefly vaporous, (as this change of volume would seem to indicate,) its approach to the sun ought to be attended by a corresponding expansion by increase of temperature. When the contrary is observed, and invariably so, it ought to be regarded as an index of the existence of other forces besides gravitation, increasing rapidly in the neighborhood of the sun; for the disturbing power of the sun's attraction would be to enlarge the diameter of a comet in proportion to its proximity. Now, the force of the radial stream, as we have shown, is as the 2.5th power of the distances inversely. If this alternate contraction and expansion be due to the action of this force, there ought to be an approximate correspondence of the law of the effect with the law of the cause. Arago, in speaking of the comet of 1829, states, "that between the 28th of October and the 24th of December, the volume of the comet was reduced as 16000 to 1, the change of distance in the meantime only varying about 3 to 1." To account for this, a memoir was published on the subject by M. Valz, in which he supposes an atmosphere around the sun, whose condensation increases rapidly from superincumbent pressure; so that the deeper the comet penetrates into this atmosphere the greater will be the pressure, and the less the volume. In this it is evident, that the ponderous nature of a resisting medium is not yet banished from the schools. In commenting on this memoir, Arago justly observes, that "there would be no difficulty in this if it could be admitted that the exterior envelope of the nebulosity were not permeable to the ether; but this difficulty seems insurmountable, and merits our sincere regret; for M. Valz's ingenious hypothesis has laid down the law of variation of the bulk of the nebulosity, as well for the short-period comet as for that of 1618, with a truly wonderful exactness." Now, if we make the calculation, we shall find that the diameter of the nebulosity of a comet is inversely as the force of the radial stream. This force is inversely as the 2.5 power of the distances from the axis, and not from the sun: it will, therefore, be in the inverse ratio of the cosine of the comet's heliocentric latitude to radius, and to this ratio the comet's distance ought to be reduced. But, this will only be correct for the same plane or for equal distances above the ecliptic plane, considering this last as approximately the central plane of the vortex. From the principles already advanced, the radial stream is far more powerful on the central plane than in more remote planes; therefore, if a comet, by increase of latitude, approaches near the axis, thus receiving a larger amount of force from the radial stream in that plane than pertains to its actual distance from the sun, it will also receive a less amount of force in that plane than it would in the central plane at the same distance from the axis. Now, we do not know the difference of force at different elevations above the central plane of the vortex; but as the two differences due to elevation are contrary in their effects and tend to neutralize each other, we shall make the calculation as if the distances were truly reckoned from the centre of the sun.

The following table is extracted from Arago's tract on Comets, and represents the variations of the diameter of Encke's comet at different distances from the sun,—the radius of the orbis magnus being taken as unity.

Times of observation, 1828.	Distances of the comet from the sun.	Real diameters in radii of the earth.
Oct. 28	1.4617	79.4
Nov. 7	1.3217	64.8
Nov. 30	0.9668	29.8
Dec. 7	0.8473	19.9
Dec. 14	0.7285	11.3
Dec. 24	0.5419	3.1

In order the better to compare the diameters with the force, we will reduce them by making the first numbers equal.

Distances.	Diameters.	The 2.5th power of the Distances.	Reduced Diameters.
1.4617	79.4	2.58	2.58
1.3217	64.8	2.01	2.10
0.9668	29.8	0.92	0.97
0.8473	19.9	0.66	0.65
0.7285	11.3	0.45	0.37
0.5419	3.1	0.21	0.10

This is a very close approximation, when we consider the difficulty of micrometric measurement, and the fact, that as the comet gets nearer to the sun, as at the last date of the table, the diameter is more than proportionably diminished by the fainter nebulosity becoming invisible. But, there may be a reality in the discrepancy apparent at the last date, as the comet was then very near the plane of the ecliptic, and was, consequently, exposed to the more violent action of the radial stream.

To attempt to explain the *modus agendi* is, perhaps, premature. Our principal aim is to pioneer the way into the labyrinth, and it is sufficient to connect this seeming anomaly with the same general law we have deduced from other phenomena. Still, an explanation may be given in strict accordance with the general principles of the theory.

Admitting the *nucleus* of a comet to be gaseous, there is no difficulty about the solution. According to Sir John Herschel, "stars of the smallest magnitude remain distinctly vissible, though covered by what appears the densest portion of their substances; and since it is an observed fact, that the large comets which have presented the appearance of a nucleus, have yet exhibited no phases, though we cannot doubt that they shine by the reflected solar light, it follows that even these can only be regarded as great masses of thin vapor." That comets shine solely by reflected solar light, is a position that we shall presently question; but that they are masses of vapor is too evident to dispute. According to the same authority quoted above, "If the earth were reduced to the one thousandth part of its actual mass, its coercive power over the atmosphere would be diminished in the same proportion, and in consequence the latter would expand to a thousand times its actual *bulk*." If this were so, and comets composed of the elementary gases, some of them would have very respectable masses, as the nuclei are frequently not more than 5,000 miles in diameter, and consequently it becomes important to examine the principle. From all experiments the density of an elastic fluid is directly as the compressing force; and if a cylinder reached to the top of our atmosphere, compressed by the gravitation of the earth, considered equal at each end of the cylinder, it would represent the actual compressing force to which it owes its density. If the gravitation of the earth were diminished one thousand times this atmospheric column would expand one thousand times,* (taking no account of the decrease of gravitation by increase of distance;) so that the diameter of the aërial globe would be increased to 108,000 miles, taking the atmosphere at 50 miles. But the mere increasing the *bulk* of the atmosphere 1000 times would increase the diameter to little more than double. Even giving the correct expansion, a comet's mass must be much greater than is generally supposed, or the diameters of the nuclei would be greater if composed of any gas lighter than atmospheric air.

It is very improbable that a comet is composed of only one elementary gas, and if of many, their specific gravities will vary; the lighter, of course, occupying the exterior layers. With such a small mass, therefore, the upper portion of its atmosphere must be very attenuated. Now let us remember that the density of the ether at a comet's aphelion, is greater than at the perihelion, in the direct ratio of the square roots of the distances from the sun nearly. At the aphelion the comet lingers through half his period, giving ample time for the nucleus to be permeated by ether proportionally dense with the surrounding ether of the vortex at that distance. Thus situated, the comet descends to its perihelion, getting faster and faster into a medium far less dense, and there must consequently be an escape from the nucleus, or in common parlance, the comet is positively electric. This escaping ether, in passing through the attenuated layers composing the surface of the

* Prin. Prop. xx Lib. Sec.

nucleus, impels the lighter atoms of cometic dust further from the centre, and as far as this *doubly* attenuated atmosphere of isolated particles extends, so far will the escaping ether be rendered luminous. It may be objected here, that a contrary effect ought to be produced when the comet is forsaking its perihelion; but the objection is premature, as the heat received from the sun will have the same effect in increasing the elasticity, as change of density, and the comet will probably part with its internal ether as long as it is visible to the earth; and not fully regain it perhaps, until after it arrives at its aphelion. Suppose that we admit that a comet continues to expand in the same ratio for all distances, as is laid down for the comet of Encke when near its perihelion; it would follow, that the comet of 1811, would have a diameter at its aphelion of fifty millions of millions of miles, that is, its outside would extend one thousand times further from the sun, at the opposite side to that occupied by the centre of the comet, than the distance of the comet's centre from the sun, at its enormous aphelion distance. Such an absurdity shows us that there is a limit of expansion due to natural causes, and that if there were no radial stream the volume of a comet would be greatest when nearest the sun.

But while the comet is shortening its distance and hastening to the sun in the form of a huge globular mass of diffuse light, it is continually encountering another force, increasing in a far more rapid ratio than the law of gravitation. At great distances from the sun, the force of the radial stream was insufficient to detach any portion of the comet's atmosphere; presently, however, the globular form is changed to an ellipsoid, the radial stream begins to strip the comet of that doubly attenuated atmosphere of which we have spoken, and the diameter of the comet is diminished, merely because the luminosity of the escaping ether is terminated at the limit of that atmosphere. Meanwhile the mass of the comet has suffered only an infinitely small diminution; but if the perihelion distance be small, the force may become powerful enough to detach the heavier particles of the nucleus, and thus a comet may suffer in mass by this denudating process. We regard, therefore, the nucleus of a comet to represent the mass of the comet and the coma, as auroral rays passing through a very attenuated envelope of detached particles. The individual gravitating force of these particles to the comet's centre, may be therefore considered as inversely as the squares of the distances, and directly as the density of the particles; and this density will, according to analogical reasoning, be as the distances or square roots of the distances;--grant the last ratio, and the gravitating force of the particles composing the exterior envelope of a comet, becomes inversely as the 2.5th power of the distances from the comet's centre.* This being the law of the radial stream, it follows, of course, that a comet's diameter is inversely as the force of the radial stream. It must, however, be borne in mind, that we are speaking of the atomic density, and not of density by compression; for this cometary dust, which renders luminous the escaping ether of the nucleus, must be far too much diffused to merit the name of an elastic fluid. May not the concentric rings, which were so conspicuous in the comet of 1811, be owing to differences in the gravitating forces of such particles, sifted, as it were, and thus arranged, according to some ratio of the distances, by the centripulsive force of the electric coma, leaving vacant intervals, through which the ether passed without becoming luminous? This at least is the explanation given by our theory. We may, indeed, consider it possible that the escaping ether, when very intense, might be rendered luminous by passing into the surrounding ether, and, as it became more diffused by radiation, at last become invisible. In this case, as the law of radiation is as the squares of the distances from the centre inversely, the rays would be more and more bent at right angles, or apparently shortened, as the power of the radial stream in-

* With reference to the resisting power of the atoms.

creased, and the apparent diameters of the coma would be diminished faster than the ratio of the 2.5th power of the distances. But whichever view we adopt, the diameter would again increase in the same ratio on leaving the sun, if we make allowance for increase of temperature, as well as for diminution of density, for the ordinary distance of a comet's visibility. We, however, regard the change of diameter, as due to both these nodes of action, as best agreeing with the indications afforded by their tails.

From the preceding remarks, it results that the density of the particles producing the nebulous envelope of a comet, renders the variations of diameter only approximate to the law of the radial stream; a comet's own electric energy, or the intensity of the escaping ether, may also modify this expression, and many other causes may be suggested. That the radial stream is the cause, in the way we have pointed out, is proved by the positions of the major axis of the short-period comet, making frequently nearly a right angle with the radius vector of the orbit in 1828. A soap bubble gently blown aside, without detaching it from the pipe, will afford a good illustration of the mode, and a confirmation of the cause. The angles measured by Struve, reckoned from the radius vector, prolonged towards the sun, are subjoined:

November 7 . .	99°.7	December 7 . .	154°.0
November 30 . .	145 .3	December 14 . .	149 .4

At this last date, the comet was getting pretty close to the sun. When the angle was greater, as on November 7th, the comet appeared to make almost a right angle with the radius vector; and in this position of the earth and comet, the longer axis of the elliptical comet was directed to the axis of the vortex, as may be verified by experiment. At the later dates, the comet was more rapidly descending, and, at the same time, the axis of the comet was getting more directed towards the earth; so that the angle increased between this axis and the radius vector, and consequently became more coincident with it. We have now to consider the luminous appendage of a comet, commonly called a tail.

The various theories hitherto proposed to account for this appendage are liable to grave objections. That it is not refracted light needs not a word of comment. Newton supposes the tail to partake of the nature of vapor, rising from the sun by its extreme levity, as smoke in a chimney, and rendered visible by the reflected light of the sun. But, how vapor should rise towards opposition in a vacuum, is utterly inexplicable. In speaking of the greater number of comets near the sun than on the opposite side, he observes: "Hinc etiam manifestum est quod cœli resistentiâ destituuntur."* And again, in another place, speaking of the tail moving with the same velocity of the comet, he says: "Et hinc rursus colligitur spatia cœlestia vi resistendi destitui; utpote in quibus non solum solida planetarum et cometarum corpora, sed etiam rarissimi candarum vapores motus suos velocissimos liberrimè peragunt ac diutissimè conservant." On what *principle*, therefore, Newton relied to cause the vapors to ascend, does not appear. Hydrogen rises in our atmosphere because specifically lighter. If there were no atmosphere, hydrogen would not rise, but merely expand on all sides. But, a comet's tail shoots off into space in a straight line of one hundred millions of miles, and frequently as much as ten millions of miles in a single day, as in the case of the comet of 1843. Sir John Herschel observes, that "no rational or even plausible account has yet been rendered of those immensely luminous appendages which they bear about with them, and which are known as their tails." Yet, he believes, and astronomers generally believe, that a comet shines by reflected light. This theory of reflexion is the incubus which clogs the question with such formidable difficulties; for, it follows, that the reflecting matter

* Prin. Lib. Ter. Prop, xxxix., also Prop. xli.

must come from the comet. But, what wonderful elements must a comet be made of, to project themselves into space with such immense velocity, and in such enormous quantities as to exceed in volume the body from which they emanate many millions of times. This theory may be, therefore, safely rejected.

From what we have already advanced concerning the coma or nebulosity of the comet, we pass by an easy path to an explanation of the tail. In the short-period comets, the density of the elementary atoms is too great to be detached in the gross from the nucleus, or, rather, the density of the atoms composing the nucleus is too great to permit the radiating stream of the comet carrying them to a sufficient distance to be detached by the radial stream of the sun. Hence, these comets exhibit but very little tails. We may also conceive, that the continual siftings which the nucleus undergoes at each successive perihelion passage, have left but little of those lighter elements in comets whose mean distances are so small. Yet, again, if by any chance the eccentricity is increased, there are two causes—the density of the ether, and the heat of the sun —which may make a comet assume quite an imposing appearance when apparently reduced to the comparatively passive state above mentioned.

According to our theory, then, the coma of a comet is due to the elasticity of the ethereal medium within the nucleus, caused both by the diminished pressure of the external ether near the sun, and also by the increased temperature acting on the nucleus, and thus on the involved ether. The tail, on the contrary, is caused by the lighter particles of the comet's attenuated atmosphere being blown off by the electric blast of the radial stream of the solar vortex, in sufficient quantities to render its passage visible. It is not, therefore, reflected light, but an ethereal stream rendered luminous by this detached matter still held in check by the gravitating force of the sun, whose centre each particle still respects, and endeavors to describe such an orbit as results from its own atomic density, and the resultant action of both the acting forces. From the law of density of the ether, the coma ought to be brightest and the radiating stream of the comet's nucleus strongest on the side of least pressure: from this cause, and the fact that the body of the comet affords a certain protection to the particles immediately behind it, there will be an interval between the comet and the tail less luminous, as is almost invariably observed. We thus have an explanation of the fact noticed by Sir John Herschel, "that the structure of a comet, as seen in section in the direction of its length, must be that of a hollow envelope of a parabolic form, enclosing near its vertex the nucleus or head." We have, also, a satisfactory explanation of the rapid formation of the tail; of its being wider and fainter at its extremity; of its occasional curvature; and of its greater length after perihelion than before. But, more especially may we point to the explanation which this theory gives of the fact, that, *ceteris paribus*, the long-period comets, when their perihelion distances are small, have tails of such exaggerated dimensions.

A comet, whose mean distance is considerable, is supposed by the theory to be composed of elements less dense, and, during its long sojourn at its aphelion, it may be also supposed that it there receives continual accessions to its volume from the diffused siftings of the system, and from the scattered debris of other comets. On approaching the perihelion, the rapidity of the change in the density of the ether in a given time, depends on the eccentricity of the orbit, and so does the change of temperature; so that, from both causes, both the length of the tail and the brilliancy of the comet measurably depends on the magnitude of the period and of the eccentricity.

If the nuclei of comets be gaseous as we suppose, and that the smallest stars are visible through them, it is an outrage on common sense, to refer that light, which renders a comet visible at noon-day, within six minutes of space of the sun itself, to the reflected light of the sun. When a small star has been seen through the nucleus of a comet, without any perceptible diminution of light, it indicates perfect transparency; but there can be no reflection from a perfectly transparent body, and therefore, a comet does not shine by reflected light. It is true that Arago discovered traces of polarized light in the comet of 1819, and also in more recent comets, but they are mere traces, and Arago himself admits, that they do not permit "the conclusion decidedly that these stars shine only with a borrowed light." But it still does not follow that a comet (even if independent of reflected light) is in an incandescent state. The auroral light is not polarized, nor any other electric light, neither is it owing to a state of incandescence, yet it is luminous. The intense light of a comet at perihelion is analogous to the charcoal points of a galvanic battery, caused by a rapid current of ether from the nucleus, and assisted by the radial stream of the vortex. This will account for the phenomenon in all its shades of intensity, as well as for the absence of any perceptible phase. It will also account for the non-combustion of such comets as those of the years 1680 and 1843. We shall also be at no loss to understand, why there is no refraction when a ray of light from a star passes through the nebulosity of a comet; and if, as we may reasonably suppose, the gaseous matter composing the nucleus be very attenuated, instruments are yet too imperfect to determine whether these also have any refracting power. On this point, however, it is safest to suspend our judgment, as there may be comets not belonging to our system, with even liquid or solid nuclei, or of matter widely different to those elements composing the members of the solar system.

In addition to what has been already advanced on this subject of a comet's light, we may appeal to the well-known fact that the visibility of a comet is not reciprocally as the squares of the distances from the earth and sun as it ought to be, if shining by reflected light. In Mr. Hind's late work on comets, the fact is stated that "Dr. Olbers found that the comet of 1780 attained its greatest brightness on the 8th of November, thirteen days subsequent to its discovery, whereas according to the law of reflected light, it should have become gradually fainter from the day of its discovery; and supposing the comet self-luminous, the intensity of light should have increased each day until November 26th; yet in the interval between the 8th and 26th of that month, it grew rapidly less." Now this theory teaches, that a comet is neither self-luminous nor dependent on the sun, but on its distance from the axis of the vortex, and a certain amount of elapsed time from the perihelion, varying somewhat in each particular case. This fact is therefore a very strong argument in favor of our theory.

Amidst the many anomalous peculiarities of comets, it has been noticed that a short tail is sometimes seen at right angles to the principal tail, and in a few cases pointing directly towards the sun. Much of this may be owing to perspective, but granting the reality of the fact, it is still explicable on the same general principles.

In speaking of the modifying causes which influence the weather, we mentioned the effect due to the position of the sun with respect to the axis of the vortex. This will be found to have a sensible effect on the action of the radial stream. The natural direction of a comet's electric stream is *towards* the axis of the vortex, and in the central plane of the vortex it will be also towards the sun. But this stream is met by the stronger radial stream from the axis, and as Mr. Hind describes it, "is driven *backward* in two streams passing on either side of the head, and ultimately blending into one to form the tail." Now, if the body of the sun be situated between the comet and the axis of the vortex, it will shield the comet from the action of the radial stream, and thus a tail may really point towards the sun.

In 1744 a brilliant comet exhibited six distinct tails spread out like a fan, some seven days after its perihelion passage; its distance from the sun at the time not being more than a third of the earth's distance. The comet was then rapidly approaching the plane of the ecliptic, and if we make the calculation for the position of the sun, we shall find that the body of the sun was on the same side of the axis of the vortex as the comet, and that the comet was then situated at the boundaries of the conical space, enclosed by the radial stream in its deflected passage round the body of the sun. In this position there are numerous cross currents of the stream, and hence the phenomenon in question. As this fact rests on the testimony of one individual, and is an occurrence never recorded before or since, many are disposed to doubt the fact, yet our theory explains even this peculiarity, and shows that there is no necessity for impugning the statement of Chescaux.

Another unexplained phenomenon is the corruscation of the tail. It has been attempted to explode this fact also, by referring it to conditions of our own atmosphere; and it is generally considered the argument of Olbers, founded on the great length of the tail and the velocity of light, is sufficient to prove that these corruscations are not actually in the tail. Now, it is undoubtedly true, that as light travels less than two hundred thousand miles in a second, and a comet's tail is frequently one hundred millions long, it is impossible to see an instantaneous motion along the whole line of the tail; but granting that there are such flickerings in the tail as are described by so many, it must necessarily be, that these flickerings will be *visible*. It would be wonderful indeed, if a series of waves passing from the comet to the extremity of the tail, should have their phases so exactly harmonizing with their respective distances as to produce a uniform steady light from a light in rapid motion. The argument, therefore, proves too much, and as it is in the very nature of electric light thus to corruscate, as we see frequently in the northern lights, we must be permitted still to believe that not only the tails, but also the heads of comets do really coruscate as described.

With respect to the direction of the tail, astronomers have been forced to abandon the antiquated notion, that the tail always pointed directly from the sun; yet they still pertinaciously cling to the idea, that although this is not always the case, the tail only deviates from this direction *in the plane of the orbit.* As this is a most important question, it is necessary formally to protest against such a conclusion. If the earth should happen to be in the plane of the comet's orbit and the tail appears in that plane, it must of course be in that plane *really* ; but if the earth is not in the plane of the comet's orbit, the tail is not *necessarily* in the same plane, whatever its apparent direction may indicate. It is true there is a tendency of every particle of the tail, moving under the restraining influence of the sun's attraction, to continue in the plane of the orbit; and in certain positions there is no oblique action arising from the force of the radial stream to cause it to deviate from that plane; yet in other positions of the comet, the action of the radial stream may be oblique, forcing it out of that plane, and still such a direction might be assigned to it as to make it conform. In the comet of 1843, P. Smythe observed a forked tail 25° long on March 3d, and from the end of the forked tail, and from its *north* side, a streamer diverged at an angle of 6° or 7° to the *north.* As this was contrary to the *direction* of the curvature, if the tail had been curved, it could only arise from a portion being driven off by the radial stream, or bent towards the plane of the ecliptic. The curvature observed by others at a later date, was concave to the south. Towards the middle and close of March, the tail became straight, and with the above exception, might be considered to move in the plane of the orbit.

The celebrated comet of Halley, as observed by Dr. Bessel in 1835, showed that a more or less well-defined tuft of rays emanated from that part of the nucleus which was turned towards the sun; and the rays being *bent backward* formed a part of the tail. The nucleus, with its emanations, presented the appearance of a burning rocket, the end of which was turned sideways by the force of the wind. And, Bessel concludes: "That the cone of light issuing from the comet deviated considerably both to the right and left of the true direction of the sun, but that it always returned to that direction, and passed over to the opposite side; so that the cone of light, and the body of the comet from whence it emanated, experienced a rotatory, or, rather, a vibrating motion *in the plane of the orbit.*" It is impossible that Bessel should here mean that this motion was certainly in the plane of the orbit; for the orbit was then viewed sideways, and he had no means of ascertaining the fact. His meaning must be that it was apparently in the plane of the orbit. If a plane be made to pass through the earth, the comet, and the sun, the tail might be placed in any position in that plane, and yet appear to be at the intersection of the two; that is, in the plane of the comet's orbit. The vibration of the tail, in this case, is another strong proof of the correctness of our theory. To make it more intelligible, we shall resort to a diagram.

In the following diagram, the comet's orbit, represented by the dotted line, is drawn on the plane of the ecliptic; it is, therefore, necessary to bear in mind, that it is tilted up from the line of nodes S N, at an angle of 17° 45′. The position of the comet, October 9th, is at C, approaching its perihelion; that of the earth at the same time at T; while S represents the sun, and S Q the line of equinoxes. Now, from a cause already explained, the tail always tends to lay behind the comet, in the direction indicated by the lower tail in the diagram at 1, and, if produced, would pass to the left of the sun, as seen from the earth: the force of the radial stream, however, will not allow this lagging of the tail, and it is straightened out by this force;

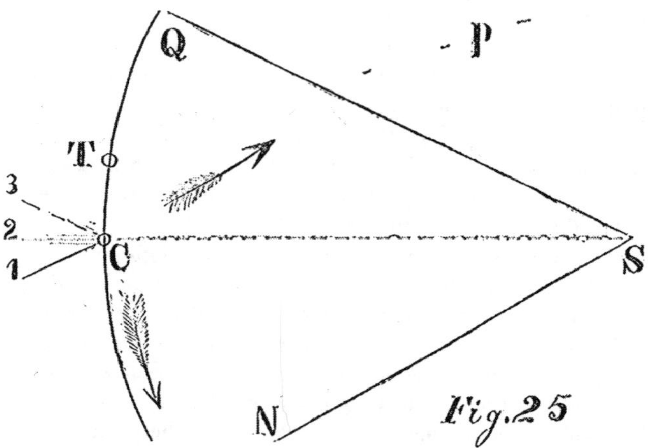

Fig. 25

but, being directed to the axis of the vortex, and not to the sun, it is not really in the plane of the orbit, but is seen in the direction of the upper tail depicted in the diagram at 3, and, if produced, would pass to the right of the sun, as seen from T. Now, there is an intermediate position of the tail, in which it will appear in the prolongation of the radius vector S C; this position is represented by the middle or central tail of the comet at 2, yet this is not in the plane of the orbit,—it only appears to be, as may be readily understood by remembering that the earth at this time is under this plane, and the comet is seen at a considerable elevation above the plane of the ecliptic. When the comet's tail becomes directed to the axis of the vortex, or in the *apparent* position of No. 3, the comet, rapidly careering on its way to the sun, again leaves the tail behind, and again it is strengthened out by the radial stream oscillating about the mean position at 2, as observed by Bessel. From this, it appears, that there is no necessity to make confusion worse confounded, by resorting to polar forces, which are about as intelligible as the foundations of the pillars of Atlas.

It may be objected that the continued action of the radial stream with that velocity we have contended for, ought to keep the tail invariably directed from the axis of the vortex; but, where there are two forces or tendencies, as in this case, analogy would teach us that a certain degree of oscillation is a necessary result. There may, also, be slight and transient changes in the direction of the radial stream. In the hurricane there are short and fitful blasts inclined to the general direction of the wind, which must arise from the inertia of the moving mass of atmosphere, causing temporary condensations and rarefractions. Be this as it may, we have assigned a cause which satisfies the phenomenon, without coming into collision with a single principle of celestial mechanics.

Prof. Struve compared the tail of this comet to a flame, or "ray of fire shot out from the nucleus, as from some engine of artillery, and driven on one side by the wind." At the same time, he saw a second emanation nearly in the opposite direction. This last might arise from a momentary fluctuation in the relative intensities of the electric radiation of the comet, and of the radial stream, owing to the probable irregularities just alluded to. Such and kindred phenomena are utterly inexplicable, without we adopt the theory we are advocating. One other feature, and we will leave the subject.

From our explanation of the solar spots, we inferred the existence of another large planet in the system. Might not the same effect be produced by a comet? Or may there not be so many comets, whose great elongation, combined with even a moderate mass, may render it impossible to calculate the position of the sun with respect to the central axis of the vortex,—always considering this last as the axis of equilibrium? In a general way, we might say that the very number of comets in all directions and all distances, would tend to neutralize each other's effects; but we are not under this necessity. A comet, moving in a parabola, does not belong to the system or to the rotating vortex; and the periodic comets, if of gaseous elements, (as seems so probable,) must, from the size of their nuclei, which the theory considers the only part constituting their mass, have far less mass than the very smallest of the asteroids, and consequently could have very little effect on the mechanical balance of the vortex, even if elongated as far as the orbit of Neptune. Did we know the influence of cold in limiting the expansibility of the elementary gases, we might approximately determine the mass of a comet, from the size of its nucleus; but this is a problem that has never yet been solved; and astronomers ought to avail themselves of every indication which promises to realize this great desideratum. The grand comet of 1556 is now probably approaching, and, from recent investigations, it appears that it will arrive at its perihelion in 1858, —subject to an error either way of about two years. An opportunity may thus be presented of determining the mass of one of the largest comets on record, which may not again occur. This arises from the possible appulse of the comet to the planet Pallas, whose mass, being so small, would more sensibly be disturbed by such an appulse than the earth. As the inclinations and ascending nodes of the two orbits approximately coincide, and as Pallas will be near the comet's path, on the approach of the latter to the sun, at the beginning of the year 1857, should the comet become visible about that time, a very close appulse is possible. It is not unlikely, also, that if the elements of Pallas were so far perfected as to afford reliable indications, that the near approach of the comet might thus be heralded in advance, and lead to an earlier detection of its presence. Would it not be a worthy contribution to science, for some one possessing the necessary leisure, to give an ephemeris of the planet for that epoch; as a very slight change in Mr. Hind's elements of the comet, would cause an actual intersection of the two orbits in about heliocentric longitude 153°? The subsequent nodal passage of Pallas will take place near opposition, and be very favorably situated for determining the instant of its passage; and, of all the elements, this would be more likely to be affected than any other.*

THE ZODIAL LIGHT.

A phenomenon, akin to that which we have just been considering, is presented by that great cone of diffused light which accompanies the sun, and which in tropical climes displays a brilliancy seldom witnessed in high latitudes, on account of its greater deviation from the perpendicular. Sir John Herschel conjectures that it may be "no other than the denser part of that medium, which, as we have reason to believe, resists the motion of comets,—loaded, perhaps, with the actual materials of the tails of millions of those bodies, of which they have been stripped in their successive perihelion passages, and which may be slowly subsiding into the sun." If these materials have been stripped, it is due to some force; and the same force would scarcely permit them to subside into the sun. Once stripped, these portions must be borne outwards, by the radial stream, to the outer verge of the system. Still, there are, no doubt, denser particles of matter, of the average atomic density of Mercury and Venus, which can maintain their ground against the radial stream, and continue to circulate near the central plane of the vortex, in all that space between the earth and the sun. But

* In making this suggestion, the author is well aware that Ephemerides of the four chief asteroids have been given annually in the Greenwich Nautical Almanac; but for the object proposed they are utterly useless. Will any astronomer contend that these Ephemerides are true to ten seconds of arc? If not, they are useless for the purpose suggested above, and the theory wants revision. And it is evident that any objection against its practicability, founded on the uncertainty of the number of the asteroids themselves, as has already been urged in answer to this suggestion, is an evidence that the objector weighed the subject in the scales of his imagination only.

if the zodial light be the denser part of that medium, which astronomers now generally recognize as a resisting medium, how happens it that it should be confined to the plane of the ecliptic? Why should it not be a globular atmosphere? Here, again, our theory steps in with a triumphant explanation; for while it permits the accumulation of such particles around the equatorial plane of the sun, it allows no resting-place very far removed from this plane. The zodial light, therefore, is not the resisting medium, but the passage of the radial stream through a diffuse nebula of atoms, brought down the poles of the vortex by the polar current, and held in check along the central plane by gravitation.

If these atoms partook of the velocity of the ether, they would not be luminous; but being held back by gravitation, they are opposed to the radial stream, and hence the light.

Many stars are also nebulous. In some cases we see the nebulosity edgewise, or along the equatorial planes of the stellar vortices; in others we look down the poles, and the nebulosities are circular, and there is an endless variety in the shape and intensity of this light. But the universe seems full of motion, and we are not justified in supposing, because a star shows no such light, that it is without rotation. The parallax of the nearest star is only one second, the whole lenticular mass of light which surrounds our sun would therefore only subtend an angle of a single second at the nearest fixed star. Seeing its extreme faintness, therefore, the effulgence of the star would render it totally invisible, provided that it *could* traverse the vast immensity of intervening space, without feeling the influence of that extinction, which Struve has proved does actually diminish the number of visible stars.

Corruscations and flickerings have also been noticed in the zodial light, and as usual, the learned have suggested atmospheric conditions as the cause, instead of trusting to the evidence of their own senses. How prone is philosophy to cling to that which is enveloped in the mist of uncertainty, rather than embrace the *too simple* indications of nature. As if God had only intended her glories to be revealed to a favored few, and not to mankind at large. Blessed will be the day when *all* will appreciate their own powers and privileges, and no longer regard the oracles which emanate from a professional priesthood, whose dicta have so often tended to darken the simple counsels of truth! To set the question of pulsations in the zodial light, as well as in the tails of comets, at rest, only requires previously concerted observations, in places not very widely apart; for it is scarcely possible, that atmospheric conditions should produce simultaneous pulsations in two distant places. If the pulsations are found to be simultaneous, they are real; if not simultaneous, they may depend on such conditions; but from the nature of the cause, we should look for them as much in the zodial light, as in the aurora borealis, regarding the different intensities.

There is also reason to suspect that the northern side is always the brightest, both in spring and autumn. On the morning of October 4th, 1853, the light was very vivid and well defined, its northern margin grazing Regulus and terminating at Mars, which was also to the north of it. Now, although the *northern side* was the brightest, the great mass of light was to the south of the ecliptic, as far down as the cone shape was preserved; but at 10° from the horizon, a still brighter mass protruded from the cone towards the north, which was all *north* of the ecliptic, and of an irregular form, extending along the horizon. The time was 4 A. M., and consequently was not due to any crepuscular light. An explanation of the general fact of the brightest light being *always* on the north side, is given in the present section, in connection with another phenomenon. If, as some suppose, the light does not reach to the sun, the annulus must at least fill all the space between Venus and the earth, but it is far more in accordance with facts as well as with our theory, to suppose it increases in density to the body of the sun.

Observations made at the observatory of the British Association, detected, in 1850, sudden brightenings of the light, altogether different from pulsations. The theory would refer these to that fitful irregularity in the momentary intensity of the radial stream, which gives the flickering and tremulous motion to comets' tails. But, the steady variations in the intensity of this light must be due to other causes. The longitude of the sun will here come in as a modifying cause; for the obstruction caused by the body of the sun, when displaced from the axis of the vortex, must necessarily exercise an influence on the force and direction of the radial stream. A sudden influx of cometary matter down the poles of the vortex, in more than usual quantities, will also tend to brighten and enlarge the zodial light; and, in this last cause, we have an explanation not only of ancient obscurations of the solar light, but, also, of those phosphorescent mists, such as occurred in 1743 and 1831, rendering moonless nights so light that the smallest print could be read at midnight.

In total eclipses of the sun, the denser portion of the zodial light is visible as a brilliant corona; but, on such occasions, the brightest stars only are to be seen, and, consequently, the fainter portions of the light must be invisible. Hind mentions as many as ten stars visible in the total eclipse of 1842. According to the same authority, the color of the corona was like tarnished silver, and rays of light diverged in every direction, and appeared shining through the light of the corona in the total eclipse of 1851. In this year on the day of the eclipse (July 28th), the longitude of the sun was about 340°, and, therefore, the body of the sun obstructed the radial stream as seen from the earth on the right side; but, in 1842, the longitude of the sun was, according to our table, about 116°, the sun's centre then being 700,000 miles from the axis of the vortex, and on the opposite side with respect to the earth; the position was, therefore, not so favorable for the appearance of these rays which, in many cases, have given the appearance of a whirling motion to the corona.

At this date, July 7th, 1842, the corona, according to Prof. Airy, "possibly had a somewhat radial appearance, but not sufficiently marked to interfere with the general annular structure. Mr. Baily, on the contrary, says, the corona had the appearance of brilliant rays; and, at Milan, long jets of light were particularly noticed. There can be no doubt but that the passage of the radial stream past the outer margin of the moon must also give rise to the same phenomena as when passing the sun, and in this we have an explanation of the fact, that, previous to the moment of first contact, an appearance resembling a faintly-illuminated limb of the moon, has been perceived near the body of the sun; as well as of those flashes of light which have been observed in the lunar disc as the eclipse advances. One important fact, worthy of note, is, that these luminous streaks are more nearly parallel than is due to a radiation from the centre. These streaks have, also, been seen bent at right angles at the middle of their height, as a flame is by means of a blowpipe, precisely analogous to cometary rays being driven backwards to form the tail, as already described, thus indicating a common origin. If the moon had an atmosphere, we should, no doubt, see a greater display; but, having no rotating vortex to protect her from the radial stream, her atmosphere must have been long since stripped off, leaving her exposed to the withering winter blast of the great stream of the solar vortex. In this connection, we may also allude to the appearance of the moon when totally eclipsed. Instead of disappearing at these times, she sometimes shines bright enough to reveal her smallest spots. This has been generally referred to the refraction of the earth's atmosphere bending inwards the solar rays. May it not be owing to the brilliancy of the solar corona, which, in 1842, was described as so intense that the eye was scarcely able to support it? This is a far more palpable cause for the production of this phenomenon, but of which astronomers cannot avail themselves, as long as they are uncertain of the origin of this corona.

SHOOTING STARS.

The continual influx of cosmical matter into the heart of the vortex in ever-varying quantities, and speedily dispersed along the central plane, according to its density, must necessarily give rise to another phenomenon to which we have not yet alluded. Scarcely a night passes without exhibiting this phenomena in some degree, and it is generally supposed that the hourly average of shooting stars is from five to ten, taking the whole year round. The matter composing these meteors we regard as identical with that mass of diffused atoms which forms a stratum conforming to the central plane of the vortex, and whose partial resistance to the radial stream occasions that luminosity which we call the zodial light. These atoms may coalesce into spherical aggregations, either as elastic gas, or as planetary dust, and, passing outward on the radial stream, will occasionally become involved in the vortex of our own globe; and being drawn inwards by the polar current, and acted on by the earth's gravity, be impelled with great velocity through the rarefied air of the upper atmosphere. That meteors are more abundant about the time of meridian passage of a vortex (or, perhaps, more correctly speaking, from six to twelve hours afterwards, when the current of restoration penetrates the atmosphere), well accords with the author's observations. It is about this time that high winds may be looked for, according to the theory; and it has ever been a popular opinion, that these meteors are a sign of windy weather. Even in Virgil's time, the same belief prevailed, as a passage in his Georgics would seem to indicate.

> "Sæpe etiam stellas, vento impendente, videbis
> Præcipites cœlo labi; noctisque per umbram
> Flammarum longos à tergo albescere tractus;"

Virgil was a close observer of nature, and commences a storm with the wind at south, "Quo signo caderent Austri;" just as we have represented the usual course when these vortices pass near the observer's latitude. It is also a well-known fact, that after a display of meteors, (and we are now speaking of ordinary displays, and not of the great showers,) the temperature falls considerably. It is not uncommon also, that meteors are more abundant during an auroral display, as they ought to be by the theory. We must, however, exempt from this influence those solid meteors which sometimes come into collision with the earth, and afterwards grace the cabinets of the curious. These bodies may be considered microscopic planets, moving in stated orbits with planetary velocity, and bear strongly on the explosive theory of Olbers, as fully detailed by Sir David Brewster.

It is a very remarkable fact, first noticed by Olbers, that no fossil meteoric stones have yet been discovered. If this fact be coupled with the hypothesis advanced by Olbers, in reference to the origin of the asteroidal group, we should have to date that tremendous catastrophe since the deposition of our tertiary formations, and therefore it might possibly be subsequent to the introduction of the present race into the world. May not some of the legendary myths of the ancient world as mystified by the Greeks, have for a foundation the disappearance of a former great planet from the system? The idea of the existence of seven planets is one of the oldest records of antiquity; but the earth of course would not be counted one, and therefore in after times, the sun was included to make up the number; just as the signs of the zodiac have been explained in accordance with the seasons of far later times than we can possibly assign for the invention of this division of the heavens. Let those who have the leisure, try how far the contraction and dilation of the asteroidal orbits, to some average mean distance, will restore them to a common intersection or node, as the point of divergence of the different fragments. The question is interesting in many of its aspects, and may yet be satisfactorily answered.

The composition of aërolites may also be taken as indications of the common origin and elementary texture of the planets, whether they are independently formed or have originally pertained to a former planet; for no hypothesis of telluric or selenic origin yet advanced, can stand against the weight of evidence against it. Their fragmentary character rather favors the views of Sir David Brewster, and when we consider that they have been revolving for thousands of years with planetary velocity, and in very eccentric orbits, through the ether of space, continually scathed by the electric blast of the radial stream, their rounded angles, and black glossy crust of an apparently fused envelope, may be accounted for, without difficulty, from the non-vitrified appearance of the interior. The composition of aërolites as far as known, embrace nearly one-third of all known simple substances according to Humboldt, and are as follows: iron, nickel, cobalt, manganese, chromium, copper, arsenic, zinc, potash, soda, sulphur, phosphorus, and carbon.

The theory we have thus given of the common occurrence of shooting stars, will render a satisfactory general account of their sporadic appearance; but there are other phenomena of greater interest, viz.: the occasional recurrence of swarms of such meteors, which defy all numerical estimates, being more like a fiery rain than anything they can be compared to. The most interesting feature of this phenomena, is the *apparent* periodicity of their return. In the following table we have set down the most remarkable epochs mentioned by Humboldt, (and no man has devoted more attention to the subject,) as worthy of notice:

About	April	22 to 25
"	July	17 to 26
"	August	9 to 11
"	November	12 to 14
"	November	27 to 29
"	December	6 to 12

Besides these, he mentions two showers, from Arabian authority, in October; one in October, observed in Bohemia; one observed by himself, in the Pacific, on March 15; one February 4, just preceding the terrible earthquake of Riobamba, in 1797. The Chinese annals also contain many showers of stars, before the present era commenced. Some were in March, more in July, and others in different months. How, then, in view of these numerous dates, can we attach so much importance to the periodicity of these showers? The great shower of 1833, in the United States, on the 12th and 13th of November, brought to mind the great shower at Cumana, observed by Humboldt and Bonpland just thirty-three years before, to a day; and it must be confessed that more than ordinary displays have been seen on this date. Yet, on the strength of this, every meteoric shower is supposed to be periodical, and has resulted in a theory which becomes more complicated as the phenomenon is more observed, and can never lead to any useful and practical results. To cite the numerous instances of discrepant results, would only encumber this brief notice with facts neither interesting to the general reader, nor convincing to those who hold a contrary opinion. The author of these pages has watched for many years, and, in view of all the facts, has concluded that the doctrine of periodicity (as held by present meteorologists) is not tenable. The celebrated August shower failed, also, this year, at least in this place, as for four hours each night, on the 9th, 10th, and 11th, there were fewer bright meteors than at the close of July.

Professor Olmsted, who has paid considerable attention to the subject, has indeed attempted to connect the great November shower with the zodial light, which last he considers a nebulous body, of an elongated form, whose external portions, at this time of the year, lie across the earth's path. (See Silliman's Journal for 1837, vol. xxxiii. No. 2, p. 392.) He even gives its periods, (about six months,) the aphelion of the orbit being near the earth's orbit, and the perihelion within Mercury's. In this way he attempts to explain both phenomena; but as the zodial light is seen unchanged all the year round in tropical latitudes, it is not the kind of body supposed by Olmsted, and the theory adds nothing to our knowledge. Others have imagined rings of nebulous matter, in which all the separate parts are moving in the same orbit around the sun, with a retrograde motion, and this, with some modifications, is the current theory of the day. The principal arguments rested on, for the support of this view, are derived from the great shower of 1833, in which a common radiant point was observed, and confirmed subsequently by the radiant of other years, in the same month of November. As this point is almost tangential to the earth's orbit at this season, the earth meets the nebulous ring moving in the contrary direction, and thus confers on these meteors the necessary velocity that is thought to be demanded by observation.

Now, our theory gives a totally different explanation of the phenomenon. We contend that a retrograde motion of such a nebulous mass, is subversive of our whole theory; and we must be permitted to examine certain points, hitherto disregarded by those entertaining antagonist views. It is supposed that the meteors in 1833 fell for eight or nine hours. The orbital velocity of the earth is more than 1,000 miles per minute, and the orbital velocity of the nebulous zone must have had a similar velocity. During the nine hours of meteoric display, therefore, the earth traversed 500,000 miles of her orbit, which would give 1,000,000 miles for the depth of the nebulous stratum. But if of such vast extent, how happened it that the only part of the earth in which these were visible in great density, was the United States, or a space embraced between the latitudes of 50° and 20° north, and the longitudes 60° and 100° west, (and these are the widest limits,) comprising only $\frac{1}{40}$ of the surface of the globe? To a calm inquirer, this difficulty seems insurmountable. The author was then in the Mediterranean, on deck the greatest part of the night,—the weather fine, and nothing unusual visible in the heavens; from other sources he has also derived similar information. Yet, were the earth then passing through a stratum of meteors 1,000,000 miles in extent, it is utterly inconceivable that other portions of the earth escaped. Much stress is also laid on the fact that these meteors in 1833, passed from east to west generally, as they ought to do, if tangential to the earth in her orbit; but on the same phenomenon occurring in 1799, when the earth was in precisely the same part of her orbit, Humboldt says distinctly, "the direction (of the meteors) was very regular from north to south." How could this possibly happen, and at the same time be moving tangentially to the orbit?

There is also another fact of importance not duly weighed in forming such a theory. In 1833 the meteors evidently differed in velocity; one class, consisting of luminous points, passed like a shower of fire with great velocity to the westward, another class were like large fire-balls with luminous trains moving with less rapidity, while a third class consisted of nebulous patches which remained stationary for a long time, and frequently emitting large streams of light. These last, at least, do not deport themselves as planetary bodies moving 2,000 miles per minute. But the fact still remains, that unusual displays have occurred about the 12th and 14th of November; and also as a general thing when there are no unusual displays, the meteors are more abundant about this time. Let us try if we can reconcile these facts with the theory of vortices.

We will first confine our remarks to the increased number of meteors about November 12th and 14th. The cosmical matter composing the zodial light, or at least the lighter parts of it, is continually driven outwards by the radial stream, just as the matter of a comet's tail is stripped from the nucleus. This matter becomes involved in the terral vortex by descending the poles, and is again passed out along the equatorial plane. The form of the zodial light, as seen edgewise, gives a lenticular form for the stratum of planetary particles composing it, and its central plane has been considered as coinciding with the plane of the sun's equator. At the orbit of the earth, this lenticular space is narrowed to a very thin stratum, but undoubtedly reaches beyond the earth's orbit with a rapidly diminishing density. As the axis of the sun is inclined about 7° to the ecliptic, and the ascending node is in the 20th degree of Gemini, the earth can only pass through the plane of the sun's equator about the 12th of December and the 12th of June. If, therefore, the central plane of the vortex coincides with the plane of the sun's equator, meteors ought to be more numerous about the dates above mentioned. But the observed times are on November 12th and 13th. Now, from actual measurements, a computation has been made by M. Houzeau, that the elements of the zodial light are materially different from those of the sun's equator. He fixes the node of the light (according to Mr. Hind) in 2° heliocentric longitude, subject to an uncertainty of 12° or 13°, and its inclination to the plane of the ecliptic, 3° 35′, subject to an uncertainty of about 2°. The truth is, astronomers have argued the coincidence of the two planes from considerations connecting the zodial light with the sun's equator, as if it were a solar atmosphere; but such an atmosphere is impossible, and it is high time such measures should be taken as will lead to some certain conclusion. If in the present state of the question, we were to take the mean, we should find the node in about longitude 40°, which is the position of the earth on November 2d. But in the absence of measurements, we will assume, for the sake of argument, that the ascending node of the central plane of the vortex was, in 1833, in 50° heliocentric longitude, and consequently the earth was passing through the meteoric stratum or central plane of the zodial light, on the night of November 12th. The opposite period of the year is May 12th—a date, it is true, on which no great shower of stars is recorded, but sporadic meteors are very plentiful at that time, and what is more important to observe is, that the 11th, 12th, and 13th of May, are the three noted *cold days* which we have before mentioned. Thus truly indicating that the earth is then in or near the central plane of the vortex along which the radial stream is at its maximum of power at any given distance from the axis.

But the question occurs, does the node of this plane remain stationary, and is there no variation of the inclination of the axis of the solar vortex? We have found from observation, that the axis of the terral vortex is continually oscillating about a mean position by the action of the moon; and reasoning from this analogy, and the constant tendency of a material vortex to preserve a dynamical balance, the same tendency must obtain in the solar vortex under the action of the great planets, whose orbits do not coincide with the central plane of the vortex. The ascending node of Jupiter's orbit is in longitude 98°, Saturn's 112°, Uranus' 72°, Neptune's 131°; so that this plane does not correspond with the plane of greatest inertia discovered by La Place, and from the non-coincidence of these planes with the central plane of the vortex, must produce the same oscillation in the axis of the solar vortex, as the moon does in the terral vortex, but to what amount, observation can alone determine. Jupiter and Saturn will of course exert the greatest influence, and when these two planets are in conjunction, the ascending node of the central plane of the vortex will vary in longitude perhaps sufficiently to bring the meteoric maximum at the ascending node into October on the one hand, and to the close of November on the other, and at the descending node to April 25th on the one hand, and the close of May on the other.

The great showers of stars which have been recorded, must be therefore considered as an accidental exaggeration of a perennial phenomenon, attaining its maximum when the earth passes through the central plane of the vortex, whose ascending node in 1833 we will suppose was in longitude 50°. This theory will therefore account for those great showers which have occurred about the 24th of April, as well as those occurring in October and November; for it is far more consonant to all analogy, to suppose the influx of planetary atoms into the solar vortex to be in irregular, than in regular quantities. Yet, whether in the one case or in the other, the matter will pass along the central plane of the vortex, either diffusely scattered or in denser clouds, and will be encountered by the earth when near the nodes *more frequently than at other times.* The phenomenon of 1833, may then be attributed to the earth encountering an unformed comet on the 12th of November; but we must reflect, that the medium of the vortex is also in motion, and the cometary matter drifting along with it; and that this motion corresponds with the earth's motion. By becoming involved in the terral vortex, it will in a measure be carried along with the earth in her orbit as a temporary occupant of the terral vortex. But we are here met with the objection that the radiant being nearly stationary amongst the stars, demonstrated conclusively, that the source of these meteors did not partake of the earth's motion. There is no difficulty in this. We suppose as a general thing, that the meteors descended to the surface of our atmosphere down the axis of the vortex (at least in the greatest numbers), and the geocentric longitude of this axis was nearly the same during the whole time of the display. We say nearly, for the motion of the moon in her orbit in nine hours, would change the longitude of the axis three or four degrees, and this is about the change in the position of the radiant noted at the time. This objection, therefore, falls to the ground; for the axis of the vortex, although carried along with the earth in her orbit, was unaffected by the earth's rotation, and would therefore appear nearly as stationary in the heavens as Gamma Leonis. But it is again urged, that the moon was near conjunction with the sun, and consequently the central vortex was on the opposite side of the globe. This is true; but the outer vortex must have been near the meridian about three hours after midnight, or about the time when the radiant was vertical and the display the greatest. When the axis was to the eastward, the stars would shoot westward, when on the meridian, they would pass in all directions, but principally to the south, on account of the inclination of the axis of the vortex; but this would only be true for places situated to the southward of the central latitude. During the great shower of stars seen by Humboldt, in Cumana, the direction was to the south uniformly. Now, the latitude of Cumana is above 10° north, yet still too low for the general limits of the vortices; but from the same inclination of the axis (from 30° to 36° to the surface), the meteors would pass far south of the limit, and might even reach to the equator. The latitude of the *outer vortex ascending* on November 12th, must have been near the line of greatest display, from the position of the moon at the time. We thus see why the phenomenon was limited to so small a fraction of the earth's surface; why these meteors should be intermingled with nebulous patches stationary in the heavens for an hour together, and why, notwithstanding these facts, they were independent of the earth's rotation.

We have yet another objection to answer, viz.: the planetary velocity of some of these bodies. Let us be understood. The velocity of a solid aërolite is due to gravitation, and is planetary, on the other hand, voluminous collections of cometary dust united by accident, and remaining so by mere inertia, are borne passively on the ethereal currents with *electric* velocity, and probably never penetrate far, even into the attenuated atmosphere, which may be supposed (from the facts connected with the aurora) to extend far above the denser stratum which refracts and reflects light, and from which the assigned limits of our atmosphere have been derived.

It is generally considered that sporadic meteors are more numerous in the summer and autumn than in the winter and spring, and we have, likewise, in the tenth of August, a date which corresponds to many great displays and meteoric showers, both in recent and remote times. This would seem to vitiate our theory; for we cannot suppose that there are two *central* planes in the vortex intersecting the ecliptic in longitude 320° and 50°. We must remember, however, that as these great displays are accidental, and as the stratum composing the zodial light is manifestly of sufficient thickness to envelope the whole orbit of the earth, that it does not necessarily follow that the dense portions to which meteoric showers are due, should be always confined to the central plane of the vortex. And, besides, we have similar displays recorded in other months, which invalidates the theory of a regularly-recurring phenomenon. We shall, therefore, only aim at explaining why meteors are generally more abundant in summer and autumn than in the opposite seasons.

The axis of the solar vortex, considered as cylindrical, must be admitted to run out to a great depth on either side from the sun, and reach far into that unoccupied space intervening between our system and the nearest fixed stars, and from these opposite points the solar vortex is supplied with that stream of ether which passes down either pole to restore a partial equilibrium in the density of the ether of the vortex, rarefied by centrifugal force. As certain portions of the heavens are crowded with stars, and other parts comparatively vacant, we may expect a similar inequality in the distribution of that cometic dust, which causes a certain amount of extinction in the light of the stars, and, therefore, seeing that the two extremities of the axis of the solar vortex are so widely separated, it would not be wonderful if different quantities of such matter were brought down into the vortex from these extremities.

From recent observations made by H. R. Birt, at the observatory of the British Association, it would appear that the brightest portion of the zodial light is always north of the ecliptic. Others have also remarked the same, and if we couple this fact with the suggestion just made, we are justified in suspecting that a greater quantity of cometic dust comes down the northern pole of the vortex than down the southern. This matter, in passing outward, does not, of course, immediately attain to the central plane of the vortex, but is more thickly distributed along a plane parallel to this plane. And the same will be observed by that matter coming down the southern pole; it will be, in a certain degree, retained in a plane south of the central plane, but still parallel with it. This would account for the greater brightness of the northern side of the zodial light. It would, also, account for the greater frequency of meteors in summer and autumn than in the opposite seasons From May to November the earth is above the central plane of the vortex, and, consequently, on the northern side; but after passing the node in November, she is on the under or southern side, and the meteors are less frequent. With this general explanation we shall close. If what we have advanced be an approximation to the truth, the theory itself affords ample indications of what observations are requisite to prove or disprove it; and, on this account, a theory is of great benefit, as suggestive of many questions and combinations of facts which otherwise might never be thought of.

We have thus taken a cursory glance at the prominent physical phenomena of the world, and attempted to link them together in the bonds of one all-pervading principle. We have fearlessly taken a new path, and claim originality for the whole, disclaiming all intention of retailing second-hand wares, or of compiling an ingenious theory from heterogeneous scraps. If it be true, or if it be partially true, let those professionally engaged in such pursuits enter the wide field of investigation we have discovered for them; for if the whole theory be true, it only shows in a clearer light that the great work which has been fancied so near completion is scarcely yet begun; while the prospect of an ultimate and final completion of the temple which so many zealous votaries are erecting, is rendered mournfully hopeless by the contemplation of what yet remains to be performed.

SECTION SIXTH.

THE POLAR ICE.

We shall conclude these pages by again referring to our theory of the weather, in connection with an event which every friend of humanity and every lover of natural science is bound deeply to deplore.

From the present position of the lunar nodes and apogee, the vortices of our earth do not ascend into very high latitudes. Now, according to the principles laid down, the frequency of storms tends to lower the temperature in the warm regions of the earth, and to elevate it in the polar regions. Let us suppose the northern limit of the vortices to be in latitude 70.° There will be, in this case, a greater prevalence of northerly winds *within* this circle of latitude, to supply the drain to the southward, and the back currents by passing above will descend at the pole, partaking of the temperature due to that elevation. The character of the arctic seasons may therefore be considered as partly dependent on the average direction of the wind. Suppose again, the extreme limits of the vortices to be about latitude 80°, the relative areas of the two circles are as 4 to 1; so that in this last case the exclusive range of the northerly winds is limited to one-fourth of the first area. South of 80° the wind will frequently come from the south, and by mixing with the local atmosphere of that latitude, will tend to ameliorate the small area to the northward. And the greater atmospheric commotion when confined to such a small circle of latitude, must assist materially to break up the polar ice; which would tend still more to equalize the temperature.

By referring to our table, we see that the mean conjunction of the pole of the lunar orbit and the moon's apogee, was in longitude 128° on April 10, 1846, and let it be remembered that when the conjunction takes place due south or in longitude 270°, the vortices attain their greatest latitude north. When, on the contrary, the conjunction takes place due north or in longitude 90°,* the northern limits of the vortices are then in the lowest latitude possible.

Sir John Franklin sailed in May 1845, and was certainly at the entrance of Wellington sound, near latitude 75°, April 3d, 1846, as the dates on the graves testify. That season, according to the theory, was a cold one; for the vortices could not reach so far to the northward in that year, and consequently there were no storms, properly speaking. It would probably be late in the summer of 1846, before the expedition was liberated, and as the prevailing winds would be from the northward, he would have little choice, but to stand to the westward if the state of the ice permitted. In his instructions he was to use every effort to penetrate to the southward and westward of Cape Walker, and he probably conformed to them under the circumstances, and passed the winter in the ice, in that neighborhood. And in 1847 we do not anticipate, from the theory, that he would make much progress westward.

In 1848, Sir James Ross was sent out with the first relief-ship; but was not able to reach the entrance of Wellington channel because of compact ice from there to Leopold Island. This was about the beginning of September—a time when the northern channels are usually the most open. On the 11th, they ran the ships into Port Leopold, and the next day the ice

* The reader will of course understand these as celestial longitudes, and the latitudes as terrestrial.

shut them in for the winter. From the character of the season, we may infer that if Franklin did not enter Wellington channel in 1847, as is most probable, neither did he in 1848. Perhaps he was not able to get his ships far to the westward, as we infer from the theory. Still, as the time was not very protracted, he would wait patiently another season and husband his resources.

In 1849, Sir James Ross cut his ships clear of the ice August 28th, and crossed over to Wellington channel, where he found the land-ice still fast, showing that this season was also a bad one in accordance with the theory. On the 1st of September he met the first gale of wind, at which time the *Inner Vortex* was at its extreme north latitude, and rapidly extending its limits by the motion of the perigee.

This vortex describes a smaller orbit than either the central or the outer vortex, and consequently reaches into higher latitudes. But the time was badly chosen, as the whole series of years since Franklin left has been unfavorable for the early rupture of the ice. Sir James Ross having been drifted out of Lancaster sound by the gale, finally bore up for England towards the close of September 1849.

The same year, the North Star with additional supplies was working up Baffin's bay; but on account of the unusual quantities of ice, and the frosts "which glued the floes together," she was unable to force a passage through the middle ice, and wintered on the east side of Baffin's bay, in latitude 76° 33'—her thermometer marking 64° below zero, as the coldest of the winter. In 1850, the perigee of the moon attained its northern limit, but the position of the node was bad; still this year and 1851, were the best of the series. The North Star succeeded in getting out of the ice on the 1st of August—a very early date for that high latitude—and on the 8th had crossed over to Possession bay; but being prevented by the land-ice, she bore up for Pond bay and there landed the provisions. The same year (1850) several vessels entered Lancaster sound. Sir John

Ross also reached Melville Island; from which it is evident that this season was far better than any preceding. According to Captain Penny, this year a floe of ice at least two years old, filled Wellington strait; but was diminished in breadth at a subsequent visit. He also saw a boundless open sea from the *western* entrance of Wellington strait; but of course the ships could not reach it, for the floe before mentioned. Following the indications of the theory, we consider it almost certain that Franklin went to the westward and not through Wellington channel; that he made but slow progress until 1850, when finding the sea more open to the northward, and attributing it more to local influences than to any change in the season, he considered it a better course to extricate the expedition, by pushing on towards Behring's straits than to attempt the frozen channels he had already passed through. But the seasons again getting worse after 1850, he was again arrested in the polar basin by the ice and islands off the northern coast of America.

Regarding the old and new continents as in reality a connected body of land, with a polar depression, we may expect that the great range of American mountains is continued in a straight line, from the mouth of the McKenzie river, obliquely across the Polar sea, and connects with the Ural; and that along the axis of the chain, protuberant masses will emerge above the sea level, constituting an archipelago of islands, from Nova Zembla to the McKenzie; and that these islands, causing an accumulation of ice, and arresting its general tendency to the southward, is the barrier which Sir John Franklin was finally stopped by, in a situation where he could neither advance nor return. With the map before us, and the data afforded by former voyages, and guided by these theoretical views, respecting the prevailing direction of the winds and the character of the seasons, we should locate Sir John Franklin near latitude 80°, and longitude 145°, in 1851; and as the seasons would afterwards become more severe, we may consider that he has not been since able to change his locality, and dare not desert his ships.

No mere stranger can feel a deeper interest than the author, in view of the hard fortunes of these hardy explorers, and he would not lightly advance such opinions, did he not suppose they were in some degree reliable. In 1832, he himself crossed the Atlantic, for the purpose of offering himself to the Geographical Society of London, intending to be landed as far northward as possible, with a single companion,* from which point he purposed to follow the coast line on foot, with cautious discretion as to seasons, confident that, with arms and ammunition, he could support himself for many years. It has always been a grave error in all these northern land expeditions, that they have been too unwieldy, too much encumbered with the comforts and luxuries of civilization at the outset, and too much loaded with a philosophical paraphernalia, for a pioneering survey,—and cherishing too fondly the idea that the wide shores of the Arctic sea could be explored in a single season. Had the British government established a few posts in the Arctic regions in the beginning,—one, for instance, in Lancaster sound, another in Behring's Straits, and a third near the mouth of the Coppermine, volunteers of sufficient scientific attainments might have been procured, to banish themselves to these inhospitable regions for a term of years, if assured of triennial supplies; and in this way, by summer boat-parties and winter expeditions, over land or ice, the explorations could have been gradually extended, and a greater knowledge of the polar regions might have been acquired, with an immense saving both of life and money. In 1832 the author's plan was deranged, by finding that Captain Back was about setting out in quest of Ross, who had then been some four years absent. This officer had all his party engaged when the author waited upon him in Liverpool,

* Mr. William McDonald, of Canada.

and no notice was taken of a modified plan which he forwarded to the Society at his suggestion. It was therefore abandoned.

The above fact is alluded to, in order to show the author's sincerity in expressing his belief that, with a previous preparation of mind and body for a sojourn in those frigid climes, a sufficient subsistence may be derived from the country itself. Advantage must, of course, be taken of the times of abundance, and due preparation made for the season of scarcity. Averaging the extremes, there is little doubt but that both land, and air, and water, afford an abundance of food for man in the Arctic zone, and that, when spurred by necessity, it is within his power to obtain it. We ought not therefore to despond, or give up efforts to rescue those who have well earned the sympathy of the world, by what they must have already suffered. *These northern seas will yet be explored.* The very difficulty of accomplishing it, will itself give it a charm, which in this restless age will operate with increasing power. And should efforts now be relaxed, and in some future time the evidence be brought to light that some of the party yet existed, long after all efforts to rescue them had been abandoned, the fact would be a dark spot on the escutcheon of England, which time could not erase.

Since these pages were written, accounts have been received from Captain McClure, of H. M. ship Investigator, which fully confirm the preceding remarks on the character of the seasons in the Arctic circle; and, more recently, despatches have been received from the discovery-ship, Amphytrite, in relation to the past season in Behring's straits, which also confirms the theory.

The Investigator (now supposed to be frozen up in lat. 74° 5′ N., and long 117° 54′ W.,—the last despatch being dated April 10, 1853) passed round the northern shores of America into the channels communicating with Lancaster sound, in 1850, but was unable to extricate herself in 1852, and, probably, yet remains in the harbor she made in the winter of 1851, in the position above named. No trace of Sir John Franklin's expedition was, however, found, and, indeed, according to our theory, the Investigator was not on the most promising ground. We contend that Franklin has penetrated the pack of apparently perennial ice, which is continually pressing to the southward, and blocking up the passages between the northern islands, or skirting the coast line of the continent; which pack has since increased, and effectually stopped all egress from the open central portions of the polar sea. If Sir John Franklin is ever heard from, this pack *must be penetrated*, and a powerful steamer ought to be sent immediately by the British government, to be ready in Behring's straits early enough to take advantage of the first openings, and make a bold push *due north*, so as to get as speedily as possible into the open waters to the north of the pack.

If the author could make himself heard at Washington, he would also urge the government to lose no time in following our own expedition under Dr. Kane, who, if he finds a clear entrance from Smith's sound into the Arctic sea, may be induced to push on, and endeavor to make his way through the pack towards Behring's straits, and thus fall into the same snare as Franklin. According to the theory, the higher the passage into the Arctic sea, the less will it be incumbered with ice, and, consequently, Smith's sound is the best both to enter and return by; and had the author not already smarted enough by having his professions derided, he would have submitted these views to the patrons of that expedition before it sailed.

The scientific world is, in reality, chargeable with the disastrous results of Franklin's expedition. The polar basin is hemmed in by the coast line of Europe, Asia, and America, in about latitude 70° north, for the greatest part of the entire circumference. And this coast line, and the islands adjacent, will cause the polar ice to accumulate and form a frozen belt along these shores, in consequence of the constant tendency of the earth's rotation to press the ice to the southward. The fact that an open passage exists between this belt and the shore in summer time, is no objection, as the tides, river currents, and warm land breezes, may very well explain this. The learned have insisted, and do yet insist, that the earth's rotation can produce no motions in the Arctic sea, and, under this delusion, Franklin has passed into the comparatively open waters inside the pack, perhaps has lost his ships; yet it is very possible that the party may have escaped, and derived a subsistence from the more genial waters of the central portion of that ocean unto this day.

We have already alluded to the difference of level between the Atlantic and Pacific waters. It is well known that the currents in the Spitzbergen and Greenland seas is to the southward, and that Parry, in his attempt to reach the pole, was foiled by this very current, frequently setting him back in twenty-four hours more than his party could travel in the same time over the ice. Through Baffin's and Hudson's bay the northern waters are also continually bearing their frozen freight southward. We are, therefore, entitled to ask, what supplies this immense drain? Behring's straits are only about sixty miles wide, and twenty-five fathoms deep; the supply, therefore, through this channel is totally inadequate, yet there is no other channel into the Arctic sea where the current is inward. We have already explained the reason why the current through Behring's straits is an exception to the general rule, yet still confirming the principle by referring it to the configuration of the land enclosing the Pacific ocean. The whole south Pacific lies open to the pole, and the inertia of the immense mass of mobile waters pressing northward, and continually contracted by the form of the American and Asiatic coasts, is not balanced by a contrary impulse of the waters of the north Pacific, inasmuch as this ocean becomes narrower as it extends northward, and the only passage to the frozen ocean is through the narrow straits of Behring. The axifugal force of rotation due to the northern waters is, therefore, overborne by the vast preponderance due to the southern waters, and, hence, the northern Pacific may be considered as relatively at a higher level, and there will be a current northward through Behring's straits, as we find it. The same cause accumulates the waters under the equator, thus giving a higher level to the Pacific than to the Atlantic at the isthmus of Panama, where the difference of level is found by actual measurement to be five or six feet. This fact has never before been explained; but the cause is too obvious to admit of question.

That the sea is deeper than was formerly admitted, is now fully confirmed. We have before alluded to the results obtained by Captain Denham, of H. M. ship Herald, who found bottom at 7,706 fathoms, or about nine English miles. Now, whether that spherical shell, which we have contended to be the true form of the solid earth, be continuous and entire; or, whether it may not be wanting in localities of limited extent where the ocean would be absolutely unfathomable, we know not; but if such be the internal constitution of our globe, there will be, no doubt, many channels of communication between the internal and external ocean, and, as a consequence of the earth's rotation, the axifugal current of the Arctic sea may be supplied by an upward current from the interior of the globe; and this current may have a higher temperature than the surface waters of that sea, and thus the middle portions may, in truth, remain open the whole year round, and be teeming with animal life. According to Captain Penny's observations in 1850, whales and other northern animals existed to the westward, where he saw the open sea stretch out without a bound before him.

It has been a question mooted by some, that Franklin's ships might be overtaken, at an early stage of the voyage, by a storm, and foundered amidst the ice. The theory would give a negative answer to this question. Stiff gales may prevail far to the north when the vortices do not reach so high; but no storm, properly speaking, will be found far beyond their northern limit. After the coming winter (1853), the vortices will gradually penetrate farther and farther to the northward, and the years 1857, 1858, and 1859, will be highly favorable for northern discovery, accompanied, however, with the necessary draw-back of tempestuous weather.

CONCLUSION.

Our theory has thus extended itself beyond those limits which we at first had drawn, and our apology must consist in the necessity existing for reconciling the most remarkable phenomena of meteorology to its principles. Yet, after all, what has been said is but an outline of what remains, but this outline is a part of our theory of the weather, and it could not well do without its aid. In some points we may not have correctly interpreted facts; but the facts remain. The numerical elements of the theory may also be in error—we know not; but we think that they are as perfect as the many contingencies on which they depend will permit. What is *certain*, however, is of ample value to compensate for trivial errors. We have hitherto experienced but little courtesy from those intrusted with the keys of knowledge, and cannot consequently anticipate a very lenient verdict. But we now tell them before the world, that they have a duty to perform, and an examination to make, and a decision to come to, "whether these things are so." Our theory may be called an ingenious speculation, but WE CHALLENGE THE SCIENTIFIC TO PROVE IT—NOTHING ELSE. The theory furnishes them with tests of daily occurrence, to prove or to disprove it. By such a trial we are willing to be judged; but let it be conducted in the spirit recommended in the opening address before the American Association for the Advancement of Science, to expose all false developments, and to do it generously and without prejudice; and to remember, "that the temple of science belongs to no country or clime. It is the world's temple, and all men are free of its communion. Let its beauty not be marred by writing names upon its walls."* The *great* objection, of friction and resistance of an all-pervading medium, which will be urged against it, we regard as rather the offspring of a bewildered imagination, than of scientific induction. We can discover no such consequences as final ruin to our system through its agency; but even if such were discovered, we may answer, that nature nowhere tells us that her arrangements are eternal; but rather, that decay is stamped with the seal of the Almighty on every created thing. Change may be one of the great laws of matter and motion, and yet matter and motion be indestructible. The earth was called into existence for a specific object, and when that object is accomplished, we are assured that another change awaits her. But when earth, and sun, and planets, are again redissolved into their primitive state, their atoms will still float on the ever-rolling billows of the great ethereal ocean, to be again cast up, on the shore of time, whenever it pleaseth Him to say, "Let there be light."

* Prof. Pierce's Address, 1853.

APPENDIX.

Since the author's arrival in New York for the purpose of publishing his outlines, the third and fourth volume of the Cosmos has been placed in his hands, containing the latest uranological discoveries and speculations. It is now more than twenty years since he began to investigate the subject he has treated of, and fifteen since he first announced to the world, that he had satisfactory evidence of his theory being true. Luckily, perhaps, he has been cut off from the great streams of knowledge; and he may confess that it was with pardonable feelings of gratification that he discovered in 1853, by the acquisition of the two first volumes of the Cosmos, that the philosophic mind of Humboldt had also pondered deeply on the planetary peculiarities of size, density, distance, inclination of axes and eccentricities of orbits, without eliciting any satisfactory relations.

From the tenor of the third and fourth volume of this learned summary of scientific knowledge, it is evident that the question of a medium filling space is more and more occupying the learned world; but the author is unable to discover any consistent theory respecting it. The increasing interest attaching to it, however, is evidently preparing the world for some radical change in preconceived views. The explanation given by this present theory to many prominent phenomena, is so totally contrary to that of the learned world, as to leave it untouched by anything yet advanced. What the fifth volume of the Cosmos will contain, is not yet known in this country, neither has the author been favored with any glimpse of the progress of science as developed before the British Association; he supposes, however, that he yet stands alone in the position he has defined.

As a question of practical importance, the reader will find in the work cited, the various opinions of the temperature of space. Both Fourier and Poisson regard this as the result of radiated heat from the sun and all the stars, minus the quantity lost by absorption in traversing the regions of space filled with ether.* But why should we regard the stars as the source of all motions? Why cannot physicists admit the idea of an infinite space filled (if we may use the expression) with an infinite medium, possessing an unchangeable mean temperature long before the formation of a single star. A star equal to our sun at the distance of Sirius, would give about one million of million times less heat than our present sun, which is only able to give an average temperature to the whole globe—about twenty degrees above freezing—then let us remember that there are only about fifty stars of the first and second magnitude, which give more light (and by analogy heat also) than all the rest of the stars visible. Such labored theories as this of Poisson's is a lamentable instance of the aberrations of human wisdom.

We would also call the reader's attention to a late conclusion of Professor Dove, viz.: That differences of temperature in different longitudes frequently exist on the same parallel of latitude, or, in other words, are laterally disposed. This may be thought adverse to the theory, but it should be borne in mind that the annual mean temperature of the whole parallel of latitude should be taken when comparing the temperatures of different years.

Another fact cited in the Cosmos apparently adverse to the theory, is the idea entertained by Sir John Herschel, that the

* See *Cosmos*, p. 41, vol. III.

full-moon dissipates the clouds. This question has been fully examined by Professor Loomis before the American Association, and he concludes that there is not the slightest foundation for the assertion—taking as data the Greenwich observations themselves.

SCIENTIFIC WORKS.

APPLETON. Dictionary of Mechanics, Machines, Engine Work, and Engineering, containing over 4000 Illustrations, and nearly 2000 pages. Complete in 2 Vols., large 8vo. Strongly and neatly bound, $12.

APPLETON. Mechanics' Magazine and Engineers' Journal. Edited by Julius W. Adams, C. E. Published monthly, 25 cents per No., or $3 per annum. Vol. I for 1851, in cloth, $3 50.

ARCHITECTURE AND BUILDING, Treatises on. By Hosking, Tredgold, and Young. Illustrated with 36 steel plates. 4to. $3 50.

ALLEN, Z. Philosophy of the Mechanics of Nature. Illus. 8vo. $3 50.

ARNOT, D. H. Gothic Architecture, Applied to Modern Residences. 40 Plates. 1 Vol., 4to. $4.

ARTISAN CLUB. Treatise on the Steam Engine. Edited by J. Bourne. 33 Plates, and 349 Engravings on wood. 4to. $6.

BOURNE, JOHN. A Catechism of the Steam Engine. 16mo. 75 cts.

BYRNE, O. New Method of Calculating Logarithms. 12mo. $1.

BOUISSINGAULT, J. B. Rural Economy in its Relations with Chemistry, Physics, and Meteorology. 12mo. $1 25.

CULLUM, CAPT. On Military Bridges with India Rubber Pontoons, Illustrated. 8vo. $2.

DOWNING, A. I. Architecture of Country Houses. Including Designs for Cottages, Farm Houses, and Villas; with Remarks on Interiors, Furniture, and the best modes of Warming and Ventilating; with 320 Illustrations. 1 Vol., 8vo. $4.

———— Architecture of Cottages and Farm Houses. Being the first part of his work on Country Houses, containing designs for Farmers, and those who desire to build cheap Houses. 8vo. $2.

GRIFFITHS, JOHN W. Treatise on Marine and Naval Architecture; or, Theory and Practice Blended in Ship-Building. 50 Plates. $10.

HALLECKS. Military Art and Science. 12mo. $1 50.

HAUPT, H. Theory of Bridge Construction. With Practical Illustrations. 8vo. $3.

HOBLYN, R. D. A Dictionary of Scientific Terms. 12mo. $1 50.

HODGE, P. R. On the Steam Engine. 48 large Plates, folio; and letter-press, 8vo. size. $8.

JEFFERS. Theory and Practice of Naval Gunnery. 8vo. Illus. $2 50.

KNAPEN, D. M. Mechanic's Assistant, adapted for the use of Carpenters, Lumbermen, and Artisans generally. 12mo. $1.

LAFEVER, M. Beauties of Modern Architecture. 48 Plates, large 8vo. $4.

LIEBIG, JUSTUS. Familiar Letters on Chemistry. 18mo. 25 cents.

OVERMAN, F. Metallurgy; embracing Elements of Mining Operations, Analyzation of Ores, &c. 8vo. Illustrated.

PARNELL, E. A. Chemistry Applied to the Arts and Manufactures. Illustrated. 8vo. Cloth, $1.

REYNOLDS, L. E. Treatise on Handrailing. Twenty Plates. 8vo. $2.

SYDNEY, J. C. Villa and Cottage Architecture. Comprising Residences actually built. Publishing in Nos., each No. containing 3 Plates, with Ground Plan, price 50 cents. (To be completed in 10 Nos.) 1 to 6 ready.

TEMPLETON, W. Mechanic, Millwright, and Engineers' Pocket Companion. With American Additions. 16mo. $1.

URE, DR. Dictionary of Arts, Manufactures, and Mines. New Edition with Supplement. 8vo. Sheep, $5.

———— Supplement to do., separate. 8vo. Sheep, $1.

YOUMAN, E. L. Class-book of Chemistry. 12mo. 75 cents.

———— Chart of Chemistry, on Roller. $5.

EDWARD L. YOUMANS.

A Class-Book of Chemistry;

In which the Principles of the Science are Familiarly Explained and Applied to the Arts, Agriculture, Physiology, Dietetics, Ventilation, and the most Important Phenomena of Nature. Designed for the Use of Academies and Schools, and for Popular Reading. 12mo. 75 cents.

"No attempt has been made to popularize this important science, and to place it on the same favorable basis with geography and astronomy; hence, the idea is prevalent that chemistry is one of those dry and difficult subjects which belong exclusively to professors and lecturers, and which can not be successfully taught as a branch of common education. In the treatise now before us we are shown that the fundamental laws of chemistry are as definite, as clear and simple, and as capable of being understood by juvenile minds, as those of numbers, which are taught in every school.

"We regard this new Class-Book of Chemistry as one of the most valuable text books that has been prepared for schools during many years. A knowledge of the science of which it treats is of great importance to every one, and is daily becoming more and more popular. This work popularizes to a greater extent than any other we have ever seen on this subject, and renders interesting to the minds of pupils, as well as to the general reader, one of the most useful of sciences.

"A peculiar and valuable feature of this treatise is its application of chemistry to the common occurrences of life, and its treating of familiar things, and presenting facts and truths alike valuable and entertaining, in a style free, as far as possible, from technicalities on the one hand, and puerilities on the other."—*Student.*

"An elementary work on Chemistry well adapted to either purpose, of aiding in the initiatory step towards a profound study of the science, or of giving that general knowledge deemed essential in ordinary education. No better illustration could be given of the progress of the science of Chemistry in these later years than the fulness of information in this elementary book on Organic and Animal Chemistry, branches of the science which but a few years ago were as sealed books even to the chemical philosophers themselves. The book is clear and demonstrative in style, and easily intelligible to the beginner and general reader."—*Tribune.*

EDWARD L. YOUMANS.

A Chart of Chemistry;

In which the Fundamental Laws and Facts of the Science, Affinity, the Composition and Decomposition of Bodies, combining Equivalents or Definite and Multiple Proportions, the Atomic Theory, Crystallization, Fermentation, Isomerism, the Nomenclature and Formulæ, are Illustrated to the eye in a clear and simple manner.

*** This Chart, which is adapted to the above Class-Book, is nearly four feet by five in size, and contains about one thousand diagrams, in sixteen different colors. That it may be brought within the reach of every school, it is sold at the low price of five dollars being the cheapest Chart, considering its cost, that is published in the United States.

The following distinguished Chemists and Educators have highly commended this Chart as a valuable auxiliary to all Students:—

Professors B. L. Silliman, Jas. R. Chilton, John W. Draper, Jas. B. Rogers, W. H. Hopkins, John Torrey, W. H. Ellett, Thos. Antisell, Gray, Hon. Horace Mann, Supt McKeen, N. Y. City, Supt. S. S. Randall, Albany, Supt. T. L. Holmes, Brooklyn, Geo B. Emerson, Boston, &c., &c.

17

PROF. SURENNE.

The Standard Pronouncing Dictionary of the

French and English Languages. In Two Parts. Part I.:—French and English. Part II.:—English and French. The First Part comprehending words in common use—Terms connected with Science—Terms belonging to the Fine Arts—4000 Historical Names—4000 Geographical Names—1100 Terms lately published, with the PRONUNCIATION OF EVERY WORD, according to the French Academy and the most eminent Lexicographers and Grammarians; together with 750 *Critical Remarks*, in which the various methods of pronouncing employed by different authors are investigated and compared with each other. The Second Part containing a copious vocabulary of English words and expressions, with the pronunciation according to Walker. The whole preceded by a Practical and Comprehensive System of French Pronunciation. $1 50.

"This work must have been one of very great labor, as it is evidently of deep research. We have given it a careful examination, and are perfectly safe in saying we have never before seen any thing of the kind at all to compare with it."

PROFS. SPIERS AND SURENNE.

Complete French and English Dictionary.

In Two Parts. I. English and French. II. French and English. One volume imperial 8vo., 1400 pages. (*Nearly ready.*)

This Work has been newly composed from the French Dictionaries of the Academy, Laveaux, Boiste, Bescherelle, Landais, &c.; and from the English Dictionaries of Johnson, Richardson, Walker, and Webster. It surpasses all others in correct and philosophical analysis of shades of meaning, in fulness of definition, and clearness of arrangement; and contains many words, particularly such as are connected with modern science, not to be found in any other work of the kind. A number of new features have been introduced by the American editor; he has given the pronunciation of every word, French and English, according to the best standards, and most approved system; he has explained clearly, though briefly, the shades of meaning which distinguish French synonymes, thus guarding the scholar against error in their use; and has brought in, in alphabetical order, the leading parts of every irregular verb in the language, thereby removing the greatest difficulty which those beginning the study of French have heretofore experienced.

Embracing all these advantages, this work is believed to be the most complete and valuable French and English Dictionary extant, and as such is presented to the public in the confident hope that it will meet with general favor.

PROF. SURENNE.

An Abridged Dictionary of the French and

English Languages. In Two Parts. I. French—English. II. English—French. With Vocabulary of Proper Names. For the Use of Schools and for General Reference. One vol. 18mo., of 558 pages. Price 90 cts.

"In compiling this abridgment of the larger work, all the words have been retained except those which have become obsolete, or whose technicality precluded their insertion in a popular Dictionary. At the same time, due regard has been paid to the introduction of such new words and definitions as the progressive changes in the language have rendered necessary; and for this purpose the best and most recent authorities have been anxiously consulted. It is, therefore, confidently anticipated that the volume will prove not only a useful auxiliary to the student, but also a convenient Pocket Companion to the traveller wherever the French language is spoken."—*Preface.*

PROF. G. J. ADLER.

A Dictionary of the German and English Languages;

indicating the Accentuation of every German Word, containing several Hundred German Synonyms, together with a Classification and Alphabetical List of the Irregular Verbs, and a Dictionary of German Abbreviations. Compiled from the Works of HILPERT, FLUGEL, GREIB, HEYSE, and others. In two Parts: I. German and English—II. English and German. One large vol. 8vo., of over 1400 pages. Price $5.

"In preparing this volume, our principal aim was to offer to the American student of the German a work which would embody all the valuable results of the most recent investigations in German Lexicography, and which might thus become not only a reliable guide for the practical acquisition of that language, but one which would not forsake him in the higher walks of his pursuit, to which its literary and scientific treasures would naturally invite him. The conviction that such a work was a desideratum, and one which claimed immediate attention, was first occasioned by the steadily increasing interest manifested in the study of the German by such among us as covet a higher intellectual culture, as well as those who are ambitious to be abreast with the times in all that concerns the interests of Learning, Science, Art, and Philosophy.

"In comparing the different German-English Dictionaries, it was found that all of them were deficient in their vocabulary of foreign words, which now acts so important a part not only in scientific works, but also in the best classics, in the reviews, journals, newspapers, and even in conversational language of ordinary life. Hence we have endeavored to supply the desired words required in Chemistry, Mineralogy, Practical Art, Commerce, Navigation, Rhetoric, Grammar, Mythology, both ancient and modern. The accentuation of the German words, first introduced by Hernsius, and not a little improved by Hilpert and his coadjutors, has also been adopted, and will be regarded as a most desirable and invaluable aid to the student. Another, and it is hoped not the least, valuable addition to the volume, are the synonymes, which we have generally given in an abridged and not unfrequently in a new form, from Hilpert, who was the first that offered to the English student a selection from the rich stores of Eberhard, Maas, and Gruber. Nearly all the Dictionaries published in Germany having been prepared with special reference to the German student of the English, and being on that account incomplete in the German-English part, it was evidently our vocation to reverse the order for this side of the Atlantic, and to give the utmost possible completeness and perfection to the German part. This was the proper sphere of our labor."—*Extract from Preface.*

PROF. G. J. ADLER.

A Dictionary of the German and English Languages

Abridged from the Author's larger Work, for the use of Learners. In two Parts: I. German and English—II. English and German. One vol. 12mo., of over 800 pages. $1 75.

"The larger work of Adler, of which this is an abridgment, has become an authority on the German language. It is now well known and in extensive use among German scholars. In making this abridgment, the author has gone over the entire ground of the larger work again; revising, condensing, or adding, as the case might require. All provincialism, synonymes, and strictly scientific terms, have been excluded from these pages, and every thing that might prove unnecessary, or embarrassing to beginners, or to travellers and others, for whom a smaller volume is better adapted. Some other changes have also been made, which were deemed important to render the work still more acceptable for educational purposes. It can hardly fail to become as universally approved in the sphere for which it is designed, as the larger work has been by more advanced German scholars."—*Courier & Enquirer.*

"Professor Adler, who fills the department of the German Language and Literature in the University of this city, is an accomplished scholar, and has done vast service to the cause of spreading a knowledge of the Teutonic language in this country. His larger work, of which this is an abridgment, is the very best extant for advanced students. The work before us is abridged and simplified in several respects, to adapt it to the wants and capacities of beginners."—*Christian Intelligencer.*

SEOANE'S NEUMAN AND BARETTI.—BY VELAZQUEZ.

A Pronouncing Dictionary of the Spanish and

English Languages; composed from the Spanish Dictionaries of the Spanish Academy, Terreros, and Salva, upon the basis of Seoane's Edition of Neuman and Baretti, and from the English Dictionaries of Webster, Worcester, and Walker; with the addition of more than Eight Thousand New Words, Idioms, and Familiar Phrases, the Irregularities of all the Verbs, and a Grammatical Synopsis of both Languages. By MARIANO VELAZQUEZ DE LA CADENA, Professor of the Spanish Language and Literature in Columbia College, N. Y., &c., &c. In Two Parts—I. Spanish—English. II. English—Spanish. One volume imp. 8vo., of about 1400 pages. Strongly and neatly bound, price $5.

The great desideratum of an accurate, comprehensive, and well-digested Dictionary of the Spanish and English languages is now first realized in this work by Professor Velazquez. The value of Neuman and Baretti's Dictionary was greatly enhanced in the edition by Dr. Seoane; but it needed still greater improvements than Seoane has given it, and the lapse of twenty years has made its deficiencies painfully apparent. Professor Velazquez has availed himself of all the valuable material accumulated by his predecessors. He has also enriched his pages from the latest edition of the Dictionary of the Academy—published subsequently to Seoane's revision—and from the great work of Cabrera, Terreros, and the indefatigable Salvá. Many familiar words not found in the Dictionaries, but constantly in use in Cuba, in Mexico, and in South America, are now first given, as well as a long catalogue of mercantile terms, collected from reliable sources. To these Professor Velazquez has added the many words and phrases, the much-needed corrections, and the thorough revision suggested by his long experience as a teacher of his mother tongue. Besides these improvements in the Vocabulary, the work is now made a Pronouncing Dictionary. The pronunciation of every Spanish word is given in a manner which will enable an English scholar to pronounce them at sight. The method of pronouncing English words in this Dictionary merits the particular attention of every one whose mother tongue is the Castilian. It is based upon the method so much admired and recommended by the learned Don Lorenzo Hervas, in his "*Catálogo de las Lenguas*;" namely, by giving to every elementary sound in the language a corresponding alphabetical character, and by restricting each of these characters to one single sound. By the help of this method, so superior to notation with figured vowels, no person willing to devote half an hour to the dozen new alphabetic characters need be at a loss to pronounce correctly every English word in the Dictionary. The new and improved orthography sanctioned by the latest edition of the Dictionary of the Academy—now universally adopted by the press—is here given for the first time in a Spanish and English Dictionary. Another new and most useful feature of the work is an "Outline Grammar of the Spanish Language," and a "Grammatical Synopsis of the English Language," each containing a grammar in miniature, and all the irregular verbs of both languages. The volume is thus rendered complete, and made to answer all the purposes of a grammar and a Dictionary.

Nearly ready, in one volume 12mo.,

AN ABRIDGMENT OF THE ABOVE.

This Abridgment is a miniature copy of the great octavo work by Professor Velasquez, and contains all its most important additions and improvements. Expurgated of the antiquated orthography, and the manifold errors and absurdities so common in Spanish and English Abridgments, it is intended as a reliable work of reference for business men, and for all the ordinary uses of a Dictionary. The scholar who wishes to become well acquainted with the Spanish and English classics, will hardly be satisfied with any thing less than the octavo edition; but as a pocket companion for beginners, for travellers, or for the use of those who consult a dictionary for practical purposes, this abridgment will be found superior to any other work yet published.

GEORGE R. PERKINS, A. M.,

Professor of Mathematics and Principal of the State Normal School.

Course of Mathematical Works.

I. PRIMARY ARITHMETIC. Price 21 cts.

The first part is devoted to MENTAL EXERCISES, and the second to *Exercises on the Slate and Blackboard.*

It has been received with more popularity than any Arithmetic heretofore issued.

II. ELEMENTARY ARITHMETIC. Price 42 cts.

Has recently been carefully revised and enlarged. It will be found concise, yet lucid.

In this work *all of the examples or problems are strictly practical,* made up as they are in a great measure of important statistics and valuable facts in history and philosophy, which are thus unconsciously learned in acquiring a knowledge of the Arithmetic.

Wherever this work is presented, the publishers have heard but one opinion in regard to its merits, and that most favorable.

III. PRACTICAL ARITHMETIC.

The Practical Arithmetic is designed not to supply the place of the Elementary Arithmetic, but is designed for the use of such institutions as require a greater number of examples than are given in that work.

IV. HIGHER ARITHMETIC. Price 84 cts.

The present edition has been revised, many subjects re-written, and much new matter added; and contains an APPENDIX of about sixty pages, in which the philosophy of the more difficult operations and interesting properties of numbers are fully discussed. The work is what its name purports, a HIGHER Arithmetic.

V. ELEMENTS OF ALGEBRA. Price 84 cts.

This work is an introduction to the Author's "Treatise on Algebra."

VI. TREATISE ON ALGEBRA. Price $1 50.

This work contains the higher parts of Algebra usually taught in Colleges, a new method of cubic and higher equations as well as the THEOREM OF STURM, by which we may at once determine the number of real roots of any Algebraic Equation, with much more ease than by any previously discovered method.

In the present *revised edition,* one entire chapter on the subject of CONTINUED FRACTIONS has been added

VII. ELEMENTS OF GEOMETRY, WITH PRACTICAL APPLICATIONS. $1.

The author has added throughout the entire Work, PRACTICAL APPLICATIONS, which, in the estimation of Teachers, is an important consideration.

An eminent Professor of Mathematics, in speaking of this work, says: "We have adopted it, because it follows more closely the best model of pure geometrical reasoning which ever has been, and perhaps ever will be exhibited.

VIII. PLANE TRIGONOMETRY,

And its Application to Mensuration and Land Surveying. Accompanied with all the necessary Logarithmic and Trigonometric Tables. 1 vol. 8vo.

It is a commendable feature in all the mathematical works of this author, that they are prepared in such a manner as will lead the pupil to rely upon his own abilities in studying the principles they contain; commencing with the simplest elements he is led on step by step throughout. This volume is prepared upon the same logical system. It contains much that is new and valuable, especially on the subject of land-surveying.

www.ingramcontent.com/pod-product-compliance
Lightning Source LLC
LaVergne TN
LVHW010254110826
845151LV00004B/1469

* 9 7 8 1 4 2 5 5 2 2 0 5 6 *